WILD RIVERS, WILD ROSE

WILD RIVERS, WILD ROSE

SARAH BIRDSALL

University of Alaska Press / Fairbanks

Published by
University of Alaska Press
P.O. Box 756240
Fairbanks, AK 99775-6240

Cover and interior design by 590 Design.

Cover photo by Sarah Birdsall.
Map by William Barstow.

Library of Congress Cataloging-in-Publication Data

Names: Birdsall, Sarah, author.
Title: Wild rivers, wild rose / Sarah Birdsall.
Description: Fairbanks, AK : University of Alaska Press, [2020] | Summary:
"In 1941, Anna Harker is attacked by an ax-wielding assailant in the gold-bearing
ridges bordering the Alaska Range. It is this moment of savagery that propels the
people of Wild Rivers, Wild Rose. Anna's lover, Wade Daniels, learns of the deaths of
Anna's husband and their farmhand, and he rushes to the hills to look for Anna and
hunt the murderer. As she lies dying on the tundra, Anna relives the major events
of her Alaska life while searching her memories for what could have led to the
violence. And, decades later, an outsider named Billie Sutherland steps into a
community still haunted by the murders. Plagued by her own ghosts, Billie delves
into the past, opening old wounds. In this gripping novel by Sarah Birdsall, lives are
laid bare and secrets ring out in the resonant Alaska Range foothills" — Provided
by publisher.
Identifiers: LCCN 2019042774 (print) | LCCN 2019042775 (ebook) | ISBN
    9781602234062 (paperback) | ISBN 9781602234079 (ebook)
Classification: LCC PS3602.I738 W55 2020 (print) | LCC PS3602.I738
    (ebook) | DDC 813/.6--dc23
LC record available at https://lccn.loc.gov/2019042774
LC ebook record available at https://lccn.loc.gov/2019042775

*Dedicated to the memory of Talkeetna writer and historian Roberta Sheldon,
whose magnificent true crime book,* The Mystery of the Cache Creek
Murders, *brought to light the facts and evidence surrounding four brutal murders in Alaska's gold-bearing Peters Hills, shedding light on and documenting a story that has long haunted the northern Susitna Valley.*

While this story is inspired by the landscape, history, stories, and people of Alaska's northern Susitna Valley, it is a work of fiction and not intended to be a factual portrayal of any of the above, historically or otherwise.

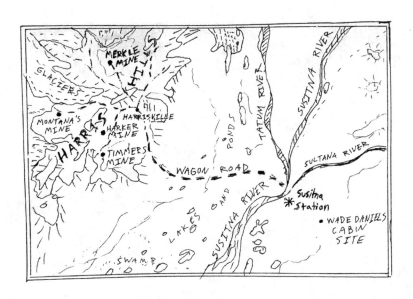

Anna Harker

THIS MUCH I KNOW: It was an ax. I felt the weight of the blade slice through the left side of my head, missing a presumed center mark and wedging into my shoulder, taking my ear with it along the way. Then the blade, once again free, hit my right side in the back of my ribcage, and I fell facedown into the tundra. I could hear the trembling breathing of my attacker. I had felt, in fact, the vibration of his body behind mine prior to my fall, caught the whisper of his smell on the wind.

I thought, perhaps, it was Henry. That he found out, and it was too much for him, like the flood of a river when the water bursts the banks. I tried but was unable to turn over to see, so I stayed with my face in the sweet-scented tundra, the warmth of my blood flowing over me like a gentle rinse. The ax came into my back a final time, and then I felt the spongy ground move as my assailant fled the scene.

Not Henry. This I also know. He would have cried while he did it. I would have heard his sniveling; I would have heard the hurt-filled beating of his wounded heart.

Here on the tundra, where I fell with hardly a sound, I find I can move my head enough so I can breathe the air and see the sky and that sharp September ache in the blue, like a loss of innocence or a remembered pain. And pain I am aware of now, rippling through my body, but somehow I am distant from it as if my senses have dimmed like a light whose wick is turned too low.

Such a shame, such a shame, the mining season over and soon back to the village for us, me and Henry and Nate, our hand. The savoring of the sweet, swift fall, then winter in the village cabin, snow swirling outside. Mornings in the roadhouse with my mother, the warm smell of baking bread, or out on the trapline with my stepfather, the sting of the cold on our faces, the lumbering shuffle of snowshoes on our booted feet.

This I know, too: I will not see it again, the village where I grew up, the place my mother and I moved to when I was not quite three, to be with Uncle Mike and help him run his roadhouse. Uncle Mike who is long drowned and absent from within those walls, but my mother—there still, there now, taking the baking out of the wood-fired oven and readying for the few who may wander in for a late lunch or early supper. I feel myself standing in the doorway, trying but failing to tell her, my voice now beyond the mystery of words. *Mama. Mama, I'm hurt.* And Thomas Merkle, my stepfather, on his way down out of the hills from his own mine, making his way on foot with a pack on his back like they did in the old days, taking shortcuts through the wildness known only to him until his feet find the silty shore of the river and the canoe he left hidden there in the spring, the hills and the mountains now shadows behind him.

The river is where Wade Daniels would be on a day like today, himself having left his cousin's mine a good eight days ago. Is he thinking of me as he stands there at the confluence, where the Sultana finds the Susitna and which the Tatum has already joined? Will he feel something, anything, as the water rushes past? Will he hear in that low murmur the whisper of my name? I call to him, wherever he is, down down the tumble of these hills, his fishing rod in hand, looking for that rainbow, or that grayling, and having no idea, no idea, that oh, my darling, I will not ever see you again—

This is what I know.

OCTOBER 1, 1941
Wade Daniels

IT WAS HIS FAVORITE TIME OF YEAR. Fall, the rivers crisp and swift and the fish hungry. He stood on a silty bank and cast his line, thinking of Anna and trying not to think of her. It would do no good, and it made no sense. But his mind kept drifting back to it: mid-May, his cabin site, the evening light and dusky at once. Anna and her full, red lips, like ripe, soft berries. And her flannel shirt and boy's jeans—like no woman he's ever known. Her black curls loose from her ponytail and falling across one side of her face; the old leather gloves she wore, her hand across her forehead as she wiped away a newly hatched mosquito.

There was a loon on the lake, early this year, and he'd watched the slow smile spread across Anna's face as the sound of its cry rose up into the evening air. He could not love her more than he did at that moment—his Alaska girl.

But not his. There was no getting around it. Unwanted thoughts flickered through his brain, thoughts that came now more often than not—Anna and Henry, her husband, the person she ate with and slept with and who touched her in the same places he did. But it was not Henry Harker who was in the wrong; it was the two of them, him and Anna. It had to stop, they both knew, but there were invisible strings between them, like a fish net they got tangled up in and couldn't find the way out. It had to stop, and he would have to see to it. Somehow. He took a deep breath and tried to clear his thoughts, let himself listen, for a moment, to the low murmur of the three rivers merging together near where he stood, and he looked to the northwest to the Alaska Range in the distance, the mountains white and gleaming from the fresh snow that settled onto them like a coat of new paint. The sky above them was blue and sharp, but the clouds were coming in from the north and would either bring cold rain or the first snow to the river valley. His eyes lingered on the heavy gray covering slowly moving toward him on the wind, and the sight made him feel as if he had left something undone.

A tug on his line and he allowed himself a smile, watching his rod bend and the soon-coming splash on the surface of the water. He pulled gently, easily, turning his reel yet giving the fish room. Sometimes he almost hated to catch them, to pull them out from the freedom of their existence in the wild water, sun on the surface and cool quiet in the depths, but, well, this evening he would be hungry, and fresh fish over the fire sounded a darned sight better than the old pot of beans that sat cold on his stove. If the weather held he would cook it outside over an open fire. If not, he would get the woodstove going in his roughly finished cabin and fry the fish in a cast iron pan and watch whatever fell from the sky hit the surface of the lake and try not to think of Anna Harker, and the first time he saw her there.

The fish jumped, breaking the surface. A rainbow, a good eight to ten, perfect. He reeled and pulled, reeled and pulled, kneeling by the water as he brought the twisting fish to shore.

"Sorry, old boy," he said as he smashed a rock onto its skull. "See you farther up the creek."

As he reached to his side and pulled his knife from its sheath, he became aware of voices—no, a voice—someone yelling, down toward the direction of the village. He paused, looked around, and decided the voice had caught a ride on the rising wind. He slit open the trout's soft underside and pulled out the warm guts and the hard little heart, throwing them into the cold swift water and rinsing the fish clean.

But no—the voice was getting louder. He heard his name: "Wade!" He rose from the river and turned, holding the fish by the gills. It was his cousin, Jake Timmers, breathless and running. "Wade!"

He was about to answer, about to say, *What?* when Jake's words closed the distance between them. "Trouble at the mines, Wade—God awful!" He slowed and tried to catch his breath. Wade's mind raced. He and Jake had left Jake's mine a little over a week ago. Again he had the feeling of something left undone, forgotten. "Henry Harker. Nate Peterson, too—an ax, apparently. Jesus!"

He looked at his cousin, not sure he understood the words.

"No one knows where Anna is—they can't find her up there, Wade—they can't find her. God she must be dead too!"

That was the moment where he felt everything stop, the world to stone, his lifeblood red clay, his lungs empty sacks. Anna by the lake, four months past. The evening light soft on her face, that new summer sun, the beginning of that sweet smile forming on her lips—

His chest moved, then, and air rushed in and he knew he was falling forward, falling toward a world he did not want to know.

Billie Sutherland

SUCH A PRETTY FACE. She'd heard it all her life, took it with a smile but always wondered what it meant. As she grew older the meaning became more apparent: it meant the ringing phone in her parents' semi-rustic ranch-style home was more often than not for her; it meant the job as a stewardess that took her out of Alaska and around the world. It meant a marriage proposal (rejected) from a handsome airline pilot, followed by—that other. That thing she did, her face led her there as well; Billie Sutherland, and she saw herself laughing her way through an airport, tall and thin and sparkly, the wild Alaska girl, confident and vivacious, with the pretty face that also meant her family expected her to "make a good match" and have children with faces like the one that stared back at her now in the mirror of the rocking train. If they only knew. She tried smiling at the face that had taken her so far, failed, and sighed. When you fall from the sky, it's a long way down.

What is it you want, Billie girl? she asked herself, but the question was smeared with something that couldn't be changed and she couldn't erase, making any possible answer murky and dark. She looked at the stick of red lipstick in her hand and realized she couldn't decide whether or not to put it on. "Come on, Billie," she said out loud, then heard the extended whistle that signaled arrival. She put the lipstick on. That's what Billie would do.

"There you are!" Aunt Sam said as Billie made her way down the aisle between the rows of seats. Billie smiled (because Billie would smile) and helped her aunt collect their little grouping of bags, then the two women stepped off the train, along with nearly every other soul on board, into the quiet little village of Susitna Station. They were here to watch the moon pass between the earth and the sun, and Susitna Station was apparently a better place than most to watch it, with a special train to ride there and back again. When Aunt Sam asked her to come along, Billie, only newly returned to her parents' home in Anchorage, initially declined. All she did, on those first days, was walk down to the water and watch the tide wash over the gray mudflats, smoking cigarettes and shivering in the rain. In the end she went only to stop the questions. And to get out. She had to get out. That was one thing she hadn't thought of when she fled, the *then what?*

But here she was now, with Aunt Sam, standing in this village surrounded by trees and dwarfed by the majestic Alaska Range in the distance. They were in the village park, a little circle of green down a small rise from the railroad depot.

"So what do you think, Billie?" Aunt Sam stood beside her, short and stout compared to her own lean length, round faced and white haired while Billie's raven waves glinted in the sun.

"I'm not sure," she said and ran her eyes over the brief span of village in front of her. A log trading post to her left, a white clapboard inn to the right, a dusty road in between that was fringed with a haphazard assortment of small wooden buildings, some front and center to the road, some back a bit, like a confused dance between undecided partners.

"It's not like you to be unsure of anything, Birdie," Sam said.

Billie narrowed her eyes and looked over the rooftops at the sky. She could feel Sam watching her, her aunt's sharp journalistic brain searching for the story in her face. A little bit of uncertainty would have served Billie well. Or wisdom, forethought—anything. Again she saw her former laughing self, breezing through one city airport after another. Then this: the small bathroom of a plane in flight, her skirt pushed up and her legs wrapped around the tight torso of the uniformed man who thrust himself inside her. Her hands in his hair, his mouth on hers. Glued together. Then there was another bathroom, and a bathtub full of blood.

"Heavens to Murgatroid, Billie, what on earth is the matter with you? You're a bit young to be having a midlife crisis."

Billie took a deep breath. The air smelled of cottonwood leaves and grass. "Sorry, Sam," she said. "My mind was wandering. What did you say?"

"I asked you what on earth was the matter with you. Prior to that I asked you what you thought."

"Right." Billie looked around to see if she could find something to comment on that would satisfy her aunt. She pulled more of the clean summer air into her lungs. As she breathed she felt something easing inside her, felt as if the ground beneath her feet was soaking up into the marrow of her bones. She could hear a slight breeze rustling its way through the treetops, and she knew that underneath the chatter of the excited gathering, the nearby rivers muttered their ancient murmurings, the water swirling with the glacial silt of their mountain homes. Across the street to her left, on the other side of the trading post, she saw the glint of a silver bush plane on the edge of a dusty airstrip, shining in the disappearing sun.

She wanted to sit down on the cool grass and have everyone else go away. Just sit. She could see herself doing that, sitting here in this park, with nothing but the quiet. She felt a sudden desire to stay. She'd quit her job, given up her Seattle apartment, and right now couldn't bear the thought of returning to her old bedroom in her parents' house and the questions that waited for her. Or the possibility of the phone ringing, ringing for her. "It seems nice," she managed to say.

"All right. Nice it is." Sam sat down on a rough bench made from peeled and split logs. For a moment Billie could imagine her aunt young again, a working woman in a man's world who got her first job as a reporter pretending to be just that: a man. Now Aunt Sam and Uncle Howard, Billie's mother's brother, owned the newspaper they once worked for. Alaska let people do that, reinvent their lives.

"I might want to stay, Sam," Billie said quietly. She sat down on the bench.

"Well, we've got the whole day."

"No, I mean stay. Stay here. For awhile."

Her aunt opened her mouth, pulled in a breath, but then seemed to think better of whatever it was she was going to say. Her eyes darted around, and Billie could see how she was trying to determine if this would be a blessing or a curse as they sat in the tiny puddle of a village, bordered by rivers and rail. Finally she said, "This town's day has come and gone, Billie. You'd be bored before the sky starts getting dark again at night. Can't be more than 150 people here, probably less. Most days I'll bet there's not a soul to be seen."

"For some reason that suits me right now."

"They'll get over it, you know, you giving up that job." She was referring to Billie's parents.

Billie cracked a small smile. "Isn't that funny, Sam. No one—not even you—wanted me to take it in the first place."

"I just thought you had a better brain than that. But the traveling I could understand." Sam looked around at the scattered crowd. Excitement seemed to be growing. "I think we're making some progress. No—don't look! We have to wait until totality, then we can see it."

"All right, all right." Billie averted her gaze. They sat quietly as the darkness grew. The sky turned a beautiful blue, like a deep dusk, the kind you find on an Alaska winter afternoon. Billie felt the shadow falling over the world, felt, too, the absence of the sun.

Later, the eclipse in the waning stages, they wandered down the short stretch of the village's main street, past the meandering mixture of old and new buildings, log and clapboard, smaller echoes of the dominant trading post and inn. "Have you lost your mind?" Aunt Sam said.

"No, Sam, I haven't," Billie said, watching the dust of the unpaved roadway collect on her boots.

"I had hoped you were joking. That train's heading back to Anchorage at five o'clock and I suspect we should both be on it. Good lord—you just witnessed the sun disappearing behind the moon. What else could you possibly want in a single day?"

"I don't know."

Sam stopped. "And I don't know what's bothering you, Birdie—none of us do—but don't throw your life away."

I think I've already done that, Sam, she wanted to say but instead kept walking. Her aunt hurried to catch up.

"What on earth will I tell your mother?"

"Tell her—" Billie paused as she studied the old wooden sign on the painted log front of the roadhouse, an old weary-looking building about halfway down the length of the street. "Tell her whatever you think she wants to hear." The door opened with a jingle, and she stepped inside.

Anna Harker

I DROWNED ONCE; I remember that. I was very little—six. Young enough to have not dwelt on what had happened to me, but old enough to know, always, that it was Uncle Mike who had saved me, at the sad cost of his own life.

I say I had not dwelt on the experience of it; in fact, when I thought about it, it was little more than a blur—a whir of gray water and freezing cold, my mother's voice, somewhere, the shrill sound of it registering in my young mind as to the serious nature of what was occurring, and that hand, that hand, and a glimpse of a blue flannel shirt as Uncle Mike pulled and pushed me toward my mother's voice with what little life he had left.

A whir—vague, unclear. But now I see it as if it is occurring at this very moment as I lay here dying on the tundra.

And Uncle Mike—oh, I loved him so much! I can see him, with his sparkling brown eyes and thick dark lashes—eyes the envy of any girl—with all those laugh lines from all his laughing. Dark unkempt hair and the blue plaid flannel he always wore with his wool trousers and the tall lace-up leather boots.

Aw, come on now, Anna! You can do this!

I hear his voice as if he is here with me in this fading day. What was it we were doing? Fishing. The autumn river running blue, the fish hungry and taking our bait. I can see Uncle Mike, feel him kneeling beside me on the rocky shore of the sandbar, at the ready as my pole bent and a large rainbow trout flashed on the end of my line. *You can do this, Anna. Just hang on. You've got it.*

When my mother and I arrived in Alaska, Uncle Mike was there on the dock when our ferry from Seattle pulled into the harbor at Seward.

"Maddie!" he'd said, swinging my mother around in a circle as I watched, delighted. "And you—you must be Anna!" Then I, too, was swept up and twirled around, my eyes glimpsing gray water and light gray sky, the white wings of flying gulls.

That night we stayed in a hotel in the seaside town, and down by the wooden docks Uncle Mike showed me a sea lion, a seal-like creature with a brown open face that looked to me like a lost person in a strange costume, rolling in the water.

"What should we name him, then?" Uncle Mike asked. He knelt beside me, his arm around my shoulders.

"Wimple," I'd said.

"Wimple?" he laughed. "Why Wimple?"

My mother came and knelt on the other side of me, and I felt her arm around my waist.

I shook my head and giggled—I didn't know. But I always remembered that friendly, round brown face and those soft ancient eyes—I see it now as if I am there again—and when Uncle Mike drowned, I thought of Wimple and wished that he could swim from the ocean to the wild river that swept my uncle away, find him, and bring him home.

I remember the morning after finding Wimple, at a table in the hotel, my mother and Uncle Mike discussing the journey ahead. Or maybe I remember the story only because my mother told it to me so many times, all the details of our first Alaska days with Uncle Mike. We were to ride the train to the town of Anchorage, spend the night, then ride a boat up the wide, gray, glacier-fed Susitna River to Susitna Station, the place that was to become our new home. Uncle Mike had lived there the last five years, having left my mother and their parents behind to chase dreams of gold in the North. But he soon found that the mining life wasn't for him—it was lonely in the hills, he said, and he preferred town life, such as it was, and he built a log roadhouse along the dirt road that served as the village's main street, offered nightly lodging and meals that he hoped would improve once my mother was onboard.

Now my mother's voice screams at me through the layers of water that are wrapped around me and pulling me down. "Anna! Anna!" I hear her as if I am back in the water, the water holding me, and the more it holds me, the better it feels. But no—I'm here on the tundra, bleeding, thinking. When I was drowning I was also thinking, and I remember how vividly I recalled that first Christmas at Susitna Station and the doll from the Sears Roebuck catalog that Uncle Mike had ordered for me, and how the box had sat under our scraggly spruce Christmas tree that we'd decorated with popcorn strings and gingerbread men and dried cranberries. On Christmas Eve the sky was clear and the stars sparkled and seemed so close to us, but in the morning we awoke to thick, heavy snow swirling down upon our already white frozen world. "Oh!" my mother had said, as she looked out the window at the slowly emerging day. "A moose! No—two. A big one and a little one!" I ran to the window, Uncle Mike lifting me up so I could see. Our little village, all soft and fuzzy with the falling snow. Cabins, tents, all with chimneys puffing streams of white-gray smoke. And the mama moose, standing in the middle of the snowy street, trying to see where she was and determine why she was there, then leading her little one through the piling snow toward the river.

I was thinking that, when I was drowning in the river, just as I am thinking that now, dying on the tundra.

We had gone upriver the day I drowned, in a flat-bottomed boat owned by Uncle Mike, one that he used to ferry miners across the Susitna River so they could head up to the gold country, to the country where I am now. It was supposed to be a fun day. Uncle Mike said my mother needed to get out of the roadhouse before winter came. The colors of the leaves on the birch trees were "coated with gold," he'd said, the river like liquid gems in shades of blue and the fish hungry and plentiful. We went upstream, past the confluence of rivers that framed the boundaries of the village.

The water had dropped from the levels it had been during the summer, the glaciers that fed the rivers no longer melting, and a tangle of dead cottonwood trees hidden beneath the water lifted the bow and tipped us over and into the rushing current when we were on our way home.

At first I bobbed to the surface. I saw my mother and Uncle Mike, both coming toward me. The water was so cold. And then I felt myself being drawn into it, like someone—something—was there beneath me, gently pulling me down.

It was all blue and green and gray, the water thick and slow. I felt panic, my heart like a wild bunny kicking in my chest, and all I wanted to do was breathe, breathe. And I did and it hurt. Then nothing hurt anymore, and I saw my grandparents at the ferry docks in Washington saying goodbye to my mother and me, and I remembered that first Christmas with Uncle Mike. I remembered Wimple and wondered if I could find him there, in that water. Then there was Uncle Mike's hand and his blue flannel shirt, and I was moving sideways to the current, and then I saw myself on the beach with my mother, her face twisted with grief and fear. The boat was still in the river, captive of the fallen trees. And Uncle Mike was gone.

I see his hand now, and I feel him touch my bloody face. *Shh, Anna,* he says. *Everything will be all right.*

Wade Daniels

HIS HAND SHOOK SO VIOLENTLY the whiskey spilled right out. John Summers, the barkeep, refilled the glass then lifted it himself to Wade's lips. "Come on, young fella, drink up. This'll settle you a bit." He felt the burn of the whiskey in his throat. All around him the barroom of the Clearwater Inn buzzed with a sound like flies on a carcass. He shook his head and pushed his way through the bodies and the noise to the backdoor. He walked to the side and vomited into a patch of wild rose bushes, the hips where flowers once bloomed now brown-red and dry, barely hanging on. He straightened and breathed. Think. Think. Henry Harker and Nate Peterson killed by an ax. Both able-bodied men, taken down, one not able to help the other. And where was she?

Maybe she's the one with the ax, someone—who?—said. Stupid bastard. But had Jake, then, looked at him? Had Jake known?

He knew Anna, he told himself, but a little voice inside him asked, did he? Did what happened between them lead her to do something unthinkable? He shook his head, muttering to himself, No, no, no.

"Wade—" And here was Jake now, his high forehead lined with concern as he pushed his thick coppery hair back away from his face. "Hey, buddy, you okay?"

Wade nodded. "It just hit me wrong, you know."

"Hits us all wrong."

"Let's get going. Let's get up there."

"Can't. Got to wait. The truck that came down from the hills is already heading back with Merkle and a few other men. And Fairfield's got to get there first—that kid's going to fly him up. We'll follow."

"She's out there somewhere, Jake. She needs our help. What about your motorbike? Couldn't we take that?"

"First—Anna. Well, she's pretty self-sufficient. She knows those hills better than anyone. But who knows if she's even alive?"

Wade grimaced, and swallowed against the bile rising in his throat.

"And the motorbike. Not running so well. Anyway it could only take one of us, and how would we get it across the river?"

Wade breathed, tried to think. "I don't understand. Who found them again?"

"Montana. He ran to the roadhouse, then Tom Hartley drove down."

"Did Montana look for Anna?"

"He says he scanned the hills but didn't see her."

"There's a lot going on in those hills. Dips, crevices, holes in the tundra."

Jake nodded, and Wade gulped the cold, crisp fall air and followed his cousin back into the crowded barroom. Now Anna's mother and the Harkers were in there, Mrs. Harker yelling and screaming as if it were the village's fault somehow, her husband trying to console her. Maddie Merkle leaned back against a wall, a man's wool coat wrapped around her, her hand gripped over her mouth as if to keep her own cries at bay.

"You tell me where your daughter is!" Mrs. Harker screamed at her. "I knew she was no good! I knew it! I knew it!"

"My daughter *loves* her husband!" Maddie responded, moving forward but held at bay by the hands that reached for her. "She might not have been good enough for you, but she is good enough for your son!"

"You tell me why—why did she do this, why did she?" With this Mrs. Harker's knees gave out, and the hands that had held Maddie rushed to this new crisis, as Mr. Harker seemed unable to hold up his wife. Maddie covered her face and slid down the wall to the floor.

Wade turned from the scene. Out the window he saw two figures walking quickly toward the village airstrip. It was Ben Fairfield, the village commissioner, and the local pilot, young Atlee Virtanen, who everyone called the Flying Finn. Wade slipped unnoticed out the door and hurried to catch the men.

"Take me," he said, breathless, when he came up beside them.

Fairfield shook his head. "Sorry, Wade. I've yet to assess the situation."

"I can help."

"I know, everyone wants to help. But I've got a job to do."

"I know the territory. I've done some tracking before. I can help."

"What's that?"

"Back in Vermont. I helped the state police once, find a missing kid. I can help. If Anna's missing, I can help."

"It's a crime scene up there. I need to do what I can before all hell breaks loose."

Wade pointed at the sky, at the gathering clusters of gray. "It's going to snow soon, Ben. Up there. Maybe even tonight. When it snows up there, it snows. I can help you."

Fairfield looked at the sky, pushed his glasses up his nose, and turned to the Finn. "Can we fit him in?"

The Finn nodded and looked at Wade. "You might have to hike out, but we can get you there."

"That's fine."

"What about your gear?" Fairfield asked.

"I don't need anything."

"All right." Fairfield nodded. "I guess we can worry about supplies later. Truth is I'm not excited about being on the scene by myself, though I imagine everyone at the roadhouse will be wanting to come with us. Or not. I don't know. There is a killer out there somewhere, after all. After he drops us off, Atlee will fly down to Anchorage and hopefully bring back some proper authorities. But let's go see what we can see, secure the scene, and hope to hell the bears aren't eating the bodies."

Wade felt his stomach lurch again. He forced the image out of his mind. "We need to find Anna Harker," he said.

"Yes, and find Anna. If she's to be found."

Wade didn't question the statement, but he knew what Fairfield meant. And in his own mind he was coming to the horrible realization that Anna was either the killer, or she was also killed; the idea that she was hiding, or that she was wounded somewhere but living, seemed increasingly unlikely.

As the Finn started the plane and Fairfield and Wade climbed inside, they could see the crowd at the Clearwater spilling out the door. The Finn pulled down his goggles and closed the doors. He taxied the plane down the length of the airstrip and turned toward the village. The plane's engine roared as the aircraft picked up speed and the Finn pointed the nose toward the sky. Wade pulled in a deep breath, squeezed his eyes shut but managed to open them in time to see, as they flew over the Clearwater, the people all gathered around outside, his cousin Jake catching his face behind the glass and waving like crazy as the plane turned toward the northwest and whatever was waiting for them there.

Billie Sutherland

THE LIGHT INSIDE THE ROADHOUSE was soft and subdued, as if the shadow of the eclipse lingered on within the walls. Billie felt that she had slipped into a different time and imagined the people who might have sat at the empty tables: miners and trappers, talking about the weather and grumbling about the conditions on the river or the depth of the snow on the trails. She caught a glimpse of movement in the next room and stepped through the open threshold. An older woman wearing an apron over a plain cotton below-the-knee-length dress startled when she turned and saw Billie, and the thick white mugs she was carrying fell from her hands and bounced and broke across the old wood floors.

"Oh no—I'm so sorry," Billie said, rushing forward and bending down to pick up the pieces. "I didn't mean to scare you."

"Who are you?" the woman asked.

Billie looked up. "I'm Billie. Billie Sutherland."

For a moment the woman stared down at Billie, her face full of a story that whispered across her features like a glimpse of movement in a shadowy corner. Then she knelt on the floor and gathered some broken pieces, looking at Billie with dark, worried eyes. "What are you doing here?"

"I'm looking for a room." Billie glanced quickly over her shoulder to see if Aunt Sam had followed her inside. She felt like she had stepped in something, but what, she wasn't sure. "Is that all right? And I'm so sorry about the mugs. Certainly

I'll pay for them." She couldn't think of anything else to say. Billie held eye contact with the woman, and time for a moment seemed to freeze as she tried and failed to decipher the expression on the woman's face. Was it fear? How could she possibly be afraid of Billie?

The door jingled and Aunt Sam shuffled in. "Billie?"

The woman looked up, and whatever had surfaced on her face slid back into shadow. "Oh—yes, of course," she said, rising from the floor, the broken pieces in her hand. "Well, I've got rooms. Don't worry about the mugs." She was looking now at Aunt Sam, who stood on the threshold between the front room and the dining room. The two older women looked at each other for an odd moment. Then Sam broke the silence and said, "Billie, what have you done now?"

"Nothing, Aunt Sam," Billie said, rising. "What should we do with these?" she asked the woman. "They're badly broken, but we might be able to fix them with a little epoxy."

"We might be able to put them back together, but it would be hard to say whether they'd hold up to any use," the woman said.

"I'm so sorry to have startled you. I'll pay for them then."

"No need," the woman said. "I'm the one who's sorry—so silly. For a moment I thought I recognized you."

Billie's heart jumped before she realized how unlikely that would be.

"Are you ladies up for the eclipse?" she asked.

"Yes," said Aunt Sam. "It was incredible. You saw it, too, I assume?"

"I did." The woman pushed back stray strands of thick gray and brown hair that had escaped from the loose, generous French twist on the back of her head. Billie took note of the woman's finely shaped brows, straight nose, and high cheek-bones; in her youth she must have been quite beautiful. Billie wondered if that had served her well. She wore a simple gold ring on her aged, strong looking hand, but there was an air of loneliness about her and about the place that made Billie think that the giver of the ring was no longer here. "Isn't it still occurring?" the woman asked.

"It is," said Billie. "But the best part's over. I wanted to see about a room."

"For the two of you?" she asked, looking from Billie to Sam.

"One single," Billie said and Aunt Sam sighed.

"I'm sorry, Sam," Billie said quietly, then turned her attention to the door, visible from where she stood with the broken pieces in her hand, and thought about how many, many times the woman must have seen it open and close, a two-way stream of comings and goings in her life and in the life of the building. The light from the brightening day outside, where the Earth was shedding the shadow of the moon, sent a pattern of lace from the curtains in the window across a nearby tabletop. Another shadow, as lovely as the light.

Anna Harker

ONE DOESN'T THINK, USUALLY, WHEN ONE WAKES, that this will be the last time, the last morning, the last day. I woke this morning from dreams of Wade Daniels to the reality of my life with Henry: the empty half of the bed beside me, the sound of the fire in the stove, the smell of coffee. Henry moving quietly. This was to be our last day here, at the mine; we were to have left yesterday, but Henry said he wanted one more day to repair the sluice boxes and ready the hydraulic cannons for the winter ahead. Though we had already done that. I did not want to appear anxious, anxious to be out of the hills and back in the village by the rivers and Wade, so I said nothing.

I rolled over and parted my lids, blinking as I watched Henry in the kitchen, his red suspenders on his thin but sculpted shoulders, his once white Henley shirt a soft ivory, the color of light dirt. I watched him and I sighed quietly but heavily. How could I leave him? How could I stay?

But the dream was with me, and I clung to its remnants: Wade by the river as he so often is, fishing pole in hand, smiling as his light little lure spun through the air and kissed the swift, rushing water, a glint of sun catching the line. Then there it was, pulled back into the air. It was only a moment, the dream, here then quickly gone. But it was all I could remember of the sleeping hours of my night.

As I smiled inside at the thought of him, I heard a magpie outside, chattering and squawking, and I glimpsed a flash of iridescent wing out the small and cloudy window near where Henry stood. I had seen the magpie yesterday as well. Typically they are not well suited to the hills and I seldom saw them here, but they thrive in the forests below and in those of the rivers of home. The presence of the bird opened up a longing in me for those rivers and those forests, and I felt my winged friend was there for me, because of me, to take me back.

"Time to get up, Anna," Henry said. Or does he say it now?

Time to get up, Anna.

But Henry, I cannot move. You see, someone has struck me with an ax.

"Anna, come on." Henry had been trying not to be mean. But still, I could hear it in his voice: *I am up and you are not. I am doing for us, and you are not. I made the coffee, and you did not.*

And if I had made the coffee, would he have said, *How much did you put in?* And would I have said, *The same as always. Why?*

It's strong.

It shouldn't be.

Well it is, Anna. It's a simple thing, you know, making the coffee. Anyone can do it.

Is it that bad?

No, it's all right. I guess. A pause. *And you spilled some coffee grounds, there, by the stove.*

But this morning, we did not have that conversation, because I did not make the coffee. And he even sounded gentle, he even sounded nice, when he told me it was time. Why? Had he known?

Or was it because we had, oddly, come together under the covers the night before. I had tried to pretend to be asleep when I felt him along my back, his hand stroking the ups and downs of me, rubbing the thin flannel of my worn and dirty nightgown against my skin. I felt his forehead press against the space between my shoulder blades, and I felt his warm breath find its way through the cloth. Then his arms came around me and across the front of me, and I felt him tremble. One of my hands found one of his bare forearms, and I stroked the fine hairs that grew above muscles made taut and firm from the summer's hard work, his skin familiar and warm. We spoke no words as he rolled me toward him and lifted my nightgown above my head, and I felt my own breathing quicken as he kissed me in a way he hadn't in years and began to move on top of me. When he was finished he stayed there for a while, and I ran my finger through his dampened hair and heard him whisper, "Anna."

Anna.

I am back to the feel of the tundra beneath me. A noise comes from my mouth, a shapeless, wordless noise. I move my eyes and I see him, Henry. He is sitting nearby, on a large rock jutting out of the ground, his head hanging, and he is crying. I want to reach him, but I can't move. I feel his hand on my cheek.

Anna. Anna, I am sorry. I am so sorry.

You did not do this, Henry.

We were to have been gone. Yesterday. We were to have been gone.

Yes.

But I said to stay.

Yes.

I needed one more day.

Yes.

One more day of you here with me.

And one more night, to have me here, here where I had nowhere else to go. Here where I was still his wife. *If that is what you needed, then I am all to blame.*

No, you are not, Anna.

I was not with you, Henry, in the way I should have been. I caused the need.

No. I was there, too, Anna, in our life together. I looked away when I should have looked at you. I looked at spilled coffee grounds, when I should have looked at you.

He sits beside me. Does he? I cannot tell if he is here, or if he is here only in my mind. But it is a comfort; Henry and I are old friends. It feels as if there are no secrets now, at the end of all things us.

Wade Daniels

THE FINN'S PLANE LIFTED as it neared the end of the rough runway located where the rugged road into the hills ended at Harrisville, a large mining camp with a roadhouse. Trails to other camps fanned out from there like the scraggly branches at the top of an old, long stretching tree. Once in the air the Finn circled back toward where he'd left Fairfield and Wade, tipped his wing, then disappeared into the graying sky.

"He's just a kid," Fairfield said, his eyes still looking into the distance where the plane disappeared. "Hard to believe."

Wade nodded numbly, slightly aware of the shift in temperature that came with the higher altitude. "Let's go," Wade said, nodding toward the group of men approaching from the roadhouse.

Fairfield followed his gaze. "Damn," he said.

"You're the commissioner," Wade said. "Tell them to gather up some camping gear, food, and give us an hour's start."

Fairfield's eyes slid to the side behind his tiny round glasses. "Between you and me, I don't know what the hell I'm doing. We don't have murders around here."

"There are murders everywhere," Wade said, and stood back while Fairfield lifted his hand to give his orders to the small scattering of men who had not yet left the hills, any one of which could be the murderer.

"All right, everyone," Fairfield began, and Wade blocked out the drone of words and looked at the expanse of hills and felt the weight of the heavy, gray sky.

A short time later he and Fairfield were on the trail toward the Harkers' claim, studying the ground in front of them as they went. Wade knew that for the first two miles or so anything they found would be hard to tie to what happened as the trail branched off to several other claims along the way; the trail had also been freeze-dried by the nightly dips of temperature and in general would not be good for tracking. So Wade scanned the hills as they moved along, hoping they would speak to him and show him where Anna was. His most hopeful thought was that she was hiding somewhere, tucked away in a nest of brush or crouched low behind one of the ice age boulders that interrupted the tundra. But hiding didn't seem like Anna. He had seen her shoot spruce hens and had heard the stories of her taking down moose just barely in range. She knew how to use a gun. But she also knew, he reminded himself, how to swing an ax.

After about a mile Fairfield said, "Hold up a minute."

Wade stopped and turned. Fairfield set his briefcase down and wiped his glasses with a blue handkerchief. He's out of shape, Wade realized. "Let me carry that," he said, lifting the case before Fairfield could protest.

"Thank you," the older man said. "You never know how heavy something is until you carry it for a few miles." His breathing was labored, and Wade realized they had no water with them, no weapons, nothing. Water they could find, but what if they needed a gun?

As if thinking the same thoughts, Fairfield said, "I was in such a hurry to get to the scene before it was corrupted, I didn't think through what we might need."

Wade nodded. "Wish I had my rifle," he said.

"All's I got is my .38," Fairfield said, tapping the side of his coat.

"Well, that'll do," Wade said, somewhat surprised the commissioner would carry a gun best suited to kill people. "Unless we meet up with a bear."

"Bears aren't our worst problem, I'm afraid. Should we make a plan?"

"Stay close," Wade said, "and keep looking around. It's hard to sneak up on someone around here."

"That's one of the many things I don't understand."

Wade nodded, but his mind was spinning. Perhaps Harker and Peterson were distracted, and there was wind. Or perhaps whoever killed them was walking beside them, or standing with them, until the moment arrived.

"We should keep moving, I suppose," Fairfield said. "Those fellas will be catching up before we know anything, and Merkle is on his way too."

Wade had been in front, and that was where he wanted to stay to try to quicken Fairfield's pace, but he stepped behind Fairfield and now brought up the rear, to keep an eye on the landscape behind them. Miles stretched out in all directions, lonely in the increasing gray of the day. The wind whispered of snow. It was four miles to the Harker claim.

When they came to a branch in the trail, Wade pointed the way, and after a few more ups and downs in the landscape they could see the Harkers' camp, ominously still, on the side of a distant hill. Wade's heart was thundering in his chest, but he concentrated on the ground along the sides of the trail. He soon saw where something had passed through the springy tundra and its low-lying brush. "Wait," he said. The older man paused on the trail while Wade gingerly stepped off it and hunched down low to the ground.

"What have you got?" Fairfield asked.

It was easy to see: the straight lines through the brushy tundra, then the clusters of bent branches and compressions on the surface of the ground, the lowbush blueberry bushes, barren. "Someone was picking berries," he said, feeling his voice wanting to choke.

"Could have been Mrs. Harker," Fairfield said. "Make note of the spot."

Wade nodded and rejoined Fairfield, scuffing the side of the trail with his boot.

Fairfield looked back down the way they came. "Let's get to where those bodies are. Those fellows are going to be hot on our trail soon, and I'd put money on the fact that Merkle by now has caught up with them or is not far behind." Fairfield stepped aside so Wade could set the pace, the older man following as best he could.

Wade's heart beat as they neared the camp, and he felt sick and weak. Fairfield pulled his pistol out, and in silence they circled the small cabin and the similar outbuilding. A haunting hush had settled over the area, the buildings void of life and movement. The feel of the place echoed hollow in Wade's soul. Death. Death was here.

"Come along now," Fairfield said. "The worst is coming."

They found the trail that began at the back of the camp. As the landscape took a downward turn and they came over the crest of the hill, they saw the bodies of the two men up ahead. Wade felt his knees going weak as he followed Fairfield. Once in Vermont he had helped the state police track a missing boy. They found him at the bottom of a small cliff, on the slightest sliver of land beside a gurgling stream. Wade was sure the boy was gone; he was so still. But no. There was a pulse. The boy was rescued and eventually recovered.

A strange whooshing noise startled Wade back to the now. He looked frantically behind behind, then realized the sound came from above—a raven, flying low and swishing past to circle in the air above the bloody corpses. Once again Wade felt his stomach lurch. Several other ravens rose off the bodies as they approached, and a black and white magpie hopped along the bloody ground.

Fairfield stopped some twenty feet away. "All right," he said. "Take a breath my young friend, steady yourself. Pretend you are a set of eyes, nothing more. I need you to go first and look at the trail. Your eyes will be better than mine. Just look at the trail. Here—hand me that case."

Wade moved his arm and Fairfield took the briefcase, quickly opened it, and tied some strips of red survey tape on either side of the trail. Wade heard his heavy breathing behind him as he walked slowly forward, studying the trail and the terrain beside it.

"Stop," Fairfield said, and Wade could see on the ground in front of him an open palm, white and waxlike, a gold band circling his ring finger. As Wade lifted his gaze he saw first the top of Henry Harker's head, then the other arm sprawled to the right, then finally the face of the dead man, the right side of which was crushed and bloody, the glasses twisted and embedded in the mess. The other side of the face was more recognizable, the forehead clean save for red dots of blood, the nose chiseled and straight, the lips lightly parted. But the eye bulged unnaturally from the socket, as if to escape its lifelong home. Wade wobbled. Past Henry, Nate Peterson lay sprawled across the trail, on his stomach—unlike Henry who lay on his back—his head nearly split in two.

"All right," Fairfield said. "I would say they were attacked from behind, Nate first. Then Henry turns around."

Wade nodded.

"Can you get around the bodies, and check the trail on the other side?"

Wade nodded again.

"Be careful not to disturb anything."

Wade scanned the ground in front of him before each step, carefully picking his way past the bodies. There was a clicking noise; Fairfield had produced a camera and was photographing the scene. Wade tried to concentrate. The ground told him little; the trail was dry and lightly frozen. There were echoes of boot tracks—a heel here, a toe there—but nothing distinct. And hadn't he and Jake walked down this trail themselves not long ago? Any boot tracks left by the killer would be hard to separate from all the others.

Fairfield was clucking his tongue. "Looks like an ax, like Montana thought," he said. "Nate got the blade, and Henry got the blunt end. It's hard to imagine anyone sneaking up on them with all this open country. Most likely they knew their killer, and he or she was walking along behind them down the trail."

"She?" Wade felt his mouth go dry.

"We have to consider everything, son."

Wade looked at the bodies on the ground, then at the country all around them. No, he said to himself. *No.*

Billie Sutherland

BILLIE AWOKE IN THE MORNING to a spare, simple room. Her bed was narrow and hard, her blankets worn and thin. There was a single window with some old muslin curtains held up by a piece of wire wrapped around a nail on either side. The room had a small sink, topped by an old, filmy mirror. That was okay. In her reflection she seemed softened, muted, vague. Indistinct. The water from the spout was cold as she splashed her face. *Time to wake up, Billie,* she thought. *Time to wake up.*

After she dressed and wandered down the hall toward the dining room, she saw her landlady—Maddie, Madeline Merkle, who had probably been up for hours—wiping down a table then reaching for a stack of dirty plates.

"I'll get that," Billie said, rushing forward, then added, with more restraint, "I can get those." Maddie smiled and gave her a nod. They had agreed Billie would help out in exchange for a reduced rate on the room. Billie stepped forward, picked up the plates, and followed Maddie back to the kitchen, where she would start her day washing the dishes that had already gathered in the sink while Maddie finished the baking. Later she swept floors, did laundry in a gas-powered machine out back, and chopped vegetables for soup. There was little talk; Maddie didn't seem to do much of it as she tended to her duties of caring for the roadhouse as if it were a proud but aging parent, and Billie welcomed the silence, especially her own.

She found more silence that evening. After Maddie's early retirement and an hour of trying unsuccessfully to settle into a novel, Billie put her shoes back on and slipped out the door. In the light of the summer night she walked down the middle of the unpaved Main Street and saw nobody; even the Clearwater Inn was closed for the evening. Where do the people go, she wondered, and imagined little houses tucked back in the side streets and quiet corners. *A town whose time has come and gone* was how Aunt Sam described it, but Billie saw it as a living thing in a quiet moment, a state of replenishing. And she liked it like this, like a face with no makeup where the skin could freely breathe. As they hung up laundry together, Maddie had told her about the Dena'ina, many of whom had perished in the 1918 flu epidemic, and who for hundreds of years lived and fished in the summer along the banks of the Susitna River, where the village now sat. The Sultana River, whose junction with the Susitna framed two sides of the village, was the river of their mountain winter home, far off into the hills to the east. The Tatum River, robbed of its Native name, cut through the heart of the Alaska Range and joined the Susitna north of the village. The lucky land river, which spilled down through hills of gold.

Billie stepped off the road and into the village park, finding the rough log bench she had sat on with her aunt during the eclipse, when the town had filled like a balloon with air then eased back to its normal state. This. What she wanted to see when she left Aunt Sam to ride the train home without her, the town in its natural state. She pulled a cigarette from the pocket of her wool shirt then changed her mind and slipped it back into place. A cigarette seemed like an intrusion on this midnight-sun late night, though she realized the smoke might help with the mosquitoes that rallied around her now that she was still. She batted them away with her hand, noticing that the polish on her nails was beginning to chip. She wondered when another northbound might come along, other than the fast-moving freights that rumbled through and broke the silence. She had asked her aunt to include a bottle of polish remover in the box of belongings Sam had agreed to send.

Some polish, too? Aunt Sam had asked.

No.

At the sight of movement Billie looked across the street where the village airstrip lay like a wide road, beginning a stone's throw from Main Street just past the trading post and ending down where the river takes a broad curve. A tall figure in dull green coveralls strode over to the silver airplane she'd spotted yesterday. Thin with thick, dark blond hair, he walked around the plane and touched it as if it were a well-ridden horse put to bed. She felt conspicuous, like an intruder, in the softly lit night and wished someone else would appear on the street to dilute her presence. She opted to remain still, as if she were nothing more than another element in the evening's painting of the town. But the figure straightened from where he had been bending over to inspect a wheel, turned, and looked in her direction. Looked at her, she knew, as if he had felt her eyes on him. Billie didn't know what to do so she lifted a hand in greeting. He responded in kind, then walked back across the airstrip toward the ramshackle airplane hangar Billie had seen tucked behind the trading post, glancing her way as he went.

A short time later a different figure appeared, this one at the end of Main Street, down past the roadhouse near the river, and long minutes passed as the person approached, walking slowly with a tall slim stick made from a piece of diamond willow. An old man, wearing a broad-brimmed black hat. When he drew closer he stopped and looked at her with an expression on his bearded face that made Billie wonder if he couldn't really see her. Then he lifted his hand, as if he could reach across the distance between them and touch her. She let her eyes connect with his, her heart beating uncomfortably. Then the noise of a machine invaded the quiet and a beat-up station wagon came roaring into the scene from one of the few roads that went no farther than a few miles out of town. It was filled with teenagers, and as they drove past, a freckled-faced boy stuck his head out of the window and yelled, "Murderer!" as loudly as he could to the great amusement of his friends. The car turned at the village airstrip, turned again, and Billie heard it speeding back the way it came. Heart pounding, she looked at the old man, who walked steadily past. Her hands were shaking and she searched her wool shirt for the cigarette. *Murderer.* Was that meant for him, or was that somehow impossibly, possibly, meant for her?

Anna Harker

I MET HENRY, darling Henry, when I was eight years old. His family had just moved their trading post from a similar settlement down the river, coming to where the prospects were brighter as the freshly completed new route of the railroad, which ran right past the village and cut through the mountains all the way to Fairbanks, lessened the need for river travel. Settlements not along the railroad route were dying early deaths.

Henry was ten. I remember my first sight of him, weighed down with bags and trudging along the street from the river toward his new home, his two younger sisters trailing behind. He wore glasses and had straight brown hair that fell softly around his face. His cheeks were red from the weight of the bags he carried, and he wore a plaid wool jacket that was slightly too large for him.

The store—with living quarters up above—had already been built by his father and a crew of men while Henry and his mother and sisters remained behind tending the old store until the move could be made. They arrived by steamboat, and I watched them from the window of the roadhouse. Henry's head was bent forward. He must have felt my eyes because he looked and saw me there through the glass.

I see the inside of the store now and can feel myself standing by the counter. Henry sits on a stool on the other side, head bent over some writing work he is doing. His mother, a round woman not very tall and not nearly as pretty as my mother, leans toward me and says, "What can I get you?"

Her eyes are small. I can feel her judging me, my dirt-stained hands and my rolled-up jeans, a boy's flannel shirt. I catch a glimpse of her two little girls, in clean dresses, playing among some crates at the far corner of the log-walled store.

"My mother wants some baking powder," I say.

"And who might your mother be?"

"Maddie Merkle."

"Oh. You're one of the Germans, then," she says, as my mother by that time had married Thomas Merkle. "Funny, I thought they were a cleaner people."

I meet her gaze. I don't say anything, but in my mind I am washing her hair with mud, the woman who would one day be my reluctant mother-in-law, Helen. Helen Harker. Those eyes that always watched me—

She hands me a tin of powder, red with white writing, and says she will write it down on the account for the road-house. I should run along, she says, but I am looking at the boy behind the counter and her voice is faint and distant. Henry. I want to say this now: *Henry!* In the store that day he glances briefly at me, as if he is an old man at his papers, and I am just a child.

Then I am standing in the store again, years later from that one particular day. I still wear jeans and a boy's flannel shirt, though this pulls now across my chest. I look Helen point blank in the eye, level with her now. She hands me a parcel for my mother, her eyes suspicious and wary as they would always be with me, and Henry, back on that stool behind the counter, looks at me and drops his pen.

"Anna, you should wear a dress, or at least a skirt," my mother said years later as she stood in the low doorway of my little cubby of a room.

"I changed," I offered, and nodded toward the pile of dirty clothes on the wooden floor near the foot of my bed.

"Gracious," my mother said. "I've let you too long go wild. Come here." She stepped into the room and opened the door of my clothes cupboard. There was the blue dress that her mother—Grandma—had sent me for Christmas, never worn. She looked at me, her brows raised.

I shook my head.

"Anna."

"All right," I said. "How about the skirt?" There was the brown wool skirt, lightly checkered, that fell to the middle of my calves, and I could wear it with my mukluks—the ones my stepfather had made for me when I was fifteen, out of tanned and beaded moose hide—and a denim shirt.

My mother pulled the skirt from the cupboard, followed by a white blouse with a high neck—the only blouse I owned.

"Must I?" I asked.

"Please. Anna. Don't make me regret letting you dress as you pleased."

"Why is it so important that tonight I don't dress as I please?"

"You know why. Henry is home and he wants to see you." Henry was newly returned from college in Seattle, and I had not seen him for several years.

"Henry has seen me most of his life, Mama. Just as I am."

She stepped forward and pushed a wayward curl off my face. "I know. And he sees how beautiful you are."

I felt the color rise to my cheeks, then, and for the first time, felt a strange fluttering inside. The sensations repeated when, an hour later, Henry joined us at the roadhouse for the Sunday evening meal, sitting across from me at the long table we shared with the guests as well as any townsfolk who wanted to pay the small sum to partake of our food and conversation. That night at the table there were only men besides my mother and me. The mining season was to start soon, and the man we called Montana—dark and brooding and rarely at our table— and the large, pretentious John Capp were there, on their way to the mines, as well as Commissioner Fairfield, whose wife had left him the winter before. I looked across the table at Henry and saw that he was now a man.

He caught me staring and smiled back before looking quickly at my father—my stepfather, Merkle, who was talking about the upcoming mining season in the hill country and how he would be leaving shortly to begin the work on our own mine. Then Henry surprised us all and said, "I'll be leaving for there soon myself." He looked first at my stepfather then at me. Our eyes met.

The table fell silent. The men looked at Henry. "Where will you be?" John Capp asked.

"Up Ramshackle. I bought a claim from my father."

I felt the effect of his words prickle around the table. I could not help but glance at Montana; it was well known that he had lost his own Ramshackle claim to Henry's father in payment for a grubstaking debt. The man turned his face toward the window by the door. Surely, I thought, if he had bought Montana's old claim, Henry knew whose mine his once was?

John Capp, all fuss and bluster, was of course the first to break the silence. "That's a big undertaking. You sure you're up for it?"

Henry held the older man's gaze. "I grew up in Alaska, Mr. Capp," he said. "I know those hills, and I've known enough miners during my life to know what I'm getting into." More silence followed, and I looked at my stepfather, willing him to speak, to say something on Henry's behalf. But he stared straight ahead, stirring his spoon around in his soup.

Then my mother said, "But you went to college, Henry. To become a miner?"

"There's nothing wrong with being a miner, Maddie. It does well enough for us," my stepfather said, finally breaking his own moratorium on words.

"I'm not saying anything against mining," my mother said. "But when you've bothered to get an education, you might as well put it to some use."

"No education is ever wasted," Henry said. "Education helps you do everything better, and I intend to make good use of mine."

I felt a twinge of anxiety for Henry, and I saw the glances exchanged around the table. Then Montana cleared his throat and, still staring at the window to his left, he said, "You think so?" There was the low hum of a growling sound somewhere in his voice.

"An education helps you see the complexities of situations. It simply helps you think better."

I felt color rise up into my cheeks, for the way Henry—handsome Henry, as I was beginning to think of him, he was so changed from the boy I knew—was stepping into it.

Montana's eyes glinted. "You mean to tell me if you and I were out in the wilderness together, lost in a blizzard, or up in the mine pumping nothing but mud, that you'd be better at solving our dilemma and saving our asses than say, someone like me, who actually knows a thing or two from actual experience?"

"Perhaps," Henry said, and Commissioner Fairfield choked on his soup. Thankfully Henry added, "But I would not presume to be able to best a man of the wilderness at skills learned from long experience." Here he paused but then continued when he should have stopped: "At least not initially."

If silence could be loud, it was like a freight train in my ears as my stepfather and the two other miners at the table stared at Henry with muddled expressions of disdain, disgust, and plain old flames of anger on their faces.

"You'll learn," Montana finally said, his eyes sliding in their sockets to shoot Henry a quick glance. "You'll learn."

And learn Henry did, to the surprise of everyone but me.

Wade Daniels

"HERE HE COMES. Good lord. Hang on to your hat."

They could see Thomas Merkle moving swiftly up the trail that wound through the hills. A black raincoat that was over his wool jacket was open and blowing out behind him. A half dozen men followed, like a pack of wary wolves. Wade felt his heart beating as if he had done something, as if Thomas Merkle was coming for him. And he had done something. Would Thomas Merkle be able to see that, somehow read it in his face and hear it in his thoughts?

He had motive for killing Henry. Wade saw how that would look, if his secret life with Anna came out. A love story gone awry.

Fairfield looked around. "All right," he said. "Let's finish marking it off. Quickly now." How long had they been here, examining the scene? It felt like hours but was, at the most, somewhere slightly shy of one.

It took Wade a moment to realize what Fairfield meant. The older man took a spool of string from his case, stepped back a little, and tied the end to a bush, dead leaves showering to the ground. He took several steps toward Wade then said, "Catch," and tossed the unwinding spool through the air. Wade leaned forward and caught it, then followed Fairfield's instruction to tie the string first to one spot, then the next, finally tossing it back to Fairfield to complete the rectangle. "It will have to do," he said. "We can't have those men stomping around everywhere. Did you find anything?"

Wade shook his head. "There are some boot marks, but nothing I can separate out from the others."

"Hmm." Fairfield looked around, scanning the area. "I was afraid of that. Bloody hell." He looked now at the horizon. "With those clouds moving in, that flying kid might not be able to get back up here with the help we need." He looked back the way they had come. Merkle and the men with him were nearing the buildings and moving swiftly toward them. "We need to keep those fellows out of our crime scene."

Wade nodded, wondering how they would do that, filling again with fear as Anna's father drew near. But when Merkle reached them he went straight for Fairfield, grabbing the bigger man by the coat collar and hefting him up into the air.

"Where is my *daughter*?" Merkle hissed, his voice rough with anguish and fear.

"Now, now, Tom, now," Fairfield said, as if speaking to a child. "We don't know yet. We just got up here ourselves. We'll scour these hills until we find her."

As Merkle returned Fairfield to the ground his wounded eyes caught sight of the corpses on the trail. A small sound rattled in his throat, and he made to move forward, but Fairfield stopped him with a sweep of his arm. "Don't go over there, Tom. You don't want to see. And we need to keep the site as clean as possible. I'm trying to get an investigator up here from Anchorage. The Finn should be down there now, but the weather's closing in."

"It's got to be one of us," Merkle said quietly, his eyes slicing across the gathering of men. "It's got to be one of us!" The men from the mines, some standing there now, others only recently gone. Wade was thinking the same thing. It's a big land, but a stranger in the area would have stuck out like the haystack around the needle.

Merkle turned his face toward the cold, gray sky, and Wade could see the flexing of his jaw as the man gritted his teeth against the pain. Then he shouted, "Where is my daughter!" His voice hung for a moment in the moving air, crying out against the shroud of silence that was settling on the hills. It's going to snow, Wade thought; he could feel it in his bones. *Lovey, where are you?* He looked at the miles stretching around them. *Please, please.* He let himself think, for a brief moment, of a figure appearing on a distant hill. Anna alive and unharmed. But the cold hand pressing on his heart warned away any such imaginings.

"All right, all right," Fairfield said, trying to calm the men, some of whom were retching off the side of the trail. "Pull it together, all of you. We need to leave this area alone. It's a crime scene, see? What we need to do, Tom, you and these fellows, organize yourselves and look for Mrs. Harker. She could be out there somewhere, needing us. Nobody go alone, and try to disturb as little as possible between the camp and the mine." While the men who came with Merkle discussed a plan, Merkle took off on his own, turning back toward the camp and quickly disappearing over a rise in the landscape. Fairfield shook his head. The six men who were left took off in groups of two, fanning out across the tundra.

Fairfield looked at Wade, and their eyes met. "This is going to be rough," Fairfield said, "but we have to stay focused. I'm glad you hopped on that plane. I wasn't really thinking about what I was walking into. So. Go down to the mine, and make note of anything odd. We don't have to worry about finding the kill site; that's clear enough. Beyond this mess here, and the need to find Mrs. Harker, I really don't know what to do."

How could he, Wade wondered. As village commissioner he'd probably seen a fight or two and maybe had to help settle some feuds, but Wade imagined that once the railroad was built and families began to settle in the area the occasional violence associated with the gold rush of the turn of the century dissipated and waned.

"Just take a quick look down there," Fairfield said. "I realize you don't have a gun, and I'm not going to part with mine at the moment, but come back this way before you do anything else."

Wade nodded then turned down the trail, aware of the fact the he was walking now over the echoes of the last steps taken by Henry Harker and Nate Peterson.

Billie Sutherland

THE MORNING AFTER BILLIE had witnessed the cry of "Murderer!" from the teenager in the car, she said to Maddie, "Last night there was this older man on the street—with a walking stick and a big black hat. He—" And before she could speak any further, her new landlady turned and walked away, as if Billie hadn't spoken at all. When Maddie returned a short time later, with a list of chores for Billie, she said nothing, and Billie opted not to raise the topic again.

But it bothered her, the scene on the street, and followed her all day like a persistent mosquito. That night she again tried staying in, reading in her small room, her legs stretched in front of her on the single bed and her ears picking up all the quiet sounds of the sleeping roadhouse—a creak here, a rattle there, the sound of Maddie's footsteps in the room upstairs and down the hall. After a while she gave up and walked again into the sleeping village, the light soft and dusky. The "simmer dim" they call it in the Shetland Isles, a term Billie found fitting for the extended twilight of Alaska's midsummer nights. As a child growing up in Anchorage her nine o'clock bedtimes were torturous; all she wanted was to be back outside, running around the neighborhood with children whose parents let them stay up later, or to be swinging quietly in the backyard, lost in thought. As a teen her rebellious years began with midnight escapes through her window to rendezvous with those same neighborhood kids she used to listen to through the screen that kept the mosquitoes out. And later, there would be boys, some from her small high school and some not, hidden in the trees of the neighborhood, waiting for Billie to climb out of her window. She was simmering, simmering in the simmer dim.

She'd lost her virginity in the shabby cab of her favorite boyfriend's old Ford truck. Joy. His name was Joy.

Your mother named you well, Billie would say to him.

And your mama would hardly think so, he'd reply. And then they'd laugh.

Billie left him behind, like she did all the others, when she flew away into the world. But she would see him sometimes, when she landed in Anchorage, now a brawny lumberjack of a man with a redheaded wife and a string of redheaded children. And his wife wore a smile that whispered there across her lips, a smile that signaled to Billie that Joy was still aptly named.

Now as she headed down the street she could see that the village was, again, quiet and empty, save for the pilot back at his plane. At the sound of her footsteps he looked up from the nose of the aircraft and nodded. Billie hesitated, then walked up to him to say hello.

"Is this your plane?" It was a stupid thing to say, she knew, but in her new state of being she couldn't think of anything else. Old Billie, old simmering Billie, would have sauntered up to the plane and said, *Take a girl flying?*

"Yes. Who are you?" He was looking at something on the other side of the plane and only glanced briefly at her.

"Billie Sutherland."

"And where are you from, Billie?"

"Anchorage. Who are you?"

"Atlee Virtanen."

Billie looked over the nose of the plane, the wind blowing her hair across her face. "That's an interesting name." Stupid again. She felt the old Billie inside of her wanting to turn up her lips and narrow her eyes and say, *What kind of a name is that?*

The pilot's head was still tipped downward as he fiddled with something on the outside of his open door. Then he looked up, leaned backward a little, and Billie could fully see his face: rugged and boyish at once, and she would have thought him younger than he was if not for something in his eyes. He'd been in the war, she guessed, even before she saw the jagged scar along his jawline on one side of his face. He arched an eyebrow. "People call me the Finn."

"*The* Finn?"

"Local folks gave it to me when I first got here," he said. "I figured I got off lucky. It could have been worse."

She smiled a little. "I could imagine." She rubbed her hand across the silver body of the plane, which was trimmed sparingly with green on the nose and the wings. "She's a beauty."

"Never thought of Bud as a she—or a he for that matter—just Bud," he said. When he smiled, lines dimpled around his eyes. Blue eyes, sky blue. Billie found herself smiling again, then quickly looked away.

"So, what's the story, Billie?"

"The story?"

"Why are you here?"

Maybe you could help me out with that one, the old Billie would say, but the new Billie could only shrug and pull away the hair that blew across her naked lips.

"Just grounded?" he said when she didn't answer.

51

"What?"

"Grounded plane. Taking a break. Repairs and rest."

His partial accuracy sent a jolt through her. She remembered the man in the black hat and looked over her shoulder down the street, but there was no sight of him.

"When I was out here last night—" she began.

"Umm. I saw you."

"There was a man with a black hat and a walking stick."

"We call him Montana. That's where he was from, a long time ago."

"Some kids in a car came by."

"I heard them."

She met his eyes. She knew he was waiting for her to ask, but she found she couldn't say the words. Her heart had sped up and her mouth was going dry.

"You're wondering why they called him a murderer," he said for her.

"Yes." She felt a strange relief washing through her like a cool rinse. But of course they—the teenagers—couldn't have known anything about her.

"That's a long story," the Finn said, returning to his work on the plane. "I'm probably not the one to tell you."

"Okay," she said.

"You're staying at the roadhouse, aren't you?"

"Yes."

"Do yourself a favor and don't ask Maddie about it."

She hoped he couldn't see the color rise in her cheeks as she remembered Maddie's reaction to the mention of the old man.

"When Maddie wants you to know, Maddie will tell you," he added.

"Tell me what?"

"What happened to her daughter."

Her mouth opened, but she quickly closed it. After a moment of awkward silence she said goodnight and walked back to her room.

Anna Harker

THERE IS NO SIGN OF SNOW TODAY. But it is coming soon—I feel it in the north wind blowing strong—and it will whip around these hills until they're wrapped in white and the ground and all upon it is buried beneath. I think, if no one finds me before the snow comes, then I may not be found. At first the thought flutters my heart with new panic, but then I think, Would that be so bad? Provided the late bears miss me on the way to their dens, and the snow piles on top of me and hides me from the wolves and all others who might think I would make a hearty meal. I could be a fairy-tale princess, asleep in the wild.

There is a gurgling in my throat, and I think for a moment I can speak, but warm liquid fills my mouth and I know no words will come from me. But I still breathe, I still see, and I still think; I will think, and I will think, and I will think, I will let my mind be a fire and my thought the fuel that feeds it and feeds it until the last spark disappears into darkness. I will think again about Henry, and maybe I will understand how I made the mistakes I made.

I walked with Henry by the river that night, the night of that awful dinner where Montana's anger burned like the heart of a heated coal. The daylight lingered now, as we sped toward summer, the water newly freed from its icy prison. It rushed past us, gray and brimming, with a deep, steady roar. A short distance from where we stood a second river merged with this larger one, and a short distance from that joining, a third river ran into it as well, a confluence, and now all as one swept speedily to the sea over one hundred twisting, turning miles away. It was still cool; I felt it in my cheeks and in the tip of my nose, and here and there a patch of snow continued on, dirty and soggy, sheltered from the sun that tonight was covered by a veil of thin, gray clouds.

"I thought about you so much, Anna," Henry said, walking beside me with his hands in his pockets, his hair falling forward over the top of his glasses. "The whole time I was gone. I couldn't wait to get back to see you."

"You didn't write," I noted. "I would have written back." Bonaparte seagulls—tern-like with their black-capped heads—swirled in the air above us. A small and delicately long-legged snipe pecked at the gray wet shore, hopping from one silt-covered rock to the next. Just days before the river had broken up—ice chunk after ice chunk after ice chunk churning down the gray water—and now it was as if the winter, and the quiet frozen landscape it had created, had never existed. Unlike some, I missed the winter when it was absent and did not mourn the passing of summer, though summer was a time of year I enjoyed immensely. But I felt the land more in its quiet state—there was something in the short twilight of a winter afternoon that stirred an aching inside of me, disconcerting and beautiful at once.

"It would have been impractical to write," Henry said. "I was miles and miles away and wouldn't be able to come back for years, then months, then weeks, then days. But I hoped you would still be here and would still be—" here he paused, searching for the right word, "unattached." He pushed his hair back from his forehead, a move that transformed the familiar face of the boy I knew back into that young man across from me at the dinner table.

I felt my face frown, even though I was trying to smile as I wrestled with the feelings that were at odds with each other inside me. There was something in the words he used that put a shadow over what he was trying to say to me—I would learn this about Henry, in the years to come, that he pulled everything back so that my heart would not sing too loudly. I have never been certain if he has been aware of this effect on me; it is among the many things we failed to talk about.

He looked at the river, his eyes following a piece of lonely driftwood rushing by, and then looked again at me. I saw something in his eyes then, some mix of caution and fear that squeezed at my heart and I felt a need, for his sake, to lighten the intensity of the moment we had found ourselves in.

"It's nice out tonight," I said.

"Yes," he replied, relief flooding his face. "Except for the bugs, of course." He waved his hand at the mosquitos hovering above his head.

I nodded, feigning agreement, but until that moment I hadn't noticed the detractors of the evening.

Another evening, again by the river, Henry standing before me, his hands tightly by his side. "May I kiss you, Anna?" he asked, not looking at me as the words left his lips but then sliding his gaze cautiously to meet mine.

I did not know what to say at first. I did want him to—I could feel, standing so near him, the faint warmth from his body and smell the clean, fresh-off-the-clothesline scent of his clothes. I had noticed in recent days that his shoulders, though still slender, had broadened from his boyhood frame, and I felt a strange longing to touch them, to feel the lean strength of them beneath the fabric of his chambray shirt. But I had not imagined ever being asked for a kiss; I imagined it happening suddenly, unexpectedly, with the swiftness of a trout leaping up from the waters of a stream.

But maybe I did not know how these things were done. The village had few young people, and my experience with kisses was as slim as the cracks between the logs in the walls of our roadhouse, which Uncle Mike had built well. I had only been kissed once, by a boy who had been my friend. He didn't ask.

"Yes," I said, trying to sound neutral least I scare him away. "You may."

"Thank you," he said, nodding slightly and closing the small distance between us. My heart beat fiercely and I struggled to keep my breath regular and inaudible. He was staring downward toward our feet on the river sand, a studious, quiet look upon his face. I was on the verge of feeling disappointment when his hand landed gently on the side of my face, and he took off his glasses and tipped his forehead against my own. Then his eyes lifted and looked into mine. His were gray-green, the color of lake water on a quiet, cloudy day, and I looked deeply into them, my lips parted in silent anticipation. Then he closed his eyes and I felt his warm, clean mouth find mine, and as he carefully and gently kissed me I felt the blood rushing through me like the water in the river when the ice breaks. Just as I was going to throw my arms around him he stepped back, and the kiss was over.

"You're all grown up now, aren't you, Anna?" he said, his pale cheeks flushed. He put his glasses back on. I remember how I stood there, unable to move, unable to guess what he felt or thought. Then a smile came to his face, and to my intense delight he took my hand and kissed me again.

And so we began.

Wade Daniels

> *Let us go, lassie, go*
> *To the braes o' Balquhither,*
> *Where the blaeberries grow*
> *'Mang the bonnie Highland heather;*
> *Where the deer and the rae,*
> *Lightly bounding together,*
> *Sport the lang Simmer day*
> *On the braes o' Balquhither.*

WADE HEARD THE SONG in his head, one from his childhood, his Scottish grandfather strumming an old dark-honey-colored guitar in the Vermont farmhouse where Wade grew up. His grandfather, Artie, would sing it in the spring when the snow was all but gone and the tulips Wade's mother planted were poking their heads out of the thawing ground. Every spring of his life he thought of Artie, long dead, and that song.

Now the song came back to him unwanted in this dark desperate fall, and all it brought with it was Anna.

"I will twine thee a bow'r . . . By the clear siller fountain." He had whispered the words as she lay beside him on the scratchy wool blanket he'd put over the ground between the cabin and the lake, his lips moving against her black hair. He could feel the smile forming on her face where it rested against his chest.

"What's this?" she whispered back.

"A song."

"Well go on with it."

"And I'll cover it o'er . . . Wi' the flowers o' the mountain."
This time he sang, quietly, his voice barely breaking above a
whisper. Then he said, skipping ahead, "Let us go." He heard
the shift in his voice as he said this, felt the increase in the
beating of his heart. "Lassie, go."

Anna stilled, and for a moment he swore she didn't
breathe. He'd tried to swallow against his now dry throat.

"To the braes o' Balquhither," he began, then breathed
and said, "Go with me, Anna. Me."

She was quiet a long time. Or maybe it only felt like a
long time; he couldn't tell. The world seemed to stop.

"Where would we go?"

"The mountains. The States. Anywhere."

"Anywhere but here," she said.

"It would have to be."

"I can't do that."

"I can't do this."

And so they said nothing further, and the evening took
over as the birds sang and the mosquitoes buzzed around
them and the sky above them turned a soft, easy blue, and he
stared at it wishing it would tell him what he was supposed to
do. Eventually he kissed the top of her head and sighed, and a
short time later he watched her pull her boots back on as she
sat on the ground and tried to smile.

"I guess I'll see you out there," she said as she stood.
Mining season was starting. Both Henry and Jake were already
in the hills.

"Yeah," he said. "See you out there." He stood so he could
watch her leave, her fishing pole in her hand, walking down

the rough trail, in the almost-summer night. She turned once and looked back at him, and as she did the early-arriving loon cried out again and she smiled.

The image brought a choking feeling to his throat, as if invisible hands reached up from somewhere inside of him, taking his breath away from the inside out.

Now he approached the mine's operation area cautiously, though the weight of the stillness, save for the rushing stream, seemed telling of its lifeless state. The operation was shut down and organized. The wooden sluice boxes were emptied and arranged in a tidy row; the two water cannons, out of place in this natural world, were clean and dry and tarped, ready for their winter of rest. A small storage cabin, gray and weathered, was padlocked on the outside. Shortly before they left the hills, Wade and Jake had been down here, visiting Henry and Nate, admiring the sleek cannons—antiques, actually, shipped up from California where they once worked in those distant mines of another time. The cannons—each easily operated by a single man—were envied by the other miners in the area for their power and small size. And they looked like cannons, whereas what the other miners were using looked like strange spewing serpents and were aptly called "monsters." Wade imagined the two men, tending to final details, jovial perhaps, as another successful season came to a close. That it was successful Wade had no doubt; Henry's nickname among the miners was "King Midas," though Jake would say it was the mine, not the man. "That mine oozes gold," Jake said. Then Wade remembered something else: the mine had once belonged to Montana, who lost it to Henry's father when he could not repay the store for grubstaking him. The Harkers had gotten a large number of claims that way. Henry Harker, Wade knew, likely did not have to work this mine—or any mine—practically by himself if he didn't want to.

The hills had a network of trails, connecting the mines and the camps and the waterways. Wade walked a ways past the storage cabin to where the land sloped upward away from the ditch the water made. He found a small ribbon of trail cutting through the brush that led upward to connect with a second, larger trail that wound along the crest of the rise. While it appeared someone—or something—had walked over the surface in recent days, the marks were vague and indistinct. How it all happened would depend, Wade knew, on whether the person or persons were trying to surprise Henry and Nate, or whether the assailant—or assailants—had simply walked up and said hello, then followed the two men down the trail on their way back to the camp.

He took a deep, shaky breath, then hurried back past the operation site to find Fairfield, who was now crouched low to the ground, examining the wounds on the fallen men. "Anything?" he asked when Wade appeared.

"No. Everything looks orderly, like they'd cleaned up." He wanted to add, "to leave," but he found he couldn't say the words aloud. "Montana—you know this used to be his claim."

"Yes," Fairfield said. He huffed. "I think some of those fellows are on their way to his cabin now. I couldn't stop them. But they should be searching for Mrs. Harker, and they damned sure shouldn't try exacting any justice on someone who might only have had the bad luck of stumbling on the scene."

Wade knew how that went, though, how it was when someone discovered a crime. It made you the first suspect, and Wade could never see the logic in that.

"On that note, go see what you can do about locating Mrs. Harker. It's going to be getting dark soon, and given those clouds I think we can give up on that flying kid making it back here today."

Wade was already on his way before Fairfield completed his thought. He rushed past the camp and back down the trail they came on. His goal was to find the berry-picking spot they had passed on the way and see if it led anywhere, but there was somewhere he needed to check first. He found the side trail that cut toward the stream where he would sometimes meet Anna and followed it, going up and down the rising and falling of the land, his heart in his throat each time a fresh section of terrain opened up before him. Finally the stream appeared, clear and bright like liquid crystal, and he hurried down to the sliver of shore. There were her tracks, all across the little stretch of beach, but no sign of anyone else, a struggle, or trouble. He sank to his knees. "Anna," he said softly to the fading footprints in front of him. "Anna." Then at once he stood up and looked around at the enormity of the country. "Anna!" he said louder, then it came out again, in a cry that fled his throat and flew out across the hills. "Anna!" He was going to yell again when a figure appeared on the crest of a nearby knoll. Thomas Merkle looked down at him from above.

Billie Sutherland

THE ROADHOUSE WAS FULL of photographs. They marched along every shelf and dresser top, marking years, nodding to a history filled with hunters on snowshoes holding aloft strings of white hares or in a dense fall forest straddling the enormous antlered head of a dead moose. Miners stood by rushing rivers of water, intent on the contents of their pan or looking up at the camera, eyes filled with hopes and dreams; trappers held wolverines fierce no longer or round fat beavers pulled out from beneath the ice. There were photos of women skinning carcasses and fleshing hides or boasting buckets of blueberries; horses, boats, dog teams, and later a car or two and bush planes and bush pilots. The Finn. There he was, no more than a tall, sandy-haired boy, arm over the nose of his plane as if it were his prom date, a smile bright and broad. Billie lifted it from the shelf above the old piano in the sitting area and pulled it close. How old had he been? How old was he now? Carefully she replaced the photo and continued her browsing. If Maddie had a daughter, there were no images of her in any of the public spaces.

Billie walked down the long hall to the back of the road-house, past the bathroom and past the small room where she slept. She looked out the window by the back door. Maddie was working in one of two large gardens that stretched out behind the building. Billie watched as she removed the chickweed and chamomile that invaded the spaces between rows and plants, swatting mosquitos as she worked. Billie thought of her own mother and how, even in their times of fiercest disagreement, pictures of Billie remained distributed throughout her parents' house, chronicling every phase of her life. She felt the silence of the roadhouse at her back. It's because something awful happened to her daughter, Billie acknowledged as she continued to watch Maddie working in her garden. And the man with the hat had something to do with it.

She found the photos the following day, as if her interest had sent a signal to the universe to show them to her. She was upstairs, mopping the dark, scarred wood floors of the hallway, the upper bath, and the guestroom, when Maddie called to her to please bring down the iron that was in her bedroom. Maddie's bedroom was to the left of the steep stairwell and faced the street. Billie gently turned the old painted metal knob of the closed door.

The room was plain, tidy, and softly colored in the gray-day light. The bed was made (unlike Billie's), and the clothes Maddie'd worn yesterday were draped neatly over a ladder-backed chair, ready to wear another day. The window was open at the bottom, where a slight breeze blew in through a stretch of screen. And there, covering the top of an old wooden dresser to the left of the window, were photographs. She crept across the floor toward them. The first one was a formal portrait of a pretty, round-faced young woman with dark curly hair. *Here you are,* Billie thought. *Who were you and where have you gone?* The other photos told pieces of a story: here she was, with a very young Maddie and a handsome young man with dark, sparkling eyes—her father? No, Billie thought, looking closer and seeing the resemblance between the man and Maddie. The brother, the one Maddie said came here first and built the road-house. The picture is of the three of them, standing beside the building, itself younger and fresher. There was a photo of the girl, older, fishing by one of the rivers, looking over her shoulder and smiling at the camera, and another of her standing in the snow with a strong-faced, broad-shouldered man beside her—Maddie's late husband, Billie guessed—the two of them holding up strings of furs. Then a wedding photograph in an oval frame, the very lovely young woman beside a handsome young man with combed-back hair and grandfather glasses.

Billie reached out and lightly touched the gilded frame, dust free and gleaming, and wondered if both these young people were gone now, swallowed by the big, whale-like mouth of life where they existed in some unseeable, unreachable world just beyond. As she turned to leave, one last item lying flat on the surface of the dark-skinned dresser caught her eye. It was a piece of tree bark—birch—curled at the edges but smooth in the center. There was writing across it, in a rushed but pretty hand—

Mama. Can't find paper so I hope this will do. All is well and we'll be packing up soon. I gave the Finn five gallons of blueberries which he promised to deliver to you—do make sure he hasn't eaten them on the way!—along with this very crude note. Henry says we have had a very good summer and by the weight of the poke bags I would wager he is correct. I love the hills as always but am so missing the rivers and the trees and trails of the valley and you and the smell of your wonderful bread baking away just for me (alas, I still can't get it right though this miserable camp stove gives me a bit of an excuse). Okay, got to give this to Atlee. I love you dearly and I will see you within the month!

And across the bottom, the name: *Anna*.

Anna. Billie looked at the wedding picture. Anna and Henry. What happened to you both?

The iron—old-fashioned and cast iron—was on the floor near the dresser. Billie grabbed it and slipped out of the room, pulling the door closed behind her. As the knob clicked shut she heard, in the quiet of the near-empty building, the sounds of Maddie moving in the dining area below. How many hours must Maddie's solitary movements be the only sound? For an instant Billie felt that aloneness and echoing quiet, and it invaded her being. In a moment, Billie would go down the stairs and emerge into the dining room, give the woman the iron and a smile. But for now she could only stand, hand still on the doorknob, as if beneath the metal somewhere there was the beating of a heart.

Anna Harker

WE ARRIVED IN SUSITNA STATION on the eve of death, my mother and I, my thoughts now going back before the time of Henry. How is it I so seldom remember this? In later years I would wonder if maybe we had brought it, carrying it along like a stowaway in our luggage, riding with us on the ferry from Seattle to Seward, on the railroad from Seward to Anchorage, and on the riverboat that brought us up the mighty Susitna. Or had it simply followed us, a slippery shadow in our wake, lying in wait to reveal itself shortly before the end of our first year?

The Spanish influenza. In truth it *had* followed us, a likely passenger in the body of someone traveling our same route before the quarantines were put in place. "Why did it come to Alaska?" I remember asking.

"It's everywhere, Anna," Uncle Mike had said.

"Why doesn't it go home?" I asked. I wanted it to leave. I wanted it to leave so I could have my mother back.

My mother had taken it upon herself to help the people in the village who were sick. "I was the only one of us who could," she would say, when we remembered that dark time. I, of course, was young and among the vulnerable; Uncle Mike had asthma. My mother had longed to be a nurse, but my unauthorized arrival in her life had caused a change of plans. So when we heard of the sick and of the dying, as rumors flew up and down a muddy late fall Main Street, she moved into the little storage shed in back so not to bring the flu home to me and Uncle Mike and set about seeing what she could do.

I watched her from the windows of the roadhouse, running from one to another so I could keep her in my view for as long as possible as she would walk quickly to the homes that needed her, carrying pots of soup Uncle Mike and I would make and set outside the back door for her to grab, or stacks of clean bedding she had washed by the river and brought home to dry on lines strung between the trees, or buckets of clean fresh water for drinking. Uncle Mike split wagon loads, and then sled loads, of firewood that my mother would haul away. Uncle Mike wanted to help further and go with her, and so did I, but instead we were sequestered to the roadhouse, our good health quarantined and hoarded.

My mother would press her hand against the window of my room at night, aligning it with mine, and sing to me through the glass:

> Hush a bye, don't you cry
> Go to sleep my little baby
> When you awake, you shall have cake
> And all the pretty little horsies.

While I was dreaming of her return, my mother was living her dream and found herself with a purpose she had not previously known, though the deaths were horrible and haunting, occurring mostly among the village's small population of Dena'ina Indians.

One night from my room, I heard a strange, frightening sound. It was familiar, yet not, and I remember I climbed out of bed and turned the doorknob, big and cold in my little hand. The hallway was long and cavernous, and I was afraid but worry for my mother spurred me onward. The lamps were still lit in the dining room, and a hunched figure sat alone at one of the long tables, shaking and making a strange sound. I stared and stared until slowly it dawned on me it was Uncle Mike sitting there, and he was crying. He startled when I put my hand on his arm.

"Anna!" he said. "What are you doing, little Bunny?"

"Uncle Mike, why are you crying? Why are you sad?" My own tears, now, had pushed their way into my eyes.

"Oh, Bunny, hey, it's all right." He pulled me up onto his lap. I dabbed at the tears on his face with the sleeve of my nightdress. "Sometimes things happen that make people sad."

"Is it the Spain?"

"You could say that, Bunny Rabbit."

"Are the children still sick?"

"Some of them. Some of them are getting better."

"Mommy's helping the children." I was jealous of the children, yet I also imagined they were jealous of me, that they knew the kind lady who brought them fresh water and soup was someone's mommy, and that the someone was me, Anna Lee.

"Yes—she is."

"Are you crying for the children?"

"A little. But there are some big people, too, who got sick."

"Did they die?"

"Some of them." At that Uncle Mike started crying again, his whole body shaking as he gritted his teeth and tried to still the jerking of his sobs.

"What some of them?"

"The chief!" he blurted. "The chief died!"

My mouth made a sound and my eyes widened with both wonder and fear. The chief! If the chief could die, then anyone could. "The chief shouldn't die," I said. "Isn't he big?"

"No, no—not so big, Anna."

"But still he shouldn't die."

"No one should," Uncle Mike said. "Not like this." I didn't know what he meant then until years later when my mother told me how many of the Natives could have been saved, if they had closed the village to people coming and going, like they did with those villages to the north of us where the Native populations were spared. Our own Native population never recovered, and the village to the south suffered greater losses. Uncle Mike picked me up and carried me back down the hallway. "You, little Bunny Rabbit, need to get some sleep," he said as he plopped me down on my bed.

"I don't want you to be sad about the chief," I said.

"Well, I can't help it. But I'll get better."

"What about the children?"

"The chief's children?"

I nodded.

"They're getting better." Uncle Mike pulled my thick wool blankets up to my chin and tucked them tight around me.

"But their daddy died."

"Yes. Yes, he did." And what Uncle Mike didn't tell me was that their mother had died as well, and the two children, George and Nellie, would have to stay now with their aunt Ruby in the woods on the other side of where the tracks would run, in a small cabin that smelled of bleach and dead animals from the hides she tanned for a living. George and Nellie, who in the previous summer had become my friends.

OCTOBER 1, 1941
Wade Daniels

I CAN'T COOK MUCH, but I can roast a mean spruce hen.

She had come out of nowhere to his cabin site, where he had sequestered himself since returning from the mines, desperately trying to get a roof over his head before the snow fell.

"Spruce hens are mean?" he said, an attempt at cleverness she only rolled her eyes at. He stood up from where he had been straddling a log, peeling off the bark with a drawknife. Anna held a small caliber rifle in her hand and a cluster of dead, fluffy birds hung from her packboard.

"Keep working," she'd said, setting down the rifle and taking off her pack. "Since I'm in the neighborhood, and since you've got a fire going, and since I've got more than I can eat, I'll cook us up a couple if you don't mind."

"No—no. I don't mind." He'd had a slab of bread smeared with bacon grease earlier in the day, and the thought of grilled meat literally made his mouth water. "So you hunt out here too?" He had met her when she'd come to swim in the lake in the spring, and over the course of the summer they'd found themselves fishing in the same stream at the mines.

"Yes," Anna said. She had taken her knife from the sheath on her belt and was squatting low to the ground, slicing through the feathered coats that covered the birds. "But I checked at the land office in Anchorage which land was yours. I believe these birds belong to the Territory of Alaska." With one smooth motion she peeled the skin from first one then a second bird. She looked over at him, her dark eyes dancing. "Same as me."

They'd both laughed. Wade remembered how they sat by the fire, pulling roasted meat free from the delicate bones of the birds, and before he knew it, she had disappeared back into the woods, leaving him full and full of hunger all at once.

Now he stood inside the rough-hewn walls of the Harkers' camp cabin, staring at the rough little kitchen where Anna must have cooked.

They had rustled up Montana who, since his frantic dash to the Harrisville roadhouse to report the finding of Henry Harker and Nate Peterson, had holed up in his cabin. Two men went to get him and brought him to the Harkers' camp. Montana was asked to sit in a chair facing the small square table, which Fairfield had cluttered with various papers. The rest of the men, numbers growing, clustered in a ring around the room, arms crossed and faces gloomy as they looked at Montana. The group consisted of the men from the Harrisville mine and those from the village who came with Thomas Merkle. No one else had made it yet, including Jake, and with the snow starting no one was expected, at least for now. There was hope the weather would lift enough for the Finn to bring help in the morning. In the meantime, Fairfield continued as best he could, and Wade stood by the door as he watched the questioning. Thomas Merkle was outside, refusing to take part.

"How was it you were over this way to begin with?" Fairfield asked. The men nodded their approval of this question, exchanged glances, eyes darting here and there. The air in the room was thick with the smell of body odor and warming wool, of lots of people breathing in a confined space. Wade felt clammy and lightheaded. He longed for fresh air and wide-open space. And he couldn't fathom that Montana had anything to do with anything.

"I was walking," Montana said in response to the question.

"But this is five miles from your claim," Fairfield pressed. "Surely you've got better things to do than wander over to another man's property."

"I thought they was gone."

"That makes it all the more curious, then, that you would come here." There was another nod of approval from the men.

"I was just walking," Montana repeated.

"Over to someone else's shut down and empty claim."

"For God's sake, Fairfield, why would I kill them then run and tell everyone they was dead?"

"Maybe so we would think just that," Fairfield said quietly, first looking at where his pen drummed against the rough surface of the table then lifting his eyes to once again meet those of the man facing him. Wade could sense how everyone felt the impact of that moment, and it was as if the air in the room fell to the floor.

Montana shook his head. "Fairfield, you know me," he said, his voice low but strong. He glanced around the room. "All of you know me."

Wade saw the color rise in Fairfield's cheeks at that; he didn't like doing this, Wade could tell, but he had to appease the other men in the room.

"This was your claim once, wasn't it?"

"Yes."

"Can you tell me how it's no longer in your possession?"

Montana shook his head. "You mean to tell me that you're the only man in this part of the territory that doesn't know how I lost this spot, or are you just asking because you have some idea that you're supposed to?"

Fairfield's mouth went tight, and he pulled his glasses off and wiped his face with his handkerchief. "Damn it, Montana," he said. He put his glasses back on and looked at the man in front of him. "I don't think you did this, but I haven't the faintest clue how to conduct a murder investigation. There hasn't been a murder in this area since 1925, and I've only been here since '29." He looked at the circle of men in the room. "Marriage certificates, death certificates, the occasional drunk and disorderly. All of you know I'm over my head here, so let's just get that out in the open and done with. Montana, these men have questions. You were on the scene and your new claim is more or less five miles away. Let's give these fellows the answers they need, then let's dig around in your memory of that day and see if there's anything helpful there."

Montana sat quietly for a moment before he spoke. "I lost the claim to old man Harker when I couldn't pay my grubstake bill. Everybody knows that. I couldn't pay my grubstake bill because this claim wouldn't work for me. And everybody knows this mine is golden now. But it wasn't just the mine and it wasn't just the gold. This place was like home to me. So I came over, when I thought they'd gone, so I could be here— see the old place again. And maybe figure out what they were doing that I didn't. But I wouldn't hurt nobody. I never cared much for Henry, but Anna—Anna, well, she's a bright spot. I wouldn't harm her. Wouldn't even harm him. I've got no reason."

A moment of silence settled upon the room, and for a moment the only sounds were the hissing of the woodstove and the rising wind outside the door.

"Did you get the feeling, when you passed through, before you found Henry, that someone was about?"

Montana shook his head. "The place was silent and still. I was sure they'd already gone."

The thick air in the room made Wade feel he couldn't breathe. His gaze kept wandering to the small bed where Anna and Henry must have slept, close together. A marriage bed, a bed where two married people slept and didn't sleep. He could almost feel it looking at him, staring him down as he stood on the other side of the room, his mind filling with thoughts he did not want to think.

"You know we have to find Mrs. Harker." Fairfield's voice was distant now as a strange ringing sound filled Wade's head. "Montana, search your mind, man. Is there anything you can remember from that day?"

"But what day are you talking about, Fairfield? The day I found them or the day they was murdered. How do we know for sure what happened when?"

'You're right," Fairfield conceded. "I can't answer that. But let's just, well—let's just pretend for a moment, all right?"

Above the ringing in his ears Wade heard Anna's voice: *Can we pretend—can we please just pretend?*

He swung around to the door, pulled the latch, and stumbled outside, like a man either dying or drunk.

Billie Sutherland

SHE HAD THOUGHT LIVING in a small town (or village, as Maddie kept correcting her) would be like gazing upon an open book. But she was finding it to be the opposite: the town was closed and quiet, *shadowed*. The old Billie would have hated it, but the Billie she was now welcomed it. The people here left her alone, and she responded in kind. There were only two questions that seemed to come her way: where she was from, and where she was staying. Even the railroad workers and train-riding weekenders, the staple of business at the road-house, asked her little more than that.

She was surprised, though, at the lack of local traffic through the roadhouse, which sat empty for the bulk of the week. Much of Maddie's income seemed to come from baked goods that were sent north on the train—boxes of bread and rolls and muffins and cakes—and it became one of Billie's duties to put the boxes in a wagon and take them up to the train depot. Here she would stand, with a few scattered persons waiting to catch a ride or waiting to meet someone arriving, and when the train pulled in, she would lift the boxes up into the baggage car and send them on their way. In that capacity she was there to collect her own box from a northbound passenger train.

The box contained, of course, a note from her mother:

Billie—

*I hope these are the things you want. Your current
wardrobe, as I'm sure you know, isn't exactly suited to
rural life, but I was able to find a few odds and ends and
combine them with some old things still in your closet.
Of course I am concerned about all these sudden changes
in your life but your father, your Aunt Sam, and Uncle
Howard have all assured me the best course of action
is to let you do what apparently you feel you must. Not
that I ever had much control over what you did and
didn't do. But your father has talked to the management
department at the airlines and was assured that when
you're ready you could very likely go right back to work.
So that's something.*

Mother

Billie read the note on the way back to the roadhouse,
one hand behind her pulling the wagon with her box, then
crumpled it into a tight little ball that she threw into the
kitchen trash upon her return.

For a week now she had not seen the man in the hat, or
the pilot, though of the latter she found a trace: an empty tea
cup on the front counter one morning when she emerged, next
to one of Uncle Howard's newspapers. Billie grabbed the pages
greedily only to find the crossword had already been done in
precise, tidy printing. When Billie asked how on earth the
paper got all the way from Anchorage, Maddie'd said, "It flew
here," as if the black and white pages had wings.

Of the mysterious Anna, she had learned nothing, only that wherever she was buried it was not in the Susitna Station cemetery, where a haphazard mix of handmade crosses, traditional tombstones, and Russian Orthodox spirit houses decorated the quiet grounds.

Then one afternoon Maddie suddenly said, "Oh no you don't, Anna!"

The name had slipped out as Billie's finger reached without thinking for a teardrop of chocolate frosting that was sliding down the side of one of Maddie's famous chocolate cakes.

"Billie," Maddie said quickly. "I mean Billie."

Billie hardly moved, her hand still in the air. She had a choice. Say nothing, ignore. Or seize the moment. "Your daughter," she said and waited.

Maddie glanced around the room, like a trapped bird looking for an open window. "Yes," she said reluctantly. "So you know?"

"A little." Was that a lie? Maybe, maybe not. The old Billie was a liar. *Liars*, the note that she didn't want to think about read. *You're both a couple of liars!*

"Ah, well, it's a small place," Maddie said, sad and resigned.

"I'm sorry. I shouldn't have brought it up."

"Well, I think I'm the one that did that. You remind me of her. Don't know why. Feisty, I guess. Anna was feisty. And couldn't keep her fingers off my cakes."

Billie looked at the counter. There were bits of her reflection, like a fragmented shadow, on the varnished surface. She covered it with her hand.

Maddie sat down on a stool and Billie felt her eyes on her. "But sometimes you're not so feisty, sometimes you don't seem very happy," Maddie said quietly. "I watched Anna go through a phase like that, the winter before she was killed. I wish I had paid more attention. I feel there was a clue somewhere, there in her face during that time, that I had missed."

Billie wondered what clues were on her own face and what they said. She looked at Maddie. "What happened to her?" she asked, her own voice going quiet, too, as if the very walls would object if she asked too loudly.

"She was hacked to death with an ax."

"Oh my God."

"Yes. Oh my God."

Anna Harker

I THINK: WILL I SEE GEORGE? Georgie-Georgie, my dear
Georgie. My first friend at Susitna Station, the first boy to put
his lips on mine. The first boy to feel the pain of my growing
crush on Henry Harker, the shopkeeper's son, and my first
friend, Uncle Mike aside, who died.

It was the summer before the flu found us in the fall, and
I was playing in the dirt by the road outside the roadhouse. The
sun was hot and the mosquitoes were fierce. My mother was
busy baking and I was angry; they were both so busy now, my
mother and Uncle Mike, and I no longer had my grandma and
grandpa to run to. "We have to make it on our own, Anna," my
mother said. "Alaska is our chance, here with Uncle Mike. We
can have our own life now." But I didn't want our own life if it
meant everyone being busy—everyone but me.

"Go find some friends," my mother said.

"No one lives here!" I replied.

"Yes, yes, they do. You just haven't seen them yet, my
darling."

So I sat in the dirt and dug angry little ditches, slapping
the mosquitoes on my arm. I looked down the street. It was
usually empty, except when I would see Uncle Mike returning
from the river when he went fishing without me or when he
was freighting a miner across to the other side, but today I saw
a little brown boy coming toward me. That's what I called him,
when I told my mother about him: the brown boy, though his

80

skin was only several shades darker than my own, and while I, too, had black hair, his was straight while mine curled carelessly around my head. His eyes were mud-dark, sparkly, and shaped like almonds; and his cheeks were round and rosy. He marched down the street toward me, barefooted and barechested, pants too short and frayed at the hem, carrying a piece of driftwood from the river. He stopped in front of me, glaring more than staring, then pointed his twisty piece of wood at me.

"I got you," he said.

"Do not!"

"Do too. I capture you."

I stood up, unsure of what this meant and what I was supposed to do about it. I thought about calling out for my mother, but said instead, "Do you want to play?"

He nodded, turned, and I followed. We went down to the river, and he showed me a little dip in the silty sand on the span of beach that had filled with water. It was his lake, he said, and we splashed in the water and threw handfuls of gray silt around and made lumpy looking castles until my mother and Uncle Mike came yelling and screaming and I didn't know why. "You told me to find a friend!" I yelled at my mother as she told me over and over I was not to leave the roadhouse, ever, ever, ever, never. But leave I would, always with George, and as we grew, sometimes his little sister, Nellie, would run after us down the street as we went fishing or spruce hen hunting or trapping weasels in the winter. We built a raft one summer, with the help of my stepfather, and while we were only allowed to pole it down the sluggish sloughs, we dreamed of taking it down the river, like Huck Finn. George had two old husky dogs named Salmon and Roe that he would hook up to a sled and give me and Nellie rides down the maze of winter trails that led in and out of the village, sometimes riding the runners and sometimes running along behind if the dogs seemed tired.

Then George's voice deepened, and I started growing fleshy lumps on my chest, and he seemed so irritated with me all the time. Years earlier we had noted the arrival of Henry and his sisters, a momentous occasion for us, and though the Harkers continued to be objects of curiosity, as I headed into my teenage years I found more and more excuses to wander into the store for a piece of bubblegum or to pick up something for my mother, though I was well aware that Mrs. Harker didn't care for the sight of me. Sometimes Henry would ring me up, putting his book down as if taking my money were some sort of imposition, and I would pop my piece of gum in my mouth, start chewing, and ask, "What's that you're reading?"

"Nothing that would interest you," he would more often than not reply, spurring me to beg my mother to find more books for me. And more often than not George would be waiting for me outside the door.

"He's such a *durak*," he would say, with a dark glance into the store as the door swung open on my way out. The word meant "fool" in Russian and was used by his people.

"How would you know? You never even go in there."

"His mother doesn't like me because I'm Dena'ina."

"His mother's stupid. Your father was a chief. You're like a prince or something!"

"Am I, Anna?" He looked me full in the face, serious now, and I saw how the years had whittled away the roundness of his cheeks and dimmed the sparkly dark of his eyes. I felt, that fall day on the steps of Harker's Trading Post, how things were shifting between us. George was changing, and I didn't want him to. We began spending less and less time together, and Nellie, growing too, helped fill somewhat the void that was emerging in my life. George spent most of his time with an older pack of boys, Dena'ina like him, and they roared up and down the river in boats with big clunky motors and stole bottles of whiskey from careless old-timers.

Then one night when I was fourteen there was a tapping on my window, and I looked out and there was George.

"Anna," he said. "Come on out, eh?"

I looked around, for those other boys. Was it a trap? I'd had my hair pulled more than once by that group, that "gang" as Nellie and I called them, the boys that stole our George.

"Just me," he said. "Those boys—they're drinking by the river."

I left my room and cautiously slipped out the back of the roadhouse where George now waited in the aisle-like space between my mother's two gardens. We still had sled dogs then, in a tidy dog yard in the far corner of the property, and they watched George with silent suspicion.

"How's things, eh?" he said.

I looked at him. "What do you care?"

"I care, Anna, yeah. We're friends, eh?"

I looked at him, wondering. I noticed he wore new shoes, black and shiny like a man's shoes. They looked too big for him.

"Aw, come on, Anna. You know we are. I'll give those boys the shove-off if you don't like them."

"Okay," I said warily.

George smiled. "Great! I'm going to kiss you now!"

And he did, clumsily at first then warmly and fiercely, and it made my heart pound in my chest and a strange feeling puddle in my knees.

"So, you want to go fishing tomorrow?" he asked as he stepped back away from me, his face grinning and glowing. "Our old spot. Maybe three?"

I nodded, stunned, wondering where he learned to do that. Suddenly Henry Harker seemed small and inconsequential.

"All right then, Anna," he said, putting his hands deep into his pockets and walking backward away from me. "I'll be seeing you, then."

I nodded again, and lifted my hand, and watched him as he turned around and continued on down the street toward the river.

But we wouldn't go fishing. The next day when I was ready for our rendezvous my mother asked, "Where are you going, Anna?"

"Fishing. With George."

She wiped a table down. "No, Anna, you have things to do around here."

"Can I do them later?"

"No. You can do them now." Her voice was firm and her face was strangely hard. I put my fishing pole down.

That night George came again to the garden. "You didn't show, eh?"

"I couldn't," I said, whispering.

"Why so quiet, Anna? Can't you talk to me?" There was a flash of something in his eyes. I hadn't realized I was whispering, the same as I hadn't realized that I kept looking over my shoulder at the backdoor of the roadhouse. His eyes followed mine.

"Okay, Anna," he said, stepping backward.

"What?" I asked.

His brows lifted. "What? You tell me."

"I couldn't go. My mother—"

"Suddenly found something for you to do."

"No," I said. "I mean yes, but—"

He shook his head, took another step back. "It's okay, Anna. Maybe we can't be friends like we used to."

"George," I said. My head was spinning. What was the right thing to say? I knew now what he meant, and I suddenly knew why my mother had stopped me from meeting him. "No," I said. "It's not like that." It couldn't be, could it? My mother was the woman who'd tried to save the Natives from the flu. Was it all different now?

"Yeah, Anna. Okay," George said.

"George, wait—" But I knew the truth, and I knew he was right.

"You like Harker anyway." He spit to the side. "I'll be seeing you, Anna."

But he wouldn't be seeing me. He would go back to his boys, and several weeks later those boys would get drunk again and play chicken with a late-night freight train, and George would stumble on the tracks in his new shoes. The news was like a dark blanket falling over me, and for years I would dream about him and think about him and see his face in anyone who resembled him, my need to say something to him burning in my chest. And for years the sound of those night freights rumbling through would wake me, then go on to haunt my dreams.

Wade Daniels

"HE WAS THE ONLY ONE UP HERE," Frank Richards, one of the men who came from the Harrisville mine, said that first night around a campfire in the cold. Fairfield and the rest of the men were still inside Anna and Henry's camp cabin, where it was warm and free of snow and wind, but after he left it Wade stayed up the trail by the fire built near the corpses while Richards and the other men came and went. Someone had to stay with the bodies, which lay still and dark underneath canvas tarps. There might yet be bears in the area, or other predators. They shouldn't be left alone.

Wade watched sparks rise and vanish into the speckled black of the snowy night. His lips were chapped and dry and cracked; he had not drunk enough water, on this day of combing the hills, of stumbling over tangles of brush and tundra, of falling down short hard shots of rocky faces that jutted out of the earth. Looking for Anna, and finding nothing. He closed his eyes against the ghostly images that swirled in the smoke in front of him. *No.*

"Here," Richards said, handing Wade a tin cup of warm water and whiskey. "Drink up, man."

Wade lifted the cup and felt the sting of the alcohol on his lips. It went down like liquid heat, radiating through him, a feeling right and wrong at the same time. He wanted to die. His body wanted to live.

"Like I was saying," Richards said, looking across the flames at Wade, "Montana—he was the only one up here on his own. All the rest of us—we knew where we were because we were all together."

"What about Ripken?" Wade asked.

"Ripken showed up at the roadhouse—early—but it was likely the same day this was going down. It looked like Harker and Peterson were heading home, so it wouldn't have been morning. The Pilsners had a full camp, everyone accounted for. No, Montana's the only one nobody saw on the days in question until he showed up at the roadhouse yelling bloody murder."

"It doesn't make any sense."

"Is there sense to be made over something like this? And it's no secret he always resented Henry, a young educated guy coming out here and instantly pulling a fortune out of the mine that didn't do squat for him."

"Henry didn't have a fortune."

"That's not what most folks say—"

"What's this? What do you know about Henry, either of you?"

The voice came out of the darkness. Merkle. Slowly the man approached the fire, the light harsh on the grim features of his face. "You go in," he said. "Get warm. I will stay with the boys."

Richards rose, but Wade shook his head and didn't move. At some point someone had brought him a wool blanket from the cabin; he pulled it up around his shoulders and felt his breath catch in his throat. Anna. The blanket smelled like Anna. He felt a swelling inside, as if grief were a river filling with rain.

He could feel Merkle's eyes on him, saw them glinting animal-like on the other side of the fire. "Where did you go today—where did you search?" Merkle asked.

Wade sipped from his cup. A shiver ran through him. "There's a stream, a half mile to the east. I thought maybe she might have gone there to fish."

"So you know her a bit, then."

"Yes."

"Anna is big on the fishing."

"Yes."

"But if these men were killed here, why would a killer go so far to find her, and how would he know where she might be?"

"I don't know."

"And where have you been, these past couple of days?"

Wade quickly realized that talking with Merkle, in the state he was now in, was like dealing with a wounded bear. He had to be careful. Again he reminded himself that he hadn't done anything, yet a dreadful feeling of guilt was hanging on him. But what happened here couldn't have had anything to do with him, or them. "I was in the village—well, at my cabin."

"What day did you come down from the mines?"

He had to think about it. "We came down a week and a half ago."

"Before this, then. Or so it would seem."

Wade almost asked, *Am I a suspect?* But Merkle answered the question before it was asked: "Everyone is suspect, you must understand. All of us who have been here in the recent days. We must have a judgment on when this happened, and we must make a map of everyone's activities. And we must find Anna. We must find her before there is talk."

Wade felt an additional thud of dread inside his chest, like a tap from a swinging sledgehammer that was edging closer. "Talk . . . about Anna?"

"She is not here," Merkle said. "She is not here, and these men are dead. Of course there will be talk. Now that I have stepped outside, Fairfield and those men will be searching the camp cabin. For the gold they imagine is there. I thought Henry foolish, you know, to let those stories grow. Henry believed in the banks. Now when they don't find the imagined stash of gold they will think, aha! The murderer is the thief that stole the gold."

"But there must be some there."

"Perhaps a poke or two. But they sent the bulk of it out with the Finn and he took it straight to Henry's banker in the city. So whatever is there now is the last of it."

"They can't possibly think Anna would do this." He shouldn't have said it—he should avoid saying her name—but he did.

Wade felt Merkle's eyes searching for a lock with his in the dark. "Perhaps. Perhaps not. But I know my Anna. If this happened and she is not to be found, then she has been killed." Merkle's voice cracked and strained as he struggled to say the last words. Wade felt the stab of them in his gut, in the constriction of his heart.

"The men now talk of Montana, but soon they will talk of Anna. If you have ideas on where she might have gone to, where she might have been when this monster found her, you need to tell me now."

Wade shook his head and shivered again as Merkle studied his face, unrelenting. *Anna, Anna, Anna,* Wade thought, *Anna, come back.*

Billie Sutherland

BILLIE'S MOTHER USED TO SAY, *Choose carefully, Billie, the wrong man will ruin your life*. At the time Billie could only see that through her limited experience. Was she talking about Billie's father, or was she talking about Joy?

But the words came back to Billie as she startled awake in her small roadhouse room. She was in a bathtub full of blood. But she wasn't. The blood was hers. But it wasn't. Maybe it would be better if both had been.

No. The wrong man won't ruin your life. It's the choices you make that will.

She could tell by the degree of darkness outside the window that it was not quite midnight. Still early. She tossed the blankets back and pulled on a sweater and a pair of man's jeans.

She slipped down the street under the cover of the shadowy light and listened to the sounds of the sleeping village. The rivers, of course, loud now in the quiet, and the soft sound of wind in trees. A few mosquitoes, their ranks thinner now in this last gasp of summer. She stopped. An owl, somewhere past the town—*who-h'WHOO, who, who*. Who indeed. Could she really become someone else?

She wondered if she would see the man in the black hat and then she did, making out his form on the bench in the village park that she had planned to sit on. She felt called to him, like the owls to the trees, and she approached the bench and sat down on the opposite end. He didn't say anything, and Billie could smell him: wood smoke. And fish maybe; maybe he'd been fishing, she thought, or processing and smoking salmon pulled from the rivers. They were quiet until Billie said, "My name's Billie."

He coughed and cleared his throat. Billie didn't look at him but felt his face turn toward hers. After a moment he said, "You know who I am."

She nodded.

"And what they say I did."

She shook her head, crossing her arms against the cool of the evening, holding her wool sweater tightly to her. That was one thing Maddie did not say, though Billie guessed. She could hear Montana breathing in the quiet, a slight rattle in his chest.

"They say I murdered three people, three young people, in the gold hills a long time ago."

She turned her face toward his, his features shadowed and grainy in the thick, darkening dusk. The night had taken on a feeling of unreality, as if it were an extension of the dream she'd had. "Did you?" she asked, her voice a whisper.

His mouth moved, but he waited a moment before replying. Then he said, looking at the road in front of them, "I answer that question every time I walk down this street. To any eyes that look at me, to the trees, to the buildings, to the rivers and the darkness. To myself, when I ask it of me. Did I do it? Can the wind in the trees be right? Did I forget something, and if I go back up there will I remember something I've been denying for what seems my whole life?" He coughed a moment, ragged and rough, then continued, "Sometimes it's like I only had one life, and it's this one, this last. Those other lives—growing up in Montana, becoming a young man and

heading out for the wilds of Alaska, then all the years here—
all the years I was simply Montana and no murderin' in front
of it. Was that me, I wonder sometimes, or is this all I've ever
been?" He leaned on his walking stick and hoisted himself up
from the bench.

Billie watched him in silence, his words swirling in the
air between them. *I was someone else once, too,* she wanted to say,
but I know what I did. Their eyes met for a brief moment, then
he turned and walked away, and the night returned to silence
save for the shuffling sound of his steps as he made his way
down the street toward the river.

Billie stayed on the bench, her insides pulled and taut
like an animal skin on a stretching board. Her heart was beating, and her hands were shaking. She couldn't go back to her
room, to the four walls and the quiet, and return to dreams
she could not control. The village was swallowed in near darkness, the simmer-dim diminished and subdued. She rose and
wandered into the street, aware now that the owl was still
hooting somewhere in the woods near the river. As she neared
the dark shape of the airplane hangar a voice in the shadows
said, "Bad night?" She made out the figure of the Finn in his
open doorway. She didn't answer, but stopped not far from
where he stood.

"Been there myself," he said. "Cup of tea?"

She looked through the dark down the street toward the
roadhouse. "All right," she said and followed him inside.

He turned on a light that illuminated a large, cavernous space littered with airplane parts and pieces. She went
behind him up a set of steep and narrow stairs to an open
loft that served as his living space. They didn't speak as he
walked over to his tiny rough kitchen and put the kettle
on. Billie took a seat at a small square table and took in the

chair and the bookcase near a window that looked out over the side street and the simple bed covered in an army green blanket, no longer made but not well slept in as if he had tried but failed to sleep. The kettle whistle blew and he filled the teapot, white with a blue onion design that Billie recognized as quintessentially English. An odd thing to find, in an airplane hangar loft in Alaska. Soon he brought the pot and two cups over to the table.

"Thank you," she said quietly.

"Sugar?"

"A little, if you have it."

He handed her a spoon and a mason jar half-full with sugar. "So," he said. "The dark's coming back. No more midnight sun for awhile."

She sipped her tea. "We still have some simmer-dim, though."

"Some what?"

"The extended twilight. That's what they call it in the Shetland Isles."

"You been there?"

"Yes. It's lovely. But I think I liked it so much because the light reminded me of Alaska."

"Travel much?"

"I did. I was a stewardess."

"Was?"

"Yes. Was." She avoided his eyes and glanced around the room. "Tell me," she said, "what kind of a name is Atlee Virtanen?"

"I'm surprised you remembered. Finnish and Amish."

"Amish? How did that happen?"

He laughed. "How do you mean how did that happen? Okay—it is a bit of a story."

"I've got a few minutes," she said. She felt the tension inside her easing as she sat there, in the small warm room and its simple bright light.

"All right." He smiled and pushed the hair back from his forehead. "My grandfather was Finnish, and somehow he got tangled up with the Amish of Iowa. It was a girl of course. His family lived nearby and he was always going past the community on a long pair of wooden skis. She—my grandmother—used to come out of her house to watch him pass. Then one day there was a blizzard, and my grandmother's family's carriage was stuck in the snow with most of the family in it, and my grandfather came skiing up out of the white and gave them a hand. He was orphaned at that point, and the Amish happily took him in, and he found a home there."

"And you were raised Amish?"

"Yep."

"But you didn't stay."

"Nope."

There was more story there, she could tell, but felt it was something she shouldn't push. Still, she couldn't help but ask, "How does an Amish kid learn to fly?"

"My neighbor, Roy Jenkins. World War I pilot, spent his time after the war working the tired-out farm his parents left him and putting everything into his plane. I would sneak out and help him whenever I could." His face was both sad and happy at the memory. "In exchange, he taught me how to fly. When he learned he was dying, he gave me his plane—not Bud, but one like it. White and green. After he passed away, I packed my bags and flew north."

They were quiet, then, for a few moments and out the window Billie could see the hint of light coming back in the sky. The dark was short-lived this time of year and easy to wait out. They drank their tea and chatted about small, simple things—the salmon run, what berries were ripe, the fact that the fireweeds were blooming out, a sure sign that winter was on its way.

"I should go," she said.

"I'll walk you back."

"I can do that myself."

"Of course you can. That's not the point." They stood and went down the stairs and out into the early morning, the light erasing the dark, and walked together down the side street that took her to Maddie's gardens and the backdoor.

"Thank you," Billie said.

He smiled. "You can come for tea anytime." He turned and went back the way they came, and Billie watched him in the early morning light before returning to her room. She climbed into bed and closed her eyes.

Aren't you afraid?

You don't scare me, Alaska.

She opened her eyes and breathed.

Anna Harker

SHHH . . . SHHH . . .

Is it someone, here at last, finding me? *Shhh . . . shhh . . .*
No, no, I know the sound and it is not here; it is miles away
and weeks away, the sound of the rivers freezing, the lead gray
water slow and filled with slivery bits of ice and slush. *Shhh,*
it goes, *shhh . . .*

The sounds of my river valley, the sounds of my village,
they are filling my head now and taking me to all those places
I remember, as if they pump through my body like my blood.
The night freights, those that haunted me for so long after they
took George's life away, the whistle I would hear from my tiny
bed in my small room, heading north beyond the village, where
the woods grew wilder, the nights grew longer, and the cold
grew fiercer. I see them rumbling through the sleeping village,
a bright light cutting the dark, the black engine one with the
night. On and on and on the rumble goes, the whistle fading,
the train now on its way. Then Uncle Mike, in the living area
of the roadhouse, his guitar on his lap, his fingers dancing and
his smiling face singing—

> *She'll be comin' round the mountain when she comes*
> *She'll be comin' round the mountain when she comes*
> *She'll be comin' round the mountain, she'll be comin'*
> > *round the mountain,*
> *She'll be comin' round the mountain when she comes.*

And there he is, in the Clearwater now, sitting on a stool, the guitar a warm glow in the dull gas lamps.

> *She'll be riding six white horses when she comes*
> *She'll be riding six white horses when she comes*
> *She'll be riding six white horses, she'll be riding six*
>   *white horses,*
> *She'll be riding six white horses when she comes.*

My mother's lap bouncing beneath me as her feet tap to the rhythm of the song while dogs beyond the walls begin to howl and bark. I hear them now, always a dog, whining or barking or howling somewhere, tugging at the end of a chain, longing to run through the night.

Then the swish, swish, swish of the wind in the summer trees, talking to me above my head, singing the songs of June, July, and August green, swish, swish, swish, *shhh...*

Shhh. Shhh, Anna.

It is Uncle Mike again. There had been a sharp, loud noise, and I startled awake in my bed. *It's only the signal,* he'd said. *Someone needs a ride across the river.* And no matter the time, day or night, Uncle Mike would pull on his boots and hop in his boat and cross that wide gray water to get whoever had fired three short rapid shots to call for him to come. After he died, there was no one to answer the call, the boat wrecked in the water and my mother refusing to take on the job, and Merkle too busy and too untrusted because he was a German. Montana had been asked, but he said no. He loved his horses, and the freighting, and suddenly there is wind in my hair and I am in the front of a canoe, Merkle's canoe, my eyes closed as we ride the wild river.

He did not let me die the day I drowned. The tree that grabbed our boat—grabbed by the river the same as it would one day grab us—would not grab Thomas Merkle in his light and swift canoe, and he would see my weeping mother on the shore and my still and lifeless body and come save me, my life re-beginning while a new life, for my mother and me, was unfolding in the shape of the handsome trapper from the north, who with great agility had brought his canoe swiftly to the shore and leapt across the distance to where I was, all as our old life swirled away with Uncle Mike's lifeless body in the wild waters of the river.

Urgently but firmly, he shoved my mother aside, my mother who looked at him puzzled and astonished, as if an angel had fallen beside her in her time of greatest need. He pumped my heart and blew air into me and the river spewed out of me, like an evil demon that had captured my soul. My lungs began to move, and I opened my eyes.

Here you are, little one, here you are, back with us now. His eyes were as blue as the water that day, his hair the color of wet driftwood flecked with strands of gold. He took a red bandana from around his neck and gently wiped my mouth.

My mother gasped and choked and managed, "My brother."

He looked at her, then at the merciless river. "I'll do what I can."

A year later we were back on the river, this man saving me now from my fear of the water, that great gray mass swirling beneath us as we flew over its surface like a bird. Then I opened my eyes and there was something in front of us, a large dark shape, something moving in the river.

A horse. Two horses, swimming for their lives. And a man in a small boat. I know now why I am remembering this. We came closer, Merkle working his oar to turn the bow of the canoe enough to let us pass. I clung to the sides, afraid of the wild breathing of the giant animal heads, the frantic look in their eyes. And the man in the boat, his dark hair moving in the wind, his dark eyes upon us as if we were trespassing there, in his water.

It was Montana, the horse freighter, who carried supplies to the miners in the hills. This is who he was before tractors and trucks put him out of business and he, too, turned to mining. The sounds of my village, those horses clomping down the street past the roadhouse, led by the dark man.

What is it, Anna? my mother asked as I climbed a chair in the dim gray light of a fall morning, the first time I saw Montana.

The dark man, I said, and the horses neighed and stomped. He saw me then, his eyes finding mine through the glass, and I scurried out of the chair.

Mama! I cried, but Uncle Mike was there, sweeping me up in his arms. *It's just Montana*, he said. *Don't worry, Bunny Rabbit.*

In the canoe that other day I looked back at Merkle and saw his eyes meet those of the dark man. I remembered that moment for many years, and now I can see what it was, there before me all this time:

The Clearwater, Uncle Mike playing. My mother's feet tap, tap, tapping.

She'll be comin' round the mountain . . .

I'm no longer on her lap and sit now on the chair, my mother twirling in front of me, in the arms of the dark man.

Wade Daniels

IT STARTED AS A FAINT DISTANT HUM. Wade turned in the borrowed sleeping bag—Nate Peterson's, most likely—and opened his eyes to the gray of the tarp above his head. He swallowed, his own spit like sandpaper in his raw and dry throat. He pulled an arm free and lifted a corner of the tarp. It was faintly light, and the snow had quit. Thomas Merkle, who, if he slept at all did so in the canvas chair he brought down from the camp, stood a hundred feet or so away, his back to Wade. When he heard movement he turned and walked over through the fresh layer of snow.

"Plane is coming," he said, not looking at Wade. "Get to the camp and wake everyone up. Have someone hoof it to Harrisville to meet the Finn and whoever he might have brought with him. They won't have long. They need to bring the sledge and the tractor from over there to get these two back to the airfield and out of here." He nodded at the bodies, the canvas tarps now covered with snow. "The window won't last long."

Wade looked at the sky, wondering what kind of man he was to have fallen asleep in the midst of the most awful day of his life. He had intended to only lie down beneath the tarp Merkle had erected, and only until he could convince the older man to take his place. There should be no sleep for him. Quickly he pulled himself free of the sleeping bag, ignoring the dull ache in his stomach. There should be no food for him either.

Too ashamed to look Merkle in the eye, he sat up and pulled on his boots. Exhaustion had crept through stealthily like a drug dripping into his veins. But Merkle said, "You slept. That is good. Anna needs us. Now go send someone to the roadhouse, and someone else to come take over here. Then get back out there and help me find my daughter."

Wade nodded and hurried down the trail, his boots slipping on the new, clean snow.

By the time Wade reached the camp, the Finn's plane was in full view. The plane buzzed low and circled over the scene several times before tipping its wing and turning toward the airstrip at Harrisville. Several men, Fairfield included, stood outside watching. He looked at Wade as he approached.

"Merkle," Wade said, catching his breath. "He said to send someone to Harrisville to bring back the sledge. The weather's not gonna last."

Fairfield nodded, and two of the men standing outside volunteered, grabbed their rifles, and sped off down the trail, a faint trace beneath the snow. "Time's wasting, boys," Fairfield said to the other men. He chose a man to go sit with the bodies and relieve Merkle and directed the others to begin their search day. "Let's walk in that direction," Fairfield said, looking at Wade. "I want to intercept the Finn and his company." Wade felt the conflict spread across his face. "We'll loop around," Fairfield said, "and look on the way." Then he reminded the remaining men to stay in pairs, adjusted his holster, and let Wade lead the way down the trail. On a distant hill, they saw Merkle crest then disappear over the other side.

"What's over that way?" Fairfield asked as they were leaving the camp, seeing the shadow of a trail, and Wade said, "A small stream, about a half mile off. The Harkers got drinking water from there." A partial truth. Anna fished there. Anna met him there.

"Let's go that way."

"I went down there yesterday."

"Oh? Well, let's go again. Someone could walk in the stream, you know, and hide their tracks."

Wade, too, had thought that. The stream was shallow and cut through the country like a liquid trail. Wade picked a different route than the one he walked yesterday, and they marched grimly through snow-covered brush and across the clearer stretches of open tundra. Roughly five inches of snow lay across the land. Wade felt the cold of it seeping through the leather of his boots and the socks that were too thin for the wintry weather in the hills.

They came to the narrow shore downstream from where the Harkers filled their buckets and where Anna and Wade would meet to fish, and Wade opted not to tell Fairfield otherwise. But the older man seemed deep in thought, looking upstream, then downstream, then at the stream's bed and bank. He began to walk along, going with the current, Wade slightly behind and falling in step. They came upon a stretch where tall dead grass had bent and draped itself over the side of the bank; Fairfield pointed to it, and together they pulled the grass back in sections, hearts beating, to examine the hollow beneath. Nothing.

"Well, Wade, what do you think?" Fairfield asked as he straightened and looked around. "What do you think's our best bet?"

There are no best bets, Wade thought but did not say. Though Fairfield was right that someone could have followed the stream in an effort to hide tracks, the truth was that the trail itself would have been easier and quicker and not likely to reveal much. The biggest danger on the trail, for someone seeking to evade detection, was the random chance of being seen. That might send a person down to a less-traveled place like the streambed. But even trying to track someone or something through the brush and across the tundra was hard enough, what with animals crossing over the country and the springy tundra leaving tracks void of definition save for the marks from the sharp hooves of caribou and moose. "I don't know," Wade said at first, in answer to Fairfield's question. He did know, but the words were hard. He gritted his teeth and pulled air in and out of his lungs several times before saying, "Look for birds."

"Birds?" Fairfield asked.

"Ravens, magpies, jays, and eagles."

"Oh!" Fairfield said. "Oh. Right. Scavenger birds. Well, why don't we get up high somewhere, see what we can see, and maybe we can meet up with the Finn and the others with the sledge." So they left the stream and cut through brush and tundra, searching the ground in front of them and any brushy tangles in the landscape they came across, working their way to high ground. Once they spotted two other searchers, on a hill several miles away, and they were beginning to wonder where they might find the trail again when they spotted, coming from the direction of Harrisville, a small group of men and a slow-moving tractor pulling the sledge, still some distance off. "Ah," Fairfield said, trying to count the men. "Help at last." In anticipation of a possible investigator or other authority figure in the group, Wade and Fairfield altered their course slightly to intercept, Fairfield for once pushing ahead, with Wade lingering behind, feeling the increase in the wind and noting the deep bank of dark clouds coming in from the north. He knew whatever help was arriving would be short staying. The Finn would have to leave with the bodies, and likely with the new figure that walked beside him, within the next several hours. He stopped following Fairfield and looked over the land. Endless. He turned back into it, hoping to cover as much fresh ground as possible before the snow came again and buried everything.

Billie Sutherland

IT WAS A STORMY, COLD MORNING—the beginning of fall, Billie thought. She pulled her coffee cup closer as if it could help and took another drag off her cigarette. She was down by the river, in a world of gray—gray sky, gray water, gray sandy silt beneath her feet. If the wind were a color today it would be gray, too, swirling through the tired, fading leaves of the giant cottonwood trees like the fallen one she sat on now, the gray bark cold and rough beneath her. She watched a small flock of mallard ducks fly past, heading south already. *You're going, I'm staying,* she thought. She would have to go to Anchorage soon to get her winter gear. Her mother was refusing to send it up on the train.

What would she say to them, what could she say to them, about why she left her life behind? *I met a man.* Not just any man, *the* man, or so she thought. Didn't think, she reminded herself. And therein lay the problem.

She pulled on her cigarette, the wind blowing her hair around. She had met this man in one of the lounges at a Midwest airport, a blizzard grounding all flights in and out. She'd slid onto a stool at the crowded bar, and he'd turned toward her, brown eyes meeting brown, hair as dark as hers but shorter and waving back from his face. They'd recognized each other and he lifted his glass.

United, he'd said.

United, she'd replied.

WILD RIVERS, WILD ROSE

They drank to United. They drank to the snowstorm. They drank to each other and found their way through the snow to the nearby hotel and slid against each other in a bathroom while the stewardess she was bunked with slept, or hopefully slept. He had a pretty face. Jimmy Johnson, co-pilot. *Such a pretty face.*

Another airport, another flight, crews switching out, and Billie recognized the back of him as she walked along, carrying her bag and chatting happily with the other girls. *Alaska*, he said when she caught up and he saw her.

Oregon, she replied.

Two ninety?

Two ninety.

Then you're with me, baby.

And somehow they had sex in the tiny bathroom of the plane, pushing against each other at thirty thousand feet.

It was a song that brought him into her mind this morning, a song that came into her dreams and lingered when she woke. They had heard it together once in New York City, when they were new to each other and it was just beginning. A folk song. Young people were playing folk songs everywhere, pounding the city streets with guitars strapped across their backs. They were in a club huddled in a dark corner, hands roaming and wandering. But while Jimmy Johnson was running his fingers up her tight skirt, her ears caught the words of the song the starved-looking young man on the wooden stage played:

Oh, what hills, what hills are yon, my love,
That the sun shines sweetly on?
Oh, yon are the hills of heaven, my love,
Which you will never win.

And what hills, what hills are yon, my love,
So dreary with frost and snow?
Oh yon are the mountains of hell, my love,
Where you and I will go.

"The Demon Lover," but she didn't know that then. She didn't know anything.

Jimmy Johnson's warm mouth nuzzled her ear. *I love you, Alaska,* he whispered. Billie closed her eyes and felt her heart expand but let a sly smile curve across her lips as she replied, *I love Alaska too.*

You know what I mean.

She'd released a short bark of a laugh and turned her face so her lips could press against his.

This morning, with the song in her head, she'd climbed out of bed, grabbed coffee and cigarettes, and went out into the wind.

"I used to put horses in that water, make them swim across."

She startled and turned. There was Montana, to the side of her and a little behind. Had he been there as she walked up, or had he only just arrived? Either way she had failed to notice him.

"I was a horse freighter, hauling food and equipment to the mines," he said. He sat down on the cottonwood log, not too close. "The river was always in the way; somehow town ended up on this side, while the path to the hills was on the other."

Billie scrambled for something to say, to keep him talking. She pushed the "Demon Lover" song back into the shallow grave it occupied in her mind. "Did they like the water? The horses."

"I would reckon not. Horses knew what could kill them, better than any man."

"Why did they do it then?"

"Why? Love. Horses are loyal, and loving. Like dogs. They loved me and they knew I needed them to get to the other side. And that I was there with them. We made it, every time. I never lost a horse to the water or the wilderness."

"I thought you were a miner."

He looked across the water, a deep breath rattling through his chest. "I didn't come to Alaska for gold, like so many did. No. I loved Montana, where I was born and raised—I just wanted more of it. Something bigger, wilder. Imagine if I had stayed." He looked at her, and she shivered. Imagine. She could imagine, for both of them. "Or if I just stayed happy with the horse freighting." His mouth moved around something, and he leaned to the side and spit brown tobacco juice onto the gray river sand. He looked back at the expanse of river, at the swaying trees on the other side.

"What happened?"

"I would say what happened was the big Ford truck that old man Harker had brought up on the railroad then drove across the frozen river. The trail was improved enough by that point that the truck could make it up into the mining country. I could see how horse freighting was coming to an end, and I'd best start thinking about something else. But it started in me before then, the gold fever." His gnarled hands wrapped tightly around the walking stick in front of him. Billie could see how they shook. Her hands had shook earlier as she poured coffee into a mug. "It started the day I saw her," he said. "Walking down the street, dirty leather boots and the wind wrapping her skirt around her legs. Her long brown hair was in a messy braid down the side, and she was tailed by her little girl, with that round chubby face and all those black curls bouncing as she hurried to keep up with her mama. When I saw them I thought, that's worth living for. That's worth working for. That's worth mining for gold for. But I wasn't quick enough. She met someone else before I could get her to give me a second look."

"Maddie," Billie whispered, and the old man nodded.

"And so you see, don't you, that I could never have touched a hair on that girl's head," he said. "The only thing I wished was that she was my own, she and her mama. So instead I looked out for her, when she was up in the hills at my old place, for all the good it did her or me." He spit again. "That's not the whole truth of it though. I was truly concerned about what I was hearing about John Cobb and his men, harassing young Henry about his tailings. Cobb had some rough looking fellows that season. But the whole truth is that my heart still yearned for the place, and that was my downfall. I went back there that day because I thought they were gone, and I'd been hanging on until they left so I could do just that. I liked to go there and visit the old place. But for me, that turned out to be the wrong place at the wrong time, kind of like the way an accident happens when things line up in a particular way." He shook his head. "Merkle—he knew, I think, in the end, that I didn't do it."

"How did he die?"

"Merkle? The way he would have wanted to. The way any of us in those days would have wanted to. Out on his trapline, drops dead on the trail. They found him with his snowshoes on." He drew a deep breath. "But Madeline, she could never look at me again," he said, returning to the murders. "Maybe she knows how I once felt and believes I did it for revenge against her." He shook his head. "Wrong time, wrong place." He looked at the sky, then looked sideways at Billie. "I should have stayed away, and I should have stuck with the horses."

Their eyes met, and for the first time she saw him smile. It was a sad smile, his eyes filled with pain, but it lifted her heart. Then the smile quickly fled. "Once a suspect, always a suspect," he said. "I've been serving time here, in this village, ever since. I can't never leave because people would think I left because I did something. So I walk around here with a shackle of suspicion clamped tight around my ankle, and I hear that ball and chain dragging behind me everywhere I go." He pulled himself up, swaying with his stick, gave Billie a nod, and went on his way.

Billie sat motionless, her mind working, looking across the moving water toward the trees and the gold country hills beyond. She felt something pulling inside of her, a longing to reach into the past and send Montana away from the hills where the Harkers died, a longing to send herself in a different direction before she entered the lounge at that midwestern airport where the blizzard had grounded the planes.

SEPTEMBER 29, 1941
Anna Harker

THERE IS A SHADOW IN MY THOUGHTS, like dark clouds
rolling in or the blackness in a corner of a poorly lit room. I
want to push it away. Who did this, who has done this? I don't
want to know. It must be someone known to me, though every
season now there are new faces on the trails, at the tables in
the Harrisville roadhouse, on the long way back to the village.
Men. I see flashes of faces, familiar and not, but there is one
thing in common for all: hunger, the need to strike it rich, to
find the big one.

Except Henry. Self-assured Henry. There was never that
raw hunger, that *I need this*. With Henry it was want, *I want this,
and therefore I am going to get it.* And he did. No wonder so many
hate him. But hate enough for this? I close my eyes, press them
tight to focus on that horrible idea, but my thoughts want to
go elsewhere, to sunny days on the riverbank, fishing with
Uncle Mike, or playing with George and Nellie. My feet wet
in a warm, shallow slough, the ancient glacier silt squishing
between my toes.

I pull myself back. Yesterday. What was it about yesterday I need to remember now? Montana. I saw him again, on
the hill overlooking our camp, watching, that big brimmed
hat on his head and that rifle in his hands. I was on my way
to pick berries to add to the sourdough pancakes we were all
so weary of; the berries, too—lowbush and blue—were losing
their effect as the fall wore on, and I added more and more to

the pancakes, the muffins, the bread, the cakes. I walked down the trail a ways—the trail that would eventually take one to the roadhouse—then wandered off it to a place among the tundra where I knew the berries grew, now wrinkled by frost and age but still edible and sweet. I knelt on the soft spongy ground, rich with colors and smells—the green and spiky Labrador tea (that we were sick of drinking), the white and brittle caribou moss, like miniature antlers among the lichens and shrubs. This day I actually saw a caribou, whose antlers mimicked the moss, on the side of a hill across the ravine where Ramshackle Creek—our creek, Henry calls it—went briskly on its way downward out of this country to join with the bigger waters coming out of the Alaska Range. I liked to imagine being a leaf on that water, spinning away, spinning away and rushing along, eventually washing up on the shores of home. I was watching the caribou, which was antlered and fine and must have a herd somewhere, waiting for its return, when I felt a presence behind me and I simultaneously rose and turned to see Montana there, on the trail I had just left, staring at me. Or was he? His eyes were under the shadow of his hat and his hair, long and thick and black along with his unruly beard, left his face nearly impossible to see. The "dark man," as I used to call him. I wondered if it was because of the blackness of his hair— which was much shorter then—and his dark eyes, or if it was instead the sullen, stormy look upon his face. I looked quickly at the hill where I had so recently seen him and wondered how he came upon me so fast, and I realized he was looking at the caribou, not at me, though certainly he saw me there. Then he lifted his rifle, and I instinctively stepped back, my heart jolting for a moment though I knew, again, it was the caribou that held his attention. Of course it was out of range, and he must have set his sights on it simply for the feel of doing so. When he lowered the rifle, his eyes landed for a moment on me. I could feel them more than see them, then he turned back to the trail and walked away. I watched him go, knowing he had a good five miles ahead of him, knowing he came all this way to look down upon our camp. The camp—the claim—that used to be his.

I went back to my picking, but found no peace in the activity that usually made me feel so calm and content. I had been seeing Montana nearly every day now, and I knew he was waiting for us to leave. What for, I did not know; perhaps he merely wanted to walk the ground he had once put all his hopes in, or perhaps he wanted to try his luck with a pan down at the water. Perhaps he simply longed to know what he did wrong, why he could not make the claim produce for him to the extent that he eventually lost it to Henry's father and the grubstake debt that had grown for several years. It was an old story in the territory: the story of broken dreams. And the country was riddled with streams named appropriately for the hopes that had been dashed along their shores: Disappointment Creek, Poorman's Creek, Fool's Creek, and Last Chance. It was rich country, but it was also cruel. Some miners, like Henry, had a strange gift for pulling gold out of ground that had failed others; some miners spent all their working lives in these hills, working one claim then another then another, always hoping, never giving up or letting go until their bodies wore away like the ground they dug year after year after year.

When I looked up from my picking I saw the caribou was gone, back over to the other side of that distant hill where I imagined the herd resting and feeding, the sound of their hooves like the heartbeat of the earth. The fading of the day brought a chill in the air and a sharp edge to the blue of the sky. I began my walk back to camp, my pot of berries in hand. Beyond the hills now streaks of deep rose washed across the horizon, and I wondered how many more miles Montana had yet to go. I wondered, too, if I should tell Henry of this sighting, but knew I would not. In the past when I would tell him, Henry responded with disinterest as if Montana were nothing more than a mosquito on the outside of a net: a slight irritant, but separate, removed.

I hear one now, a mosquito, come to feast on my blood. Or is it? It seems a distant sound, swirling in the wind, touching my ear, then fading away.

Wade Daniels

THE HELP FAIRFIELD HAD HOPED FOR came and went, as Wade had feared, as swiftly as the daylight on a winter afternoon. Mr. Brown, a small, nervous man, was a United States district attorney with tight, sharp eyes. Wade had circled back in time to meet up with the group as they neared the camp, Fairfield talking to the attorney in a low steady hum that was interrupted from time to time by the other man's brisk questions and comments. The Finn walked along with the men, his young face pale and shadowed with concern. As they neared the tarp-covered forms on the ground, Wade put a hand on the Finn's arm. "You might not want to," he said quietly, but the Finn only said, "I can take it." Fairfield and Attorney Brown motioned for the others to stand back while they peeled back the tarps, careful to carry the canvas and the night's snow that lay upon it away from the bodies. Wade felt the shudder run through the young Finn. Attorney Brown stood staring at the scene, his brows pressed low toward his eyes, his mouth set grimly.

"This is a heinous crime," he said, then produced a camera and began taking photos, much the same as Fairfield had done. Fairfield stepped aside but glanced at Wade. So far the attorney was repeating the steps they had already taken, moving with a careless disregard around the crime scene. The Finn had turned his back to it and studied the clouds that were flying in on the rising wind.

"Let's wrap them up," the attorney said, "and get them out of here before the weather closes in. The autopsies will give us more information." What information, Wade wondered, that they couldn't see with their own eyes? The tractor was summoned to come down from the camp, and Wade felt the weight of the long passing moments that kept him here instead of searching for Anna. He noticed Merkle was absent, and he felt the pull of the hills as his mind raced over every inch he had not yet covered. As the tractor chugged slowly down, pulling the heavy and ungainly sledge, Fairfield answered a litany of Brown's questions while the latter wrote the answers quickly down onto a pocket pad. Fresh canvas tarps were produced, and Wade and the Finn were called upon to assist lifting the bodies to wrap them up. They found themselves holding what was once Henry Harker. The Finn's stomach convulsed several times, and Wade saw a tear slide down the side of the young man's cheek. And Wade thought, as he looked at the unmarred side of Henry's head, how young he was, and how heavy and stiff in death. On his hand Wade saw again the small gold wedding band. Wade heard, in the continuous mutterings between Fairfield and Brown, the attorney say, "See if anyone else has gone missing or taken a sudden trip. See if Mrs. Harker had any special friends."

"She couldn't have done this," Fairfield said. "I don't doubt that she's fit, but no woman brought these two men down."

"I agree," Brown said, "so let's see if maybe she had some help."

The Finn looked angrily at the attorney, but Wade kept focus on the task at hand. The bodies were wrapped in the tarps, and after they had been lifted onto the sledge, Wade gave the Finn a pat on the back, said, "Keep your eyes open when you fly over," and walked away. He was hungry, cold, and tired, but more snow was coming and daylight fading. By this time all the different camps had been searched—his cousin's included—but the open country still held miles of possibilities. He struck out, heedless of the fact that he was going alone with a possible murderer out there somewhere, and he walked, crossing Merkle's tracks in the snow on occasion, until the light faded and the faint glow of the camp windows through the thickening snow was all that remained to guide him back.

On the evening of the following day, Wade, Merkle, and Fairfield sat huddled around the stove in the Harker camp discussing what to do. The rest of the men had left earlier in the day, noting the futility of further searches as well as the fear of not being able to leave at all if they waited any longer. But Merkle would not go, and Wade, too, could not bear the thought. Fairfield, Wade knew, felt a sense of obligation—not in the hope of learning anything new for the investigation, but to the grief-stricken and angry citizenry of the community where he represented the only official anything for miles and miles.

"They can search all they want, they will not find Anna." Merkle's hands shook as he held a tin cup of coffee made from the last of the grounds they could find. Anna would be looked for, Fairfield had told him, in the various transportation corridors leading into and out of Alaska. "She is here—here!" Merkle said. "Here in the hills. Buried now, under the snow."

"We have to look at all the possibilities," Fairfield said, as gently as he could. "That's all. I don't think anymore than you do that Anna had anything to do with this."

Though he sat right next to them, the voices of the men seemed very far away in Wade's ears. How many miles, he wondered, had been covered, and how many more left undone? Too many, and now the snow, serious and silent, was covering the land inch by inch by inch. They would never find her, he knew, until spring. There was no point in staying, and they had few supplies and inadequate gear and no snowshoes. If they left at this very moment, they would have a long, hard walk to Harrisville, likely deserted now like the rest of the camps, closed up and awaiting spring. He would find her. If he had to wait until breakup, he would wait, and he would find her and bring her home. But between now and then lay a deep black crevasse that he knew he had to plunge down into and that might grab hold of him and never let go.

"Thomas, you've got a wife, waiting for you down there, needing you to stay safe," Fairfield was saying.

"And how can I return to her without our daughter?"

"I don't know, Tom, I don't know. But if you don't come out with us tomorrow, it might be a while before you can come out, and you need to get back to Maddie, Tom—she'll be needing you. We'll keep investigating, and we'll get back up here as soon as we can. Brown said it's likely the FBI will be called in on this—someone's got to handle it. Those FBI fellows, you know, they do a pretty good job. They'll know what to do, on how best to proceed."

"They won't know anything!" Merkle spat. "They won't know the country—they won't know these people here."

"Then it will be up to us to help them with all that. But we won't do any good if we get stuck up here and end up needing someone to come and rescue us. Go home and help your wife, Tom."

Merkle rose and banged his cup down on the rough wooden counter, grabbed his jacket and slammed the door behind him on his way out. A moment of silence passed before they heard him yell out in anger and frustration and sorrow, the sound muffled and swallowed by the swirling snow.

Billie Sutherland

AREN'T YOU AFRAID?
You don't scare me, Alaska.
Then Billie opened the door to the rest of her life.

"I forget. Sugar?"
"Yes, please."
The rain beat down on the roof of the Finn's airplane
hangar. It was late August already and the rain was cold and
all the remaining green things were looking worn and weary.
August was like the Sunday evening of a long weekend, when
time was running out. Billie sat at the Finn's small table and,
again, watched him make tea.
"How well did you know Anna—Maddie's daughter?"
she asked.
The Finn looked over his shoulder. "So she told you."
"A little. Maybe enough. Horrible."
"It was," the Finn said, placing the teapot and two mugs
on the table.
"Can you tell me about her?"
"Anna?" he said, sitting down and pouring the tea. "I
guess in the big picture of things I didn't know her very well. I
was only here two years before it happened. She was beautiful,
high spirited, tough—forty below she'd be out, snowshoeing
down through town then out across the rivers, hunting ptar-

migan or scouting game tracks for Merkle. Or if the water was open she'd be out there fishing."

"What happened?"

The Finn shrugged and shook his head. "Someone took an ax and killed them—Anna; her husband, Henry; and their hand, Nate. Most people knew I flew their gold out to their bank in Anchorage on a near-weekly basis—or maybe there was someone who didn't know that."

"But people think Montana did it."

The Finn hesitated before replying. "He was there, he had motive—their claim used to be his, before he lost it to Henry's father."

"He doesn't seem like a murderer." But neither would she, she knew, and she felt the clammy hand of dread pressing down on her and wondered if there would ever be a day in her life when she would wake up in the morning without that feeling that something was wrong.

"Things happen to people," the Finn said.

"But something like that—" Billie began then stopped. She didn't know how to say it. The ability to kill three people with an ax is not a thing that *happened* to the person who did it. It had to do with something inside the person, there from the start, a seed or a marking in the center of the soul.

"Who investigated?" she asked.

"Ben Fairfield, mostly. The FBI but only briefly, because of the war."

Her mind was working. "So there's a record somewhere, of the investigation."

"A bit of a one," he said. "Come here." He walked over to the window and pointed to an area to the left of the Clearwater, where tall dry grass swayed in the evening breeze. "Ben

Fairfield's office used to be there, in that empty spot," he said. "A few years after he left there was a row of some sort at the Clearwater, and somehow a kerosene lamp got involved, and somehow that building and not the Clearwater caught fire and burned to the ground. His records went with it."

"What about the FBI reports?" she asked as they returned to the table.

"They're out there somewhere," the Finn said. "At the time the field office was in Juneau, but there's one in Anchorage now. But your uncle would know all about the case."

"My—" Who had she told?

"Don't look so frightened. I ran into him in Anchorage."

"How do you know my uncle?"

"I met him back then. He was a reporter at the time. I know your dad, too."

"Christ." Of course. Her father was the manager of Anchorage's small public-use airport.

The Finn smiled gently at her discomfort. "I'm in and out of that airport all the time. Of course I know him. Hal's a good man, and he does a good job running things there."

Alaska, Billie thought. Her parents always said it was like one big small town. Everybody knew somebody who knew somebody who knew somebody. But the Finn was right. Uncle Howard would know. Aunt Sam, too, who oddly didn't mention the murders when she was here. But Sam and Maddie had exchanged a look as if they recognized each other.

"I never really thought Montana did it, but I could never say for sure he didn't," the Finn said. "All these years later, and no one really knows."

"Any other suspects?"

"We were all suspects, I think—anyone within spitting distance. It was a strange time, all of us looking at each other and wondering. I think I slept with my shotgun that whole long winter." He sighed, long and deep, and Billie watched the rise and fall of his lean chest. "Billie, you're young, alive, and *here*—why spend your time thinking on that old tale?"

Billie shrugged and spun the sugar around in her tea. "It suits my mood," she said.

He watched her in silence for a few moments, and Billie let her eyes linger on his. "All right," he said. "If the ceiling lifts tomorrow, I've got to fly up that way and make a mail drop. You're welcome to come along."

"Thank you," Billie said, and smiled.

The next day Billie joined the Finn on the airstrip and climbed into the seat beside him. Growing up she would fly in her father's bush plane when his work allowed him time for anything. It was always a treat, and to be cherished, as, it seemed, any time with him was. Her mother always thought he put too much effort into his job, but his response was that lives and safety depended on him, though it was also true he had an inordinate love of planes.

The Finn taxied down the airstrip, away from the village, coming almost to the river before he turned around. Then the plane sped toward Main Street, lifting into the air and over the Clearwater Inn with a smooth swoop that sent a flutter of excitement through Billie's insides. Down below, the village grew tiny and toylike, and from this bird's-eye view she could see how insignificant it was compared to the miles of thickly wooded forest and the three great glacier rivers that from the air reminded Billie of braided hair, three strands weaving together into one. The Finn flew the plane above the Tatum River for a while, heading toward the mountains, then turned over the forest that soon thinned as the terrain grew hilly and higher. She could see below a thread-like ribbon of dirt road wiggling its way through the wilderness until it came to an end at a small cluster of buildings near a silvery stream.

"Harrisville," the Finn shouted back to her.

The plane circled low and headed toward an airstrip; she wondered if they would land. A man waved, and the Finn opened his door and tossed out an army green bag with several bright ropes tied to it. Billie watched it tumble through the sky until it hit the strip. The man waved again then walked toward it. The Finn tipped his wing, turned, and flew a little farther into the country. Below them trails and streams snaked through the terrain, and they flew over several large mining operations with clusters of buildings and large, monster-like dredges. Then they flew over a lonely stretch of hills toward the headwaters of those streams, and Billie's heart beat a little faster. When an old, worn building, weathered and gray, came into view, she knew. He was showing her where Anna and Henry Harker mined, and where they died.

SEPTEMBER 29, 1941
Anna Harker

I DO NOT LIKE THE MINING BUSINESS; I never have. It mars the land and brings out the worst in men. In all this wild beauty they squabble like ravens over a carcass: my claim, your claim, your tailings on my claim, your operation ruining mine.

Things have changed since the time I was young, and Merkle took me out to our own operation, across the hills from here, in wilder land deeper in the wilderness. He was a hand miner then, and he is a hand miner now: a shovel, a sluice box, a swift-running stream. He takes what he needs and leaves the rest for another year. This is our bank, he says, this is our rainy day. The other miners thought and still think that pay dirt is not there—if there was, then certainly Merkle would expand his operation, get the giants and their penstocks and hoses, get men working for him. Every season he arrives late and leaves early, his pack on his back and his rifle in his hand, coming out of the woods and disappearing back into it. *Come out with us,* the other miners say, *we have ways to make the snow melt faster and thaw the ground sooner and get the water flowing. Come early, stay late.* And Merkle would say, *I have a lovely wife,* and keep to his short season, slipping past with his secret stashed in his pack, bags of bright gold for half the effort. This season, though, he stayed on longer, not for more gold but because he knew John Cobb's men were roaming the hills looking for new claims, and he wanted to be there should they come near his. It was our fault, I suppose, or so John Cobb says, that our tailings are ruining his efforts on his claims downstream from ours. We had hoped he would find new territory, though I hoped he would not invade my stepfather's quiet world.

Like the mining business, I do not like John Cobb and I never have. I see him, ironically, the way I imagine others see Henry: snobbish. But John Cobb is a loud, bossy bully, and what's more he's a fake Alaskan, here for the summer and gone for the winter yet claiming this is his home. He has a round face and a fat mustache that hangs down over his pouty mouth. He's big and tall with small eyes and calls me "little lady." *Where can I find your husband, little lady?*

He was here four days ago, prior to his departure.

Your dams are not working, sir, and your operation continues to interfere with mine! His voice bellowed around the hills and reached my ears. *I'm out of patience with you, Harker—you've cost me thousands this season alone! It's time for a court of law to settle this, and by God by next spring I'll have you shut down!* I walked along the trail to where I could see. There was Henry, hands on his hips, the wind blowing his hair around as he stood facing Cobb, who was red faced with his legs spread wide and his fists clenched angrily at his side, his brimmed hat and flapping oilcloth jacket like costume props from a movie set. When I saw that he was turning to go I dove into a patch of alders so he would not see me as he passed, and I hid there like an animal on the run until he was gone. When I reemerged I saw Nate now with Henry, the two deep in conversation. I walked back to the camp, aware of Cobb's footsteps on the trail in front of me. The feud has been ongoing for two years now. Was it our fault that Cobb staked his claims downstream from ours?

Here, Anna, hold the pan like this, see, and move it like this, like you are washing the dirt. The gold is the heaviest, and it will sink to the bottom. The sun glints off the water, and Merkle is smiling. The stream is bright and swirling by in front of me. I swish the water in the pan, tipping it ever so carefully so the dirt and pebbles spill away. I see my gold, then, bright and gleaming, and I cry out and smile up at Merkle, who cheers and rubs his hand across the top of my head. There is a nugget, small but fair. Merkle will take it to a jeweler for me, and have a necklace made for my mother, and there I am now, on her birthday, the little ribboned box in my hand.

I hear my labored breathing, my lungs working because they don't yet know how to stop. I was thinking about Cobb, about the mining, then suddenly I went elsewhere. My mind keeps pulling me away from here. But I must think, mustn't I, think. The miners, the mines, the trails, the land. I am spinning with it all. Who would walk this way and find me here, and is this about me, or about Henry and the mine and the gold? John Cobb would like to hurt Henry, I have no doubt, but hurt him with a piece of paper from a judge. But then there are his men, and their strange dark loyalty. But do this to me? Henry is the only one with reason to hurt me. But no, no—that is not true. There is someone else with reason to hurt me and my eyes fill with tears as I see her dark, angry, and hurting face where we stopped together by the river. *You take everything, Anna! You've taken everything from me!*

Please, no—I didn't mean to, I didn't know.

Yes you did, Anna. You knew. My voice, not hers. My guilt.

I have lost all sense now of how long I have laid here. It feels like seconds. It feels like years. Think, Anna, what time was it when I came here, to this spot, to see this view? Afternoon, yes. A moment to myself before the dinnertime chores and back to packing the camp. Henry will wonder where I am, if I am not there, if he still lives. And will Montana come this way today, to stand on the ridge and look down upon us as we flourish on what was once his claim?

And a dark thought: perhaps he already has.

OCTOBER 5, 1941
Wade Daniels

THEY ARRIVED in the village at twilight, stone-faced and silent, having poled their way across the river in the boat that waited for them at the landing, tied to a piece of drift-wood on the shore. Now a silent street greeted them, and the only sounds were the weary shuffling of their feet and Fair-field's labored breathing. Merkle broke loose at the roadhouse, nodding grimly to the two men before opening the door of a building that merged with the growing dark, save for a faint light coming from somewhere deep inside. Wade did not envy the man, who had yet to face the hardest part of this day.

"Well young fella, here I am," Fairfield said when they came up to his office. "Are you sure you don't want to stay in town tonight?"

"No," Wade said, "but thanks. I need to get home."

"Don't we all." Fairfield tipped his face to the sky and Wade did the same: the snow had caught up with them, and here it was now, falling softly on the village. "Well, I guess I need not say don't go anywhere."

"No."

"And please—don't tell anyone I'm back. I'm going to lock my door, leave my lights off, and crawl into bed."

"All right."

"We'll get to the bottom of this soon as we get a little help."

Wade nodded and walked away, his legs weary and his heart heavy. He reminded himself again that they had not been set up to stay, from clothing and equipment to food. The snow would only get deeper, and without snowshoes they would get trapped. As it was they struggled through it, following the faint trail of the men who left the day before. Gradually they found ground again as they descended into the valley, and with thanks to Merkle's knowledge and secret path, they made the journey in two days and one long, cold night.

The lights came on in the inn as he passed, and he saw several figures hunched at the bar. How could they sit there, he wondered, when the world had been smashed to pieces? And another thought occurred to him: perhaps there was someone within those walls right now who knew what happened. Some-one somewhere knew. Someone most likely here among them.

He saw Jake's motorbike leaning against the corner. He could go in and ask for a ride part of the way. But he didn't want to talk to anyone and was grateful the growing dusk masked his passage through the village. He soon left the grow-ing number of lighted windows behind.

What little light left was grainy and diffused, but it held for him for half an hour until he left the roadway and started down the trail to the lake. The snow was falling heavily now, and as the darkness thickened, he strained to see the path in front of him to avoid the veiny roots that lay, slippery and exposed, across the ground. At last he could discern a dark shape: the cabin. When he reached it, he pressed his face against the cold log walls that still smelled of spruce sap and felt himself starting to break. He pulled himself away, found the door, and stumbled inside and into bed, stopping only to remove his wet coat and boots.

Slowly, the cold covers warmed, and he felt himself sinking toward sleep. He fought against it, staring into the blackness of the room. It didn't seem right, to be warm and to sleep while Anna was still out in the hills in the cold. His last thought before succumbing to exhaustion was this: *Let me wake up to the world revised. Let it all be different in the morning.*

But of course it wasn't. Twelve hours later his eyes opened to the soft gray light of a snowy day, his body still heavy with fatigue and sorrow. But that same body was calling: he needed to piss, he needed water, he needed something to eat. Slowly he pushed off the covers that had tangled around him in the night, slipped on his still-wet boots, and pushed open his door and blinked against the whiteness of the world. As he pissed into the snowy bushes, he looked at the lake, smooth and still on this quietest of days, and he felt an urge to walk into it, to let the water that once wrapped around her lovely body wrap itself around him. Anna, Anna—

He felt something move and turned to look down the trail. Someone was coming. It took him a moment to recognize the knee-length kuspuk with the longer cotton skirt beneath, the tall leather mukluks. Nellie. He didn't want to see anyone and walked back into the cabin, but she followed.

He crawled into bed and lay there as, wordlessly, Nellie started a fire in the stove and put water on to boil. "Don't," he finally said. "Don't be here."

Nellie shot him a wounded look, and he saw how the skin around her eyes was puffy and raw. "I have no one," she said, "but you."

He closed his eyes. A short time later he felt Nellie's hands on him, grabbing him and pulling him into an upright position. First she gave him warm tea. Then she gave him broth that tasted of spruce hens and vegetables. Then he slept. When he woke again she gave him soup, and after that some dried smoked fish.

"You didn't find her, eh?" she said, and Wade shook his head. He tried to keep chewing but something was breaking up inside him, and he heard a strange sound spill out of his mouth. Nellie was there at once, kneeling on the floor by the side of the rough and narrow bed.

"It's not your fault, eh? You tried. All you could do was try."

His eyes, narrow and tear threatened, met hers. What wasn't his fault, he wondered. In Nellie's world, what wasn't his fault?

Billie Sutherland

"THE HARKERS HAD A LOT OF CLAIMS—a lot of claims," Maddie said. "Emmitt Harker wasn't anyone's fool. He might have come here to supply the miners, but he knew the gold was out in the hills, not on his shelves."

Billie stood with her arms crossed over her chest, embracing herself against the growing cold of the evening, the smoke from her cigarette making her think of the warm fire inside. She and Maddie were in the gardens behind the roadhouse digging potatoes. The darkening sky was steely gray, and the evening had a tense stillness to it, like the world put on pause. Billie felt the kiss of the coming winter on her nose and on her cheeks, and she wished she'd put a sweater on underneath her plaid wool jac-shirt. She took a final drag off her cigarette and stubbed it out in an old tin can. She picked up the little shovel she was using and went back to helping Maddie.

"Oh?" Billie said, treading carefully. She shook the dirt off a cluster of potatoes, tangled by the roots.

"He'd grubstake those that didn't have the means to grubstake themselves." Maddie worked her shovel around in the ground. "He'd front them supplies. And be mighty generous about it too."

Billie heard the bitterness in Maddie's voice. She loaded some potatoes into a burlap sack.

"And then when they'd fail, or have a rough go of it, they'd have to sign over their claims in payment."

"A clever businessman," Billie noted.

"That he was. And some of those claims paid off in dividends. Then the miners who lost them to him would have to go on, knowing that if they'd just been able to hang on for another year they'd see their dreams of gold come true."

Billie thought about that, trying to imagine the feeling. "And then they'd have to live in the same village with him." Like Montana. Billie thought of his dark, sad face.

"Yep. Those that stayed."

Billie looked over her shoulder, past the rear of the roadhouse and back toward the street. All that money and all those dreams, lost and found and lost and found, swirling around this tiny village, even smaller then. Is it any wonder that the mines eventually gave birth to murder?

Maddie stabbed her shovel into the earth in such a way that made Billie turn her head with a start. "I've hated gold and hated the mines, and I've hated Emmitt Harker ever since," she said, her mouth a thin line of anger. She tossed a shovelful of potatoes over toward Billie. "And who to hate more than myself? I had caught it too, that gold fever. It's true, you know, what they say. It's a sickness. A bright boy like Henry should have been off running a business somewhere or teaching at a university, not slaving away in the mines. And not even willing to part with enough gold to hire more help up there. My Merkle, he worked our claim, but our operation was small. We took what we needed to live, because that was the point: to live. To enjoy our life in this country, not become a slave to it." Maddie's shovel stabbed and tossed, stabbed and tossed. Billie stood speechless, holding the burlap bag, the dirty potatoes collecting near her feet. "But I—I felt the clutch of the gold, which I knew the Harkers had plenty of. But I didn't want it for myself. I wanted it for Anna." Now she stopped, and tossed the shovel down onto the battered ground. She knelt and began shaking dirt off the spuds. Cautiously Billie joined her, the cold, damp earth soaking through the knees of her canvas pants. "I'd remembered how I had been poor most of my life," Maddie went on. "At the same time I had forgotten that while I had been poor most of my life, I did just fine. I did what I wanted—provided I could work around my parents—I went where I wanted and I spent time with who I wanted, though I guess you could say I made a few mistakes, but having Anna, of course, was a mistake that was the greatest blessing of my life. And then I came up here to be with my brother, lost him but found my Thomas, all on the same day.

"But I wanted something different for Anna than what I had. Don't all parents have those thoughts, that somehow for their own child things have got to be better, brighter, bigger? All Anna ever wanted was to run around the woods and fish in the rivers. I'm not saying Henry didn't love her; he did. But he wanted her to calm down. He wanted her to be pretty and docile and know how to bake a cake without wrecking the kitchen. And after they got married her choice in the summers was to go up to the mines with him and be a camp cook, or stay in town and help his parents run the store. Of course she'd go to the hills. Of course. I'd have done the same."

Billie saw tracks now in the dirt that had dusted itself across Maddie's cheeks, like streams on a map. "I could have told her she did not have to get married, not to Henry, not to anybody. I could have told her that. But that was not what a woman was supposed to do. Of all the men already here or coming through, Henry seemed the best choice, the safest, and when he laid out his first summer's yield on our table and asked my husband for permission to ask Anna for her hand, I was the one who said, 'Yes! Yes!'" In one swift, sweeping motion Maddie stood and lifted a full burlap sack and swung it over her shoulder as she left the disrupted garden. For a few long moments Billie didn't move and let the night and the cold begin to gather around her, the feel of Maddie's words echoing across the quiet.

Anna Harker

"YOU'LL LEARN," Henry often said, remembering Montana's low spoken words. He came out of that first season with enough gold to handsomely finance the next season—let alone live comfortably through the winter. And I had become, somehow, a pivotal part of his future plans, and that fall my mother and I stood in my room, repeating the scene we had performed four short months ago:

"Anna, please, a dress this time," she said, her eyes despairing at the sight of my skirt and mukluks and blouse combination again. My suspendered trousers, wet and silty at the bottom from my afternoon of fishing along the river, lay in a heap on the floor. She reached down and collected them, draping them over the small wooden chair that already held my flannel shirt. "We'll have other guests as well as Henry tonight."

I suppressed a sigh. "They certainly already know I don't wear many dresses."

"Anna, you have to grow up sometime," my mother said. "You are a lady now, you know. You can't spend the rest of your life running around the woods and the rivers acting and dressing like a boy." But truth be told I would have been happiest doing just that: running around the woods with my shotgun over my shoulder, running the dogs down the rivers in the wintertime, helping my stepfather with the traps. But was that my undoing, was that what inspired the pressure to marry

Henry, simply that I felt I had as much of a right as anyone to be out there in the wild, wearing pants and snowshoes and not caring the slightest if my hair was frosting and splitting at the ends or if my fingernails were more suited to a boy's hands than the hands of a twenty-year-old woman?

"And why can't she?" My stepfather now stood behind my mother, buttoning the cuffs of a clean flannel shirt that I was sure my mother had made him change into. "I'm not so sure I'm ready to lose my trapping partner just yet."

I had told no one about the springtime kisses with Henry by the river, though somehow they seemed to know. In the days since those kisses I had remembered how Henry smelled good and tasted good, and I imagined more kisses by the river that lasted longer and longer and left us flushed and panting. Unbeknownst to me Henry had already stopped in to see my parents this day while I was out fishing by the river, and he had poured a ribbon of gold down the length of the table and asked them for my hand. They had said yes.

My mother stepped forward and tried to organize my hair. "I am so happy for you, Anna. Henry is just right, you know. He's an Alaskan boy, but he's smart and he's educated. And you know him—we all know him—so we can trust him. That's important, you know, here in the territory."

Despite my confusion at her words, I had felt at that moment my mother's life: heading off into the unknown with a small child in tow, Alaska like the middle of the ocean, Uncle Mike the only guiding light.

I remember that dinner, my heart thumping as Henry walked in the door and took the hat off his head, his hair still damp from his bath. He greeting me cordially but not with an abundance of enthusiasm, though I was privy to a little secret smile and a gleam in his eyes. But I could feel that I was on the outside of something, and the feeling hung on me like an uncomfortable dream or like something that was wrong that I had forgotten about but couldn't quite remember.

This evening Henry brought a new friend with him, a young miner named Jake Timmers who had previously mined in areas to the north and who helped Henry over the season. He had a small nose and coppery-colored hair that waved thickly back off his forehead. As Henry introduced us, I held out my hand to shake his, and I saw him hesitate then he reached instead for my stepfather's hand and shook it firmly, leaving me feeling very much in my woman's place, adding to my feeling of unease. As I ate the fresh trout I had caught and my mother had cooked, I remembered I had seen Timmers the previous spring, getting off of the northbound train. His face was set, his eyes narrow and wary as he took in this place he had stepped into; the depot provided a fair view of the village proper. There was something unfriendly about him, I'd thought, as he brushed past without so much as a nod or hello to any of the people gathered to meet the train, and I had assumed—and rightly so—that here was another miner, whose thoughts were only of gold.

This evening he attempted friendliness, despite his refusal to shake my hand, and several times he smiled knowingly at me, adding to my sense that I was unaware of something that was impending.

"And what do you do, Anna?" he asked.

"Do? I do lots of things," I said. "What do you mean?"

"How do you spend your time?"

"Well," I said, "I help my mother run the roadhouse, I hunt and fish—"

"Anna caught this evening's meal," my stepfather interjected.

"And when I can, I like to read," I said.

"Oh, yes—reading," he said. "Are you cerebral, then?" I had the sense he thought I would not know what he meant.

"I would like to be."

"No college for you?"

"Not at the moment. I don't care to move to the city."

"Perhaps some of Henry's education will rub off on you." At that, I saw color rise in Henry's cheeks, and he frowned a little at his new friend. And the color rose in my own face.

"Were you part of that trouble at the mines in Lawry?" I asked pointedly and instantly felt reproachful glances from around the table come my way.

"What trouble's that?" Timmers responded.

"The missing miner," I said. It had happened last fall. The young man left the camp where he was working and vanished. He had departed the operation early to return to the States for college, hiking out from the mine to the railroad in order to catch the train. But he never showed up anywhere, and the miners who were left searched for him until the snow came.

"That was hardly trouble," Timmers said. "A sad misfortune, apparently."

"Sad indeed," I said. "But when a body's not found, who knows what happened?"

"Anna," my mother cautioned, but at that moment the door opened and John Capp came in, blustering and wanting food, so I took the opportunity to leave the table and serve him up a plate. He was obviously just down from the mines—his pants and boots muddy from the rough road—and he focused on his food for a while before he said, looking at Henry, "Well, young fella. We're going to be neighbors of sorts."

Henry made a motion as if his food had temporarily caught in his throat.

"I just filed on some claims downstream from that one you were working on this summer. I figured if you wanted them for yourself, you would have already snatched them up."

Henry took a drink from his glass of water, obviously taking his time to reply. "Congratulations," he said. "Ramshackle has proven good for me." He left it at that, and I suffered through the rest of the meal until at last I was down at the river, walking with Henry. The fall river was low and a clear green-gray, the silty shore smelling of salmon, spawned out and rotting. The cool breeze rattled the dry yellow leaves on the alder bushes, and out on the water a flock of ducks circled and landed and I heard the distant sound of geese. I do not remember what we talked about as we walked—some sort of chitchat I suppose, and we left the dinner inside the road-house walls. Then suddenly Henry said, "Stop."

"What?"

"Anna, stop a moment." And he came 'round to the front of me and knelt down onto the silt, taking my hand. I knew what was coming then, what it was the others knew that I hadn't. "Anna, will you marry me?"

A myriad of thoughts scattered through my brain, and I felt like the ducks on the water that had landed but whose restless movements seemed to indicate they were deciding between staying or once again taking flight. I looked from Henry to them then back again, and forced myself to focus on the warmth of his hand in mine and the serious, earnest expression on his familiar face. I suddenly realized that if I did not marry Henry, I had no idea what I should do with my life; I had been out of high school two years, had no desire, like I noted at dinner, to move to the city for college, and this was obviously what my parents thought best for me to do as I realized they knew this was unfolding and had given their blessing. And I could not imagine a world without him, the brainy boy behind the counter, and hadn't I daydreamed of marrying Henry for years? Though that thought lived far away in a land I called "eventually"—eventually this, eventually that. "Eventually" had found me now, and I realized that this was my chance, that if I did not take it, "eventually" would find someone else for Henry, and he would no longer be a part of everything I knew. "Yes," I said as my eyes rolled up to the evening sky so as not to miss the flock of Canada geese overhead on their way south—so early, I thought, why so early?

"Anna?" Henry asked, noticing my distraction.

"Oh!" I said and laughed, and pulled Henry up out of the silt where we embraced and teetered like a wobbly top before steadying and standing locked together in the stillness. I remember the smell of his skin and the distant fading honking of the geese and the humming of the river, my eyes looking past his shoulder at the swirling, moving water.

Wade Daniels

ARE YOU CLOSE TO HIM?

Jake? Used to be, but he's been gone awhile now, while I stayed at the farm.

That evening by the river, talking with Anna, before they got drunk and fell into each other for the first time. It seemed so long ago, it was almost as if it had never existed.

Wade had been home six days now—an indeterminably long six days that moved like liquid lead cooling across a floor. He spent a lot of time in his cot, staring at the wall with his back to the door. Sometimes, when he slept, he would wake to find his face wet with tears and his chest heaving as he gulped air like someone afraid of plunging into deep water. But today he pulled himself up and went outside. There were things that needed doing. The snow had settled and melted slightly, and he went about the business of readying the cabin for the real snow soon to come. He split and stacked wood. He put new moss between the logs where the gaps had widened or where the old moss had shrunk and fallen out. He repaired the bind-ings on his old wood snowshoes and picked up any tools that might get buried if left where they lay. And always the lake was there, like a clear smooth face watching him, still and serene. He was back working on the chinking between the logs when he heard a strange buzzing that took him a moment to recog-nize: Jake's motorbike. He put down his bucket of moss and walked around the cabin and waited until he saw his cousin come on foot down the last part of the trail.

"There's FBI in town," Jake said, breathless as he approached, the same as he had been on that first awful day. "Got off the train from Fairbanks yesterday. They're investigating the murders. They want to talk to you."

Without responding Wade walked inside the cabin and grabbed his jacket and hat.

"They're at Fairfield's office," Jake said when Wade reappeared. Wade nodded and began walking down the trail, Jake following behind. "They're talking to everyone who was up there, so don't worry about it."

Wade stopped. "Did they talk to you?"

"Yeah. Piece of cake. We were both here in town—case closed."

Wade looked at his cousin. "It's not a joke, Jake."

"I know that. But God, Wade—why are you taking it so hard?"

Wade swallowed against a strange anger rising inside him. Everyone should take it hard. And if Jake had seen what he saw, maybe he would. "Who else have they talked to?"

"I'm not totally sure. I think the FBI in Seattle is interviewing Capp down there—at least that's what the rumor is. Montana finally crawled his way down from the hills, and I heard they're going after him pretty hard. And well—word is they're still thinking Anna might have done it and then flew the coop."

Wade's body trembled and he felt his head shaking back and forth. "Good God, Jake. Even if she wanted to, she couldn't have done that."

Jake shrugged. "She could have had help. Maybe she's got someone else, you know?"

"But why—" he struggled for control and for the right words. "Even if she has—had—someone, why would she ruin everything? It's not like she can come back from wherever she went and get her—get her—get her life back, Jake. It doesn't make any sense. It doesn't make any sense!" He realized he was yelling now. Jake took a step back.

"Whoa there, Wade. Don't go acting like that in front of the FBI. Calm down buddy, okay? I said it's a piece of cake, but they want to nail someone, make no mistake. So stay calm and answer the questions they ask you and don't offer up anything extra. I've been through this before, remember—well, not with the FBI—but up at the Lawry mine when that fella went missing. I know what I'm talking about, little cousin."

"Did they ask you about that—the Lawry mine?"

"No—and I didn't volunteer."

"But won't that look funny, if someone else mentions it and you didn't?"

Jake shook his head. "I don't think so. That was a freak thing, and there was never any foul play suspected, and if there had been, there would be a whole camp full of suspects. But do me a favor and don't you go offering that up."

Wade shook his head. He stood for a moment pulling air in and out of his lungs while Jake waited with him on the trail. He could smell the decay of the leaves and plants beneath the thinning layer of snow. It was cold and damp, and he wiped his nose on the sleeve of his jacket as he tried to think. If the FBI knew about him and Anna, it would make no difference to anything. All it would do would be to cast more suspicion on her and raise him up on the suspect list. And what would the village think, he wondered, if people knew? There was part of him, though, that wanted to scream the truth, to serve himself up to the judgment of the law and everyone else. Let them blame him. Better to blame him than her. But that wouldn't do anything to help find the person—or persons—who did do it. And they—all of them—needed to know. They needed to know, and they needed that person to help them find Anna.

"You all right, buddy?" Jake asked.

Wade nodded.

"We'd better get moving. I don't think you want to keep those fellas waiting too long."

Wade nodded again, and they moved forward on the trail. When they came to the road and reached the motorbike, Jake offered him a ride, but Wade shook his head and kept moving on the muddy, half-frozen ground in front of him while Jake worked at starting the bike. He needed the time to think, to get himself into some kind of state of calm if at all possible. He had known this day was coming. How much would he say? His cousin's words echoed in his brain as he passed Wade on the motorbike, waving and wishing him luck, and soon the buzzing sound of it faded down the road that was wet and slippery with slushy, dirty snow. When he got to the village, he walked straight to Fairfield's office and knocked on the wooden door.

Billie Sutherland

"WELL, LOOK WHAT THE WIND BLEW IN."

"More like the train, Uncle Howard."

Her mother had won. Billie needed warmer clothes and, as her mother refused to send them up on the train, she had to make the journey south. Now she walked across the newsroom, which swarmed like a stream full of fish as reporters and editors wove through the currents of air in the big, open space. Her uncle put his arm around her shoulders and swept her quickly through the open doorway into his office.

"So what's all this I hear about you hiding yourself away in some small town up the railroad?" He pushed a wheeled chair across the room in her direction. He was a big man, though now saggy in the shoulders and heavy around the middle, his once thick hair thin and wispy and white. "Your mother blames Sam and Sam blames herself and I'm the mosquito caught between the net and the wall."

Billie sat down. "Oh for crying out loud. Last I checked I was twenty-nine years old. I can live where I want."

Her uncle responded with silence as he studied her face.

"What?" Billie asked.

"So what is it, Billie? Man trouble?"

"Man trouble?" she repeated, forcing a short laugh.

I'm married. Does that bother you?

Does that bother you?

No. But it's a long story.

I won't think about it, then.

Howard cleared his throat. "All right. I know that's none of my business. But your family is concerned. Most people don't throw their lives away for no reason."

"I'm not throwing away my life. I'm changing it, that's all."

"You don't necessarily have to change yourself to make changes in your life."

"No. But I want to."

"And you can't tell me why?"

"No."

"Talk to me, Billie."

"No."

He sighed and tapped a pen against the wooden surface of his desk. "All right. But tell the old Billie we miss her, wherever she is." He gave her a smile. "Now I suppose you can tell me what brings you into the newsroom today."

"To see you, of course. I was also looking for some information on a murder. Well, three murders actually."

"Oh," he said, the smile leaving his face as he looked for a moment back out the window. "Those murders."

"If you mean the ones at the mines, yes. The ones that happened in 1941."

"Oh I know, I know when they happened," he said. "Surely someone up there can tell you better than me."

"No one talks about it very much."

"I guess I can understand that. Why are you so interested?"

"It suits my current mood."

At that moment Aunt Sam walked in, still managing to look disheveled in a skirt and pumps and blouse. "Well look who's here!" she said. She put some newspaper-sized proofs on Howard's desk and pulled a chair out from beside the wall. "How's things in the boondocks?"

"Fine, Sam."

"I thought your mother was going to have my head!"

"Sorry, Sam."

"Billie's interested in the murders," Howard interjected.

"Oh," Sam said. "Those murders." She leaned forward in her chair and pushed up her sleeves. "People there still talking about it?"

"No," Billie said. "Not very much."

The room fell quiet for a moment, then Sam said, "Of course I recognized Madeline Merkle. I realized that somewhere along the line I had quit thinking about her. There was a time I thought about her every single day."

"Why didn't you tell me?"

"Tell you? While you were busy shoving me back on the train? If you were going to stay I didn't want to interfere. I figured I'd let you form your own relationship with the town. I thought maybe it had moved on from that old business."

"It hasn't."

"Yet they don't talk about it."

"Only minimally." Billie decided not to mention Montana.

Howard stood. "Come on. We covered it extensively. Those issues shouldn't be too hard to find."

It was damp and a little cold in the basement of the paper where Billie sat at a gray metal desk and delicately turned the pages of the old papers. The stories were all front-page news, though the event was miles away. "Murder in the Mines." "Terror in the Hills." "Two Dead in Brutal Slaying; One Missing." "Brutal

Murders Remain a Mystery." There was the wedding photo of
Anna and Henry, and a fuzzy, out-of-focus snapshot of Nate
Peterson, a few big blow-ups of the general area. Billie looked
at the roll of the hills and the gully-like valleys. And then this:
"Anna Harker Found."

> The remains of Harris Hills murder victim Anna Harker
> have been found at last. Wade Daniels, himself a miner
> who lives near Susitna Station, requested last week
> to be flown out to the crime area and was so obliged
> by local pilot Atlee Virtanen, otherwise known as the
> Flying Finn. Daniels spent several days snowshoeing
> through the hills in what was left of the snow and found
> the remains approximately a mile and a half from the
> Harkers' mining camp. When asked how he knew where
> to look, the thin and weary looking Daniels replied that
> he didn't; he simply looked everywhere within a five-
> mile radius.
>
> Mrs. Harker suffered wounds similar to those
> inflicted upon her husband, Henry Harker, and their
> hand, Nate Peterson, the details of which we will elect
> not to publish in these pages. Suffice it to say the crime
> was brutal and executed with great force if not precision,
> with the likelihood that Mrs. Harker endured great
> suffering before succumbing to her wounds.
>
> As many regular readers will remember, the
> investigation into these murders was interrupted by
> our country's declaration of war against the country of
> Japan and our subsequent involvement in the European
> situation. It is unknown at this time when or if the
> investigation will resume, which leaves the tiny railroad

community of Susitna Station left to wonder who
committed this horrible deed.

And wondering still. Billie heard footsteps on the stairs and felt her uncle's presence behind her. "Find what you're looking for?" he asked.

"A little." She turned in the chair. "It's like reading a story that has no ending." Or like walking down a trail that fades into a shadowland.

Howard handed Billie a manila folder. "You can't take the papers with you, but I kept a file of clippings."

Her heart beat. "Thank you," she said.

"I'll make a reporter out of you yet. Ready for dinner?"

"I suppose." Together, they put the old papers back on the shelves then climbed the stairs, turning off the light, and closing the door behind them.

SEPTEMBER 29, 1941
Anna Harker

I WALKED A SUMMER TRAIL with my mother, Madeline, Maddie, her tall leather boots dirty beneath the hem of her cotton skirt. She wore a wool shirt that belonged to Thomas Merkle, who had been my stepfather for a year and a half, from that December day four months after we lost Uncle Mike, and we had a small wedding at the roadhouse. It was dark and cold—winter solstice—but my mother lit every single candle from the case she had brought up on the train from Anchorage. "This is the end of the dark, Anna," she said. "Our dark. The light will come back now." There was a cake that she baked herself, a moose roast, and a small scattering of the village's residents—miners, mostly, and men who knew Merkle from the trapping trails. Many people did not come. I had thought it was because of my mother—I was growing old enough to recognize that there was something wrong with the fact that until this event she was not married; however, I was able later to discern that it had something to do with a war that had happened far away and in my small world long ago, and that Thomas Merkle was a German.

On that other day, on the summer trail, my mother talked about the light. "We need to savor this, and then remember it, all this light," she said, glancing back over her shoulder at me. I had wanted to be fishing, and I was bored, and I also knew we were on a futile mission. The fiddlehead ferns were uncurling and were past the picking stage; if my mother spent more time in the woods, she would know that. "Three months from now we'll be sliding back into the dark. It happens so fast!" she went on. She looked back at me again and smiled, her teeth white against the red of her lips. Her hair was falling out of the bun on the back of her head, and there was something about that, and the way the wool shirt hung on her slim shoulders, and her old, trail-dusty boots that made me realize, suddenly, and for the first time, that my mother was young (I had always thought she was pretty), and that not too very long ago she had been like me.

"Mama," I said and stopped on the trail.

She stopped, too, and turned. The world was new spring green—green leaves on the birch trees, green leaves on the sprouting fireweed stalks, green leaves adorned with popcorn-like clusters of tiny white flowers on the highbush cranberry bushes. And the brightest green of all was found on the fiddle-head ferns, unfurled and reaching and looking like big green feathers stuck into the ground. I saw my mother's warm dark eyes look toward them. "Oh," she said. "I guess we missed them."

"Mama," I said again.

"What is it, Anna? You were right, you know, you told me, didn't you?"

"Do I have to grow up?"

She looked at me a moment as I stood on the trail, my flannel shirt all crooked above my dirty boy's overalls, the lace of one of my leather boots undone and dragging on the ground.

"Don't you want to?" she asked.

"Did you want to?" As young as I was I could see how my return question surprised her.

She looked down at the trail then up at the new leaves waving from the tops of the trees. "I think I did," she said, looking back at me. "It all happened so fast, this grown-up business."

"Do you miss being a kid?"

"Oh, I do," she said. "But I have you. And I couldn't have you and still be a kid."

"Will it happen fast to me too?"

"Oh, Anna." She set her bucket on the ground and knelt down in front of me. "Not if I can help it. And look at you! A lady you are not. Not yet! There are years and years of play ahead of you, my dear, and we'll stretch it all out as long as we can. Now remember this day, this beautiful new summer day with everything blooming and sprouting and—"

Her voice is fading from me now, the day disappearing like water in my hand, and I hear another voice, a singing— *Where the blaeberries grow* . . . And no, no, I do not want to go to that day—

Go with me, Anna. Me.

I was afraid of losing everything, and look at where I am.

I was on the edge of a cliff. And now I have found my way off of it, though in a way I could never have foreseen. And here I linger, between the beginning and the end.

Wade Daniels

"COME IN, WADE," Fairfield said and pulled open the door. In contrast to the man Wade had grown to know in their time together in the hills, Fairfield now wore a white shirt, rolled at the sleeves, and his round face and balding, hatless head were covered with a thin film of sweat. As Wade stepped inside he was hit by the heat that radiated out from the potbellied wood-stove. He removed his wool coat and took in the two men at Fairfield's desk, both in white shirts and dark pants, their suit jackets draped across the backs of their chairs. Their city shoes were marked with mud.

"This is Agent Morgan and Agent Arnold," Fairfield said. "Go on ahead and sit in that seat there."

Wade obeyed, still holding his jacket, and faced the men.

"We called you in for two reasons," Arnold—or was it Morgan—he'd forgotten already which was which—began. "First, we're questioning all the miners who were in the Harris Hills this past season. And secondly, because you volunteered to be part of the initial search team."

Wade's brow furrowed. He wasn't sure what that last had to do with anything.

"You were in the employ of your cousin, Jake Timmers, in a mine roughly two miles from the Harkers' claim," the second agent said.

"Yes."

"From what day to what day?"

"I went up there the end of May. I came back about three weeks ago."

"Can you be more specific?"

"No."

The agents paused. Then: "Did you know the victims?"

He nodded.

"Elaborate."

Wade took a deep breath. "It's a small place. We all know each other."

"Were you friends with Henry Harker or Nate Peterson?"

"A little, I suppose."

"How so?"

Wade shrugged. "I would see Nate at the Clearwater sometimes. We went fishing once or twice."

"What was it—once, or twice?"

"Twice. Maybe three times. I go fishing a lot. Sometimes people just show up."

"What about Mr. Harker? Did you go fishing with him?"

"No."

"And why not?"

"Henry didn't fish."

And so it went, for some time, with every answer Wade gave somehow opening the door for another question. He felt his mind drift as he answered numbly, barely comprehending what he was responding to.

"And what about Mrs. Harker?" one of the men asked.

"Who?"

"Mrs. Harker, who remains missing. Did you know her?"

"Yes."

"Do you know where she might be?"

Wade felt a shudder run through him, despite the warmth in the room. "No. We couldn't find her."

"I understand you've worked with law enforcement before, in Vermont where you come from."

"Yes. But only once."

"Pretty good out in the wild?"

"Good enough."

"Where do you think Mrs. Harker is now?"

He swallowed. "The hills." The words came out softly.

"Where?"

"Up there. The hills."

"If she's there, why couldn't you find her?"

"The snow came too soon." Wade realized his hands were shaking. He tried to still them in his lap.

"Do you think she's hiding, then?"

"No."

"What do you think happened to Mrs. Harker? Do you think she was kidnapped?"

"No."

"And why not?"

He shook his head. "I don't know."

"Think about it."

He nodded, felt a tightening in his throat. "Because," he said, "I think she is dead."

"And why would you think that?"

"I feel it, that's all." He knew this was the wrong response, but it was the only thing he could say.

"Feel it?"

Wade nodded.

"Were you friends with Mrs. Harker?"

"Yes."

"Did you know her well?"

"I think so." He was alert now, like walking on new ice. He could fall through if he wasn't careful. "She liked to fish."

"Do you think she was capable of killing her husband and Mr. Peterson?"

Wade shook his head and lifted his eyes. "You've seen those bodies. You tell me."

The two men exchanged a glance, tapped their pencils on sheets of paper. The one sitting in Fairfield's chair on the other side of the desk leaned forward. "What do you think we should know?" he asked.

Wade had to think. He wasn't sure what the agent meant. "How long," Wade said.

"What?"

"How long does it take to murder three people with an ax thirty miles from anywhere and disappear?"

"You tell me," the agent leaning back in his chair said, echoing Wade's earlier remark.

Wade stared at the desk. He had thought about this, over and over. His mouth began to move, and he heard his words escape out into the world. "You lie in wait, bide your time. Maybe you're up on that little hill, right behind the operation, watching. You wait until it looks like Henry and Nate are ready to head back to the camp; you don't want to spend too much time talking to them. So you wait to show up, and when you do, they're surprised because it's late in the season and most everyone has left. They invite you back to the camp. You make sure you take up the rear as you head down the trail. Maybe the ax is hidden somewhere, where you can grab it quickly without them seeing.

"You're pretty strong and have the advantage of surprise so the murders of the men are fairly quick. But then you have to find Anna. For some reason that's important, not to leave her behind. Because that would be easiest, you know, to kill the two men then leave the way you came. But for some reason, you must also kill Anna. Was it because she saw you? Was it because, if only Henry died, she would get the mine? Or was it because you just couldn't stand the thought of her being alive." His whole body was shaking now. A little voice inside of him was telling him to shut up, shut up, but he couldn't stop himself. "Anna's not in camp. Where would she go, and how would you know where to find her? Unless you got lucky and caught a glimpse of the direction she was heading. Then you track her down. This takes longer than you'd like, because she walked quite a ways from camp, for some reason. Otherwise we would have found her. But wherever she is you're able to sneak up on her—the wind blows up there, and the tundra is soft beneath your feet. You could do it. Or maybe you just walked up and said hello, the same way you did the men. Then you've got to get out of there, and fast, because it will eventually get dark and you don't want to be anywhere near."

The room felt heavy then, as if the weight of the snow on the roof were pressing down and waiting for the walls to burst. Fairfield stared out a window at nothing, and the two FBI men looked at him. "I see you've thought quite a bit about this," one of them said.

"I have."

"Did you kill Henry Harker and Nate Peterson?"

He shook his head.

"Answer. I mean, say it."

"No."

"No what?"

"No, I did not kill those men."

"But you wanted to."

Wade's voice caught in his throat. "No," he said. No, he did not want to. But not so far down deep inside part of him had wished Henry Harker would fall off the face of the earth.

He felt their eyes on him. "I did not kill those men," he repeated.

They let him go then, and as Wade walked away down the street he could feel them watching him.

The temperature dropped that night, and the next morning a thin layer of ice lay across the surface of the lake. He walked to the edge of the shore, his boots crunching on the frozen ground, and squatted down. The ice was perfect, like a clear sheet of glass. He laid his hand on it, cold and smooth, then watched as his hand formed a fist and slammed onto the fragile ice, and the whole of it moved, as if taking a breath, a spider-web of cracks radiating out from the gash in the ice where he broke through.

Billie Sutherland

BILLIE SAT IN THE BEDROOM of her youth, smoking a cigarette and looking out the window at the old swing in the backyard. The board for the seat was weathered and gray, the rope
frayed and rough. Her father had made it years ago, and she and
her baby brother, Gus, had spent many hours of their growing
years sitting on it, sometimes swinging, sometimes not.

Gus had been there at dinner, along with Uncle Howard
and Aunt Sam, and her mother had cooked a big moose roast
with potatoes and carrots from the garden. Everyone had
been on best behavior, as if Billie were an out-of-town guest
they were trying not to scare away. Gus restrained himself
from wolfing down his food as fast as he could before excus-
ing himself to go cruising down the long straight streets
of midtown, where his girlfriend lived; Sam and Howard
discussed the latest developments in the young state's polit-
ical arena; and her parents, Hal and Clara, sat at either end of
the table, as quietly as if every word out of their mouths might
exact a hefty price. Typically the couple's words flew across the
table like ping-pong balls aimed straight at the other as their
verbal war held steady across the decades:

*You're never here, Hal. You're always at the airfield or out in the
"wild blue yonder." When you're not flying for pay, you're flying for fun,
and I feel like I'm raising these two on my own.*

You've never complained about the pay, Clara.

When a woman has mouths to feed, she doesn't complain about the pay.

You could thank me now and then.

And you could thank me.

Shortly after dinner, after Sam and Howard went home and Billie had finished washing the dishes, she heard them going at it in the deserted kitchen.

"Just leave her alone, Clara. She'll work out whatever it is."

"It must be a man, Hal. Billie never had any sense when it came to men."

Her mother and her sharp bird-like face—hawkish—the swoop of dark hair falling sideways across her forehead toward the hairpin that held it back near her ear; her father, softer, taller, rounded eyes and receding hairline, his pale, fleshy face worn and tired from his long days at the airfield.

Billie didn't tell them she was leaving in the morning. She had found her winter gear stuffed away in the upper shelves of her closet and had it packed and ready in a duffle on the floor. There wasn't another northbound train for several more days, but the Finn had given her his schedule and offered to fly her back. He would be at the airfield tomorrow, her father's airfield, and she would be there to meet him, even if she had to walk. She knew the sight of him would be like seeing a cool lake on a hot sweaty day. But she knew, too, that she had to keep that in check. She didn't know him. And he didn't know anything about her.

Her mother was right. She never did have any sense with men. Or with women.

Amelia.

Billie.

So nice to meet you! I just moved in next door and was wondering if you would like to share a bottle of Beaujolais?

I'd love to! My place or yours?

Oh—yours if you don't mind. My place is rather—well, you know what's it's like, moving in.

Of course. My place it is!

And her place it was, her treasured Seattle apartment, for many bottles shared with Amelia, her new neighbor. Amelia was thin and petite with long straight sand-colored hair and freckles across her nose. She seemed so young, but she was thirty-two already, older than Billie. Jimmy's age. Amelia was a travel writer so they considered themselves in the same field, and they talked about Greece and Italy and England and France. They talked about men, too—their "others" as Amelia called them.

Copilot, Billie said.

Pilot.

Oh? Which airline?

Continental.

Mine's with United.

Ever do it on plane?

Yes, Billie said. They clinked glasses at that.

Does he come here often—to your place, I mean.

No, not often, Billie said. *We meet up when we can where we can. But when we're both in Seattle, definitely.* Billie didn't mention hers was married. But Amelia said, *Mine was married when we first met.*

Oh. How did that go?

His wife found out and she committed suicide.

You're kidding.

No—it was quite awful, really. We nearly split up over it. But then we figured, what the hell, you know? Why cry over spilt milk?

163

I guess, Billie said, unsure of how she should respond. Then Amelia raised her glass and said, *A toast.*

Billie raised hers.

To dead wives, Amelia said.

Billie laughed, and shrugged, and clinked her glass against Amelia's.

Now Billie tried to imagine herself, her old self, on the swing in the yard. Before she knew anything. Before she did anything. That self she could no longer be.

Anna Harker

THERE IS A SCAR ON MY HAND, between the forefinger
and the thumb, where I was bitten as I tried to break up a fight
between two of our sled dogs. Merkle and I were out in these
hills, in the bitter cold of winter, checking a string of traps, the
landscape white and hard and frozen. We glided over it, him
on the big sled with the main team and me behind on a smaller
sled with my favorite dogs—Jack, River, Grizzly, Keats, and
Brontë—pulling me along. The day had been clear and pain-
fully bright, and we wore dark glasses against the glare of the
snow. It was a blue-white world, punctuated by stabs of green
where the top halves of wind-beaten spruce trees stuck out
from their tombs of snow.

As the light began to fade, I could see up ahead where we
were headed—a little patch of spruce on the side of a distant
hill where a trapping cabin Merkle had built stood half buried
and frozen. It was when we arrived at the trees that the dogs
had their fight. Merkle had removed his shovel from his sled
and was digging a trench through the snow to free the door
of the cabin; I knew without being told to begin to ready the
dogs for the night, releasing them from the lead line and tying
them to trees.

I did Merkle's dogs first. Despite being tired they seemed
agitated, and I realized one of the female dogs, a small slender blue-eyed Siberian named Gracie, was coming into heat. I
pulled her off to be somewhat distant from the other dogs, and

a big male named Wolfie, still fastened to the lead line, lunged forward, bringing the sled with him. Then Grizzly followed suit, bringing my whole team with him. Grizzly caught Wolfie and they lit into each other. Fortunately, I had already fastened Gracie to a tree and was able to rush forward into the violent, twisted tangle of dogs to try to stop them from tearing each other into shreds. Wolfie had the smaller Grizzly down in the snow, so I grabbed Wolfie by the harness and yanked him backward as Grizzly shot back up and went after him.

There was a moment of fangs and fur and awful snarls before Merkle was there, pulling Grizzly back while I still held Wolfie. Grizzly had a torn ear and Wolfie had a bloody mouth, but otherwise the dogs were all right. It wasn't until we got all the dogs separated and put in their proper places that I noticed my mitten was torn, and when I pulled it off, I saw that I had been bit.

Merkle poured some whiskey on it—the "medicine," as he said. He never drank but carried a small bottle with him to use as either an antiseptic or a painkiller in emergencies. "You'll be all right, Anna," he said. "It's not too deep." He pulled a clean handkerchief out of his pack on the sled and wrapped it around my hand, then returned to shoveling out the cabin while I fed the dogs slabs of salmon my mother and I had harvested from the river and dried the previous summer while Merkle worked the mine.

The cabin heated quickly but only had one small slice of a window, so we left the door cracked to catch what little remaining light there was. When the darkness came we closed it, and knowing how the snow surrounded us and smelling the thawing dirt floor beneath us, I felt like I was buried. This feeling was enhanced as bits of movement on the floor caught my eye: mice and shrews. Merkle saw these too and lifted the only piece of wood on the floor, beneath which a large tin can was stuck into a hole in the ground. He placed a small piece of pemmican into the can, and while we sat at the tiny square table on tree stumps for chairs I could hear the mice and shrews, one by one, falling into the can.

"Don't let them eat each other," I said, trying not to think about it as I ate thawed-out stew and bread packed for us by my mother.

"The biggest one will win," he said. "Isn't that the way of the world?"

"No," I said. "It doesn't have to be."

"It is the way of the humans and their countries," he said, "and the way of nature and her forests. I prefer the forest."

"Is that why you left Germany?"

"There is plenty of forest in Germany," Merkle said. "Beautiful, majestic, ancient forest." He scooped spoonfuls of stew with one hand and held his bread with the other, tearing pieces from it with his teeth. "The land my family owned, with a big forest of many acres, I could have lived there forever."

Those last words puzzled me and made me feel jealous, somehow, of that country far away. I watched him eat, the dim kerosene light softening and sharpening his features at once as all became either shadow or gentle, yellow light. "Why did you leave, then?"

He quit chewing for a moment, his eyes looking down at his half-empty bowl, and I could tell that he was thinking. "The country stayed beautiful," he said, "but the people began to change. I found I could not change with them."

I had never really thought about Merkle's life before his became part of my mother's and mine. "What about your family?" I asked.

"My older brother was killed in the war, and my parents looked at me and saw him instead."

I didn't know at the time exactly what this meant, but I realized suddenly that if Merkle had never left his German family behind, I surely would have died the day we lost Uncle Mike. "You saved my life," I said, and as he looked across the crude little table and his blue eyes met mine, I could see he knew what I was referring to.

"No, Anna," he said softly. "It is you and your mother who saved mine."

Save me again, I think now. *Find me before the snow comes and bring me home*. Otherwise I will be buried like the cabin. I see the scar I received that long-ago day, my arm sprawled in front of me on the tundra, and it winks at me as my hand, which I cannot feel, twitches like a thing with a life of its own. *Save me again*.

Wade Daniels

WHY DID HE EVER get involved with Nellie, he wondered.
Was it because Anna sprung a leak inside of him that made him
burst out all over? He couldn't have Anna, but he could have
Nellie. And she wanted to be with him, then and now, more
than he ever wanted to be with her.

But there was a time, admittedly, when he considered
Nellie. He would never have let things go as far as they did
if there wasn't that possibility; he was not that bad of a man.
She was beautiful in a gentle, quiet way; her skin the color of
a cup of builder's tea rich with milk and sugar; and her hair
the shiny black of ravens' wings. He felt like he could love her,
her and her soft, easy kisses and gentle ways. He watched her
now, moving around his cabin, still looking after him in the
wake of the horror in the hills. A deep shame burned in him as
he remembered the two of them, drunk from the New Year's
Eve party at the Merkles' roadhouse, stumbling back to her
cabin on the other side of the railroad tracks and into her soft,
warm bed. She lifted her thick sweater and her calico kuspuk
over her head. Her long john shirt was thin and worn, but she
had embroidered little flowers around the neckline, flowers
the color of wild roses strung together with a delicate green.
He lifted this up and over her head, and when she was free
of it, she grabbed it back and held it to her chest. He laughed
and fell backward against the pillows. Then she threw the shirt
down into his face and laughed, too, and they rolled around

together, laughing and pulling at each other's clothes. It was only when she cried out in pain that he had realized she was a virgin. The awareness of that had weighed on him and filled him with a tenderness for her at the same time. And when morning came, and her dark eyes danced with happiness, he knew that he had gotten himself into something that would be difficult, at best, to put behind.

She was making fry bread now, dropping the dough into the fat that bubbled in a pot on the stove, turning it over and over until lightly browned on all sides. She'd lined a flat pan with a clean flour sack and put the done pieces onto that, and the pile grew into a golden mound. It smelled good. In normal times Wade would have eaten several pieces already, waiting eagerly for Nellie to scoop each new batch out of the pan, but all was changed now, forever.

She put several fresh pieces onto a plate and brought it over to him. "You need to eat, yeah? This is real good." She stood before him as he sat on his cot, and he looked up into her deep dark eyes.

"Why aren't you crying?" he asked, studying her face. He saw the shadow of his words there as she realized his meaning.

"Why you say that, eh?"

He shrugged and shook his head. "I'm sorry. I just—" He couldn't finish. She sat down beside him.

"I loved Anna, and Henry," she said. "Nate—I didn't know so much, but he seemed nice, yeah? But Anna, she was my big sister. And Henry—he was the boy we all wanted, so smart, you know. When I was little I thought Anna would marry George and I would marry Henry, and we would do all kinds of things together, and be a big family. Now they're all dead, and I still want a big family. I think now, maybe in *yuyanq*—the sky—is where my big family is, waiting, and I have to wait until I find them there."

He still, even in the midst of his current pain, recognized the fact that he had let Nellie down. It was like a cloud in his cluttered brain. But there was also something she was saying, that glinted in his mind like a flake of gold at the bottom of a stream. "We don't know that she's dead," he said.

Nellie studied his face. She seemed unruffled by his words. "She's dead, yeah," she said softly. "Where else would she be?"

Wade held her eyes as long as he could, then looked away. Nellie stood up and put the plate of fry bread on the table. Keeping her back to him she said, "I lost people, you know that. I've cried enough in my life to fill all the rivers. And I cried for Anna, and I cried for Henry. But I can't cry all the time anymore. I'm stuck here in this life, and I need to keep going." She looked over her shoulder then. "You're stuck here in this life, too, and you need to keep going." She pulled her coat off a chair. "You need more wood, eh? I'll split some before I go."

"No. Please. I can do it."

"You don't want me to do it, then you get up and get outside, and do it yourself. That's where I'll be, chopping. When you come outside to do it, I will stop." She grabbed her mittens and walked out the door.

Wade sat for a few moments, trying to think. He wanted to be left alone. He was sick of Nellie. He was sick of Jake. Always checking on him. *Why are you so worked up about it?* Jake had said, on his last visit here, and it was all Wade could do to keep from punching him. He had to pretend, but every day it seemed harder, not easier. There were some wounds, he was learning, that time would not heal.

He heard the sound of the ax outside, coming down on wood. Chop . . . chop. *Stop!* He wanted to yell. Stop. But he pulled himself up and found his boots and his coat, in a heap on the floor by the door. As he shoved and tugged himself into his outerwear he looked out his window and saw Nellie lifting the ax. She swung it hard down into the wood, which fell from the block halved in two. She picked up another piece and set it down on the chopping block, swiftly, then just as swiftly she raised the ax again and brought it back down. As he watched her, thoughts and images flashed through him, like lifting the lid on a box of snakes. "No," he said aloud, wanting to shove them back down. "No."

Nellie would not do that, even if she could.

Billie Sutherland

IN THE QUIET OF HER ROADHOUSE room Billie pored over the clippings her uncle gave her, some that she'd read in the newspaper morgue and some from other newspapers, yellowed and fragile, from both in-state and out-of-state publications. Billie noted the names that appeared: Montana Hines, John Cobb, Wade Daniels, Atlee Virtanen, Thomas Merkle, Madeline Merkle, Emmet Harker, Helen Harker, Ben Fairfield. There was always the same issue when it came to possible suspects: the distance and the difficulty of the location. She realized the second most likely suspect (after Montana, who was already there) would be the Finn. He could fly in, kill everyone, and fly back out. But there was his flight log, and the fact that he was seen that day in a community two hundred miles to the north.

You're my prime suspect, she imagined herself saying to him, and the thought brought a smile to her face until it triggered her memory:

I can't be here.

What?

I can't. Think of how it would look. I'd be a prime suspect. And so would you.

What?

And then the screaming began again in her head.

"We have to quit meeting like this."

Billie startled at the words. She looked up from the folder of clippings, which she'd brought with her.

"I'm kidding, Billie," the Finn said as he sat across from her, the teapot full and warm.

Yes, indeed.

You are such a bad, bad person.

Yes, indeed.

Show me how bad.

Yes, indeed.

"You okay?" The Finn poured their tea.

"Yes." *Oh, what hills, what hills are yon, my love?* She could hear the song again. She took a deep breath and focused.

"Is that your uncle's folder?"

"Yes."

"Find anything new?"

"I don't think so." She pushed the folder across the table and watched as he flipped it open and let his eyes wander over the clippings.

"Bad memories," he said.

Billie glanced over her shoulder at the window. "What if the person who did it was still here, walking among you, living and breathing?"

"Then it would be Montana," he said.

"Or you."

"I'm afraid I'm not the murdering type."

"That's what they all say." She gave him a quick glance and short smile, then saw how her hand shook as she reached for her mug. *Don't worry, Billie, no one would think you did anything. You're not the type.*

"You all right?" he asked again.

She nodded.

He watched her. She made an effort bring the cup to her lips.

"I shake sometimes too," he said quietly. "Remnants of the war."

"Some excuse."

"I suppose there's all kinds of wars."

"I suppose."

"It helps to focus on the present. You know what they say, the past is dead and gone."

She laughed before she could stop herself, and was aware of the strange, strained sound she made. He reached across the table and grabbed her hand, holding it firmly in his.

Anna Harker

OUR WEDDING NIGHT, mine and Henry's. We'd planned
the wedding to coincide with a southbound train, so we could
ride into Anchorage and spend several nights in a real hotel.
I hadn't been into the city in so long and was surprised to
see how much it had changed and grown. So many shops, it
seemed, lining the streets. Henry held my hand and carried our
small suitcase. My shoes were pinching my toes, and I couldn't
wait to kick them off my feet. I didn't know where we were
going; it was a surprise.

Had we married, I would later wonder, because we were
two of the few people our age in the village? Would we have
even noticed each other if we had lived in a city such as Anchorage, which to me on that day seemed as full of people as the
streams are full of water in the spring? But now I think yes, yes;
there was more to it—more to Henry—than I have thought in
the days since Wade.

Our wedding was down at the river, which Henry's
mother didn't like but which was the one thing I insisted upon.
It was partly sunny, and in the distance the mountain range
winked in and out of the clouds. There was silt in my shoes,
and I would have got rid of them right then but conceded
that would not make a good fresh start with my new in-laws,
though there was not to be a fresh start with Helen and Emmitt.
I would always be the fatherless inappropriate girl with the

disreputable mother and the stepfather from "that country."
Ah, well. It all seems so silly now. But it didn't then.

My maid of honor and only bridesmaid was Nellie, who
was growing now into a lovely young woman but who was
so tragically alone since George's terrible death, save for her
aging aunt. Henry's best man was Jake Timmers. I found that
odd—surely he could have found someone else—but he noted
many of his friends now were his college friends, miles away,
the best of whom, Nate Peterson, would join us in the spring
and help at the mine. The ceremony was brief, and there was
an afternoon reception at the roadhouse where we ate fresh
grilled trout and cake and drank some cheap champagne that
my parents had managed to have brought up from Anchorage.
By the time we got on the train my head hurt, but I leaned
against Henry and dozed as the train rumbled its way through
the miles of wilderness until it reached the city that I always
knew was there but which always seemed another world away.

"We have arrived, Anna," Henry said, and my eyes opened
to his.

And so we walked newly married down the streets of
Anchorage. "Look at all the cars!" I said, my head turning
from one side of the street to the other to take them all in. I
had not been to the city since I was thirteen, when Mama and
I accompanied Merkle on his yearly end-of-winter trip to sell
his furs. It had been much smaller then, and what I remembered most about the visit were a group of children who played
in the street and threw soggy snowballs at each other, and I
wondered if I might see Henry among them, as that was one
of the winters his parents had sent him away to school. But
I remembered, too, the feeling of wanting to go home. The

stores didn't interest me, and I missed my dogs, and after a few days I had given up hope of seeing Henry playing in the streets.

"Someday we'll have one, Anna," Henry said about the cars. "I can promise you that." He looked at me quite seriously and only then did it really hit me who he was now: husband. Someone I belonged to, and who belonged to me, and with whom I might someday be the owner of an automobile. For an instant the idea sent a thrilling shiver through me and I had to stop myself from kissing him in public, which I knew he would not like and which I was unsure was legal to do in a city. Then I remembered something and laughed. "We have to get a road before we get a car," I said. Though there were indeed roads in Susitna Station, there was no road to us yet, and those few who owned cars and had them brought up by the train had to content themselves with driving on what was like a small island surrounded by trees.

"The road will come," he said. "And when it does, Susitna Station will never be the same."

"Oh." That wasn't necessarily a welcome thought, though I could see that for Henry, it was.

The sidewalks were wide, the streets paved, and it was not lost on me the eyes that turned toward us and the smiles that fell upon us as we walked along. My dress was not fancy enough nor was Henry's suit to announce our recent nuptials. There was something else about us, something on our faces or the way we strode down the side of the street as if the world were suddenly ours. And it was, I see that now, to have life and youth and love, and as Henry led us toward the beautiful Anchorage Hotel, I could not even begin to let myself imagine that was where we were to stay, but there was something else that was ours: Gold. And I felt its power as Henry led me across the street toward the tall white building that towered above us and glowed in front of us.

"The magic of gold," Henry whispered as he loved me that night, our small-town, simple skin sliding across sheets of heavenly silky smoothness. It was paying for our nights in this grandest of places. It would buy our breakfast in the morning, delivered to our room, dinner and champagne before another night in the large bed in the lovely room, which would be followed by several more luxurious days before it also paid for our train ride home. Henry carried a pouch of gold in the pocket of his pants. That night in the hotel he pulled a pinch of it out from the pouch and sprinkled it over my naked body.

"Henry, don't," I said.

"Why not?"

"It's wasteful."

"I don't think so," he said, rubbing the flakes across my now-glittering flesh. "It looks beautiful on you." He parted my legs and lay down on top of me, bringing his face close to mine. "There's more where that came from, Anna," he said, "and I'm going to dig it all out of the ground."

As I waited for a kiss, or for him to thrust himself inside of me, I watched his eyes slide away from mine and look at something near the top of my head: the bag of gold, still clutched tightly in his hand.

Wade Daniels

WINTER FELL ON SUSITNA STATION like the remains of an avalanche that slid down from the hills. Wade sat in the Clearwater and watched it come, swirling all around the building he sat in, swirling all around the quiet town. Across the horseshoe bar, out the window and across the street, Wade could discern in the thickening white the figure of Emmitt Harker sweeping the snow off the store's front porch. What must he think, Wade wondered, what must he feel? Mrs. Harker had been rarely seen in the days since the murders, and several weeks ago went to Washington State where her two daughters were living. Would she come back, would Emmitt follow her there and leave this place behind? This place that had been so good to them before it turned like a rabid wolf that tore their hearts from their chests and ate them while they watched. How does one recover from that?

He had an image, then, of a day like today, years down the road or years "farther up the creek," as the old-timers say, when sitting like he was now someone might say to him, "Have you heard about Emmitt Harker?" and slide a Washington newspaper down the bar for him to look at, where he would see Emmitt's life condensed into a column of type on the obituary page, Alaska and this town a paragraph in black and white. But there would be this: *preceded in death by his son, Henry.*

Would Wade himself, though, still be here then? He couldn't see what his life might be like. He couldn't see how anything would ever feel different than the way the world felt at this moment: shrouded and sad, all gray and white, falling all around him.

The door opened and Montana stepped in, the snow clinging to his shoulders and his hat. Wade and the two other men at the bar all watched him walk in and sit down in the corner by the window where he always sat. Wade noticed how the others kept looking at him and the way Montana stared out the window, his jaw set tight against the staring, looking thin and gaunt. Wade looked away. He knew Montana couldn't have done what was done. Still, he could feel John Summers, the barkeep, ignoring Montana. He wiped the bar and washed some glasses and wiped the bar some more. After about ten minutes Montana grabbed his hat, shook the wet off it, and went back out the door, ending the standoff that was a daily occurrence now in these dark times.

Wade watched him through the window as he walked out into the snow. He went over it again in his mind. Montana kills them, waits a day, goes back to the scene, rushes to the Harrisville Roadhouse to report the discovery. Plenty of time to clean his ax (with the wrong-sized blade), burn or bury any bloodied clothing. (Though Wade and everyone knew Montana had little clothing: two pairs of trousers, two long sleeved shirts, two short, one set of long johns. Raingear, a wool jac-shirt. All accounted for and nothing recently washed.) Himself not recently washed. There would be blood, wouldn't there be, taking human beings down with an ax? "It's not him, it's not," Wade said, slipping off his barstool. "You're wrong, all of you, to think it."

"Then who, Wade, just answer that," Summers said, snatching up Wade's empty glass.

"It could be any of us," Wade said. "Any one. Any one of us could have slipped away for a few days, hotfooted it up there, then come back."

"But Montana had reason," Summers said. "Emmitt Harker took that claim from him, and he's been angry ever since."

"It doesn't make sense that he would do it," Wade said.

"It doesn't make sense that any of us would, Wade. But somebody did. Somebody." And then the circle of men around the bar did what they've been doing ever since: looking around from one face to the other, wondering.

Wade pulled on his wool hunting cap and walked out into the snow. Montana had all but disappeared down the street; Wade could barely make out his form in the swirling snow and grainy light. Wade shoved his hands into the deep pockets of his wool coat and hurried after him.

"Montana!" he said. "Hey—wait up!"

The older man stopped and looked over his shoulder at Wade as he approached. "What?" Montana said.

Wade breathed in the cold air and looked up at the thick and delicate flakes cascading down. His mind went involuntarily to the hills, to the thick white blanket this would add onto, burying Anna ever deeper. "I don't think it was you," he said, still watching the snow.

Montana answered with silence, and finally Wade looked at him. "I'm not just saying that," he said.

Montana spit out into the snow, brown and syrupy from the wad of chew in his cheek. "It was someone completely crazy, or someone who wanted that mine," Montana said, his face gray and angry in the fading light of the winter day. "I wanted that mine back. But I wouldn't touch a hair on either of their heads. Anna and Henry. I watched them grow. Now that mine is as dead to me as they are. Who would want it after that?"

"Something went wrong," Wade said, "with somebody."

"Gold! Gold's what went wrong. It gets ahold of you and wraps its shiny sharp fingers around your heart, leads you around by a ring in your nose. It's about the gold. Has to be."

"But that doesn't make sense, either. Like you say, who would want the place now? That and Anna—they both—had family."

Montana shrugged. "Maybe it was a crazy person then. I don't know. The only thing I know is that I didn't do it, and I'm the only one who knows that for sure."

Wade was going to say more, but as he looked to his left he saw a face in the window of the roadhouse. Maddie, looking out at the two of them. Whatever it was he was going to say caught in his throat. Montana made a small noise, like a wounded bird, then turned and walked away, disappearing into the snow.

Two weeks later, Wade was again in the Clearwater, and on this day the patrons were so silent you could hear every time someone took a sip of their whiskey or beer. The radio was on, and those nearest to it leaned toward where it sat on the bar. If anyone dared to speak, even whisper, they were met with a quick, sharp *Shhh*. The radio's reception was bad, faint and full of static, through which floated the voice of a man far away. Now and again the people in the barroom looked at each other, the confusion evident on their faces. Then the Flying Finn burst through the front door, and before anyone could shut him up, he said, his cheeks flushed from the cold and from the excitement of his news, "We're going! We're joining the war!" and a swarm of voices buzzed through the room. Wade looked out the window, at the quiet winter street, so far away from the struggle in Europe and the devastation in Hawaii. But like a great hand that reached across the miles of the world, the war had found him, and he would be plucked from this village, from this life he built for himself that was so brutally chopped into ruins by the swinging of an ax, and he would be all too willing to go.

Billie Sutherland

NELLIE. Billie had seen the quiet, dark-eyed woman bring bags of blueberries and cranberries to Maddie, who in turn simmered and strained the blue and red harvest into jars of jam and bottles of juice and ketchup. Nellie's hair was thick and black with a few strands of white and was twisted into a round, soft bun pinned to the back of her head, and today she wore a thick wool scarf that framed her still young face. She stood quietly by the river, gazing off somewhere in the distance as the twilight began to gather. Billie had seen her walking this way as she picked rosehips for Maddie, and she came out of the brush and onto the river sand not far from where Nellie stood. The older woman turned and smiled at Billie, tilting her face down shyly, and Billie felt instantly welcome.

"Whatcha making?" Nellie asked, looking at the can of rosehips.

Billie shook her head and pulled dead leaves out of her hair. "I'm not making anything," she said. "I'm going to give these to Maddie, and I'm sure she'll turn them into something wonderful."

"Probably some jelly," Nellie offered.

"Oh," Billie said. "Maybe."

"Probably. It'll be good, eh?"

"Everything Maddie cooks is good," Billie said. "I'm Billie."

Nellie smiled and nodded. "I know. Everyone knows, eh? The lady from Anchorage who has the Finn flying in circles!" She giggled a little. "I jokes. My name is Nellie."

"I know," Billie said. "And I know I'm new, and all of you have known each other for a long time."

"It's not bad, to be you. So much attention! It would be a fun thing. Me, I've always just been here. I've never been new." She was still smiling, but Billie could see a sadness on her face.

"Where do you live?" Billie asked.

"Oh, I have a place, on my family property. It's over that way," she pointed back toward the village, "on the other side of the railroad tracks."

"I've seen you walking from there," Billie said, and then as Nellie looked back toward the river a silence settled around them.

"I'm kind of sad today," Nellie said finally.

"I'm sorry," Billie said.

"It's the time of year. It always makes me sad."

"Summers are too short, aren't they?" But Billie was well aware of the day.

"I like the winter," Nellie said. "I don't mind."

Billie waited while Nellie stood solemnly staring at the water. Then she asked, "You were friends with Anna Harker, weren't you? That's why you're sad, isn't it?"

Nellie nodded and pulled something out of her pocket. "I found something today, see?" She stretched her hand toward Billie. It was a wild rose, pale and delicate. "Late bloomer, eh? I almost didn't want to pick it. But I thought Anna must have made it happen, from the other side. That she was saying hello. And I remember how her mama always throws a rose into the river on her birthday, and I thought maybe Anna bloomed the rose so I could throw it into the river on her death day. Maybe there's some meaning in it, you know? Like that her birthday and her death day are not so different." Nellie attempted to smile but her lips trembled instead. "I've tried not to be sad in the fall, but it's hard sometimes."

"I think it's okay to be sad," Billie said.

"I liked everything so much better when she was alive. And then the war happened for us, too, right after." Nellie lifted the rose to her lips, kissed it, and tossed it into the gray water. They watched it spin away until they couldn't see it anymore.

Still watching the river, Billie said, "Did you lose many to the war?"

"Not many," she said. "But enough."

Billie looked back at Nellie's face and saw how she blinked back tears. "It was a sad time, all around," Nellie said. The wind coming down the river was cold, and they had been standing still long enough to feel it. Billie's hands were white and icy where they held her can of rosehips and she saw Nellie pull herself a little more into her wool coat.

"Winter's coming, yeah?" Nellie said. "Early this year."

"Yes," Billie said. She looked at the gray water and the gray sky, the nearly leafless trees and the gray-green spruce. She felt a chill inside, at the weather, at herself, at this new gray place she was in. She looked at Nellie. "Would you like to go back to the roadhouse and have some cocoa?" Billie asked. She wanted light and warmth and company; she wanted to do something nice for someone, for Nellie, for Maddie, and lift the heavy cloud that lay over everything today.

Nellie's eyes brightened, but then she looked back at the river and seemed to think about it for a moment. "Cocoa's good, yeah?"

"It is," Billie said. "Come on. It's getting cold out here."

They turned away from the water and walked quietly to the roadhouse. When they entered, Maddie was sitting alone at one of the wooden tables in the growing dusk.

"Hi!" Billie said, putting her can of rosehips onto the counter with a show of emphasis. "It's pretty chilly out there. I found Nellie by the river and thought we should all have some cocoa." She tossed her jacket onto a stool and whipped her way around the counter to the cookstove. She flicked the light switch on the wall and the room brightened somewhat. Nellie shuffled over to the table and took a seat across from Maddie. Billie filled a pot with canned evaporated milk and water and put fresh wood into the fire chamber.

"Hello, Mrs. Merkle," Billie heard Nellie say.

"Oh, Nellie, aren't you ever going to call me Maddie?"

"Maybe someday," the younger woman answered, and reached her hand across the table as Billie spooned cocoa and sugar into three large mugs, watching the two sad women at the table.

Anna Harker

I COULD SEE THE SUNLIGHT above me, rippling down through the green water, and I was rushing toward it, not knowing the world would change when I broke through to the other side. I can see now, how water was there at so many events in my life: that great body of ocean water that carried my mother and me to Alaska; the river water that stole away dear Uncle Mike; and the river I stood beside when Henry first kissed me in the spring and later in the fall when he asked me for my hand, his knee down in the damp, gray silt.

On the day I now remember, nearly three years into my marriage, I was swimming in my favorite lake, a clear, tree-ringed pool several miles from town. The lake was fed by a stream that ran both in and out and was often a good, quiet place to fish for trout. I had no reason to think I was not alone, save for the bugs above and the fish below, and I surfaced gasping for air as the water was tingling and cold. I shook the water from my face and hair and turned toward the shore. Where only moments ago there had been nothing and no one, there stood a man in water that reached nearly to the top of his waders, fishing. For a moment I forgot the cold and the inconvenient fact that my clothes lay in a tangled heap on the shore nearby as I watched the up and down flick of his pole and the line going up and back and out, teasing the surface of the water. He was backlit by the soft early evening sun that kissed golden across the tiny ripples caused by the whisper of wind that moved quietly though the trees.

I saw the fish break through, rising into the air, lunging after the little speck that flew at the end of the fishing line. Then with a splash it went back into the water and dove, though the arc of the pole showed the fish had met its match. It was as he stood there pulling and reeling that the man noticed me. For a few moments his attention went back and forth between me and the turmoil at the end of his line, as if he couldn't quite believe what he was seeing. And I had been in the water too long and needed to leave where the fish so badly wanted to stay.

But the lake ran shallow toward the shore, and to get to my clothes I would be forced to stand and walk and didn't relish the thought. So I swam a little closer, teeth chattering, as he backed his way out of the water and landed his fish, whose writhing and twisting was promptly ended by a swift blow to the head with a rock.

Still squatting by his catch, he looked back at me. "Aren't you cold?" he asked.

"Freezing!" It was really too early for a swim. The lakes needed time to warm, but time was something I had little of, since I was soon to join Henry at the mine.

"Well, why don't you come out?"

I crossed my arms over my bare chest while my legs pumped wildly to keep me afloat. "You're standing near my clothes."

He looked to the side then, at my messy little pile at the edge of the trees, and looked back at me. "I won't look," he said.

"I don't think so!"

"No? Should I go off into the trees where you can't even see if I'm looking or not? Trust me."

"I don't even know you."

"Well, it is trust me or get hypothermia. Now come on out before I have to go in and save you."

"You might be some crazy wild man!" My numb arms began pulling me forward though the water.

"Really? I think if crazy and wild are what we're worried about, I'm the one who should be wary."

"Why would you say that? I'm the one trapped out here in this freezing water with no clothes."

"Exactly."

"What?"

"Exactly," he said again. "I think I win the sanity debate today. Now I'm going to mind my own business and gut this fish."

I swam until the lake bottom scraped my breasts, then stood slowly, covering myself as best I could, shivering and shaking but also wanting to laugh. I rushed toward my pile, my underwear sticking to my wet skin as I pulled them on as best I could, following with my old wool pants. My flannel shirt went on the wrong way and I had to pull my arms out and start all over, and then my shaking blue fingers were useless with the buttons.

"Are you all right?" he asked.

"Yes. Why?"

"You're taking a long time."

"I can't button my shirt," I said.

"Are you decent enough for me to turn around?"

"Yes."

He rose from the water's edge where he was rinsing his fish and faced me, approaching slowly as if I were a wild animal he wanted to pet, wiping his wet hands on his canvas pants. "Let me get that for you," he said. "I will be good. I promise."

"All right," I said reluctantly, but as he drew closer I could see how he was young, like me, and he seemed like someone who could be my friend. He met my eyes, and his warm, soft looking lips smiled quietly inside the frame of his barely there mustache and beard, light brown like the hair that fringed down the sides of his wool-felt hunting cap.

"I'm Wade," he said. "Wade Daniels. I just filed on this property here."

"Oh—oh no," I said before I could think.

He stopped, hands on my shirt dangerously near my breasts, and looked at me with questioning eyes.

"I'm sorry," I said. "It's just that I like to swim here."

I saw the relief on his face. "That's it?" he said. "I won't stop you. And welcome to the happiest day of my life—" he paused, leaving a space for me to fill.

"Anna."

"Anna. I was so excited to catch my first fish from my own shore that I didn't realize you were a human and not some water rodent I would eventually have to trap."

"A water rodent?" I said and felt the laughter shake its way through me. And I felt a quickening of my heart, a sensation that thrilled me and filled me with dread all at once. I knew something had worked its way in there, like a wild, native plant in a garden full of transplants. It was something that wouldn't easily be removed. I could try and I could try, and in the coming years I did and I did, but the roots of love had twisted themselves deep within me.

Had that somehow led to this?

Wade Daniels

THE DARK DAYS OF DECEMBER crept on. Wade cut wood
and split wood and fed the fire; he opened and reopened his
water hole in the lake. By the middle of the month he pulled
his traps. Something happened. He caught a lynx, uncommon
and unexpected. As he approached the set he could tell there
was an animal there, tucked back under the windfall, silent
and unmoving. Dead perhaps? More and more he approached
his traps with dread. This is what we do, he'd kept remind-
ing himself. We mine, we trap, it's the way of things around
here. But he did not like the sight of blood, nor the glazed,
distant stare of dead eyes. It took him back into the hills. He
even passed by a bull moose, still and broadside and perfect
for the shooting, and now his meals consisted of beans and
bread and rice.

On the day he caught the lynx, two weeks ago now, he
knew that was the end of something for him. He crouched
down to peer beneath the fallen log into the little cave carved
out of the snow and his eyes met those others. Gray-green and
strangely calm. It just looked at him. Wade knew what he had
to do but found he almost couldn't bear it. His hands shook
as he raised his rifle, and the cold bit through him.

"I'm sorry," he whispered. "I'm sorry." The rifle cracked
the stillness of the frozen woods, and blood splattered across
the snow.

Now, the traps pulled, there was nothing to do but wait. For what? He almost didn't know, but he did. Find Anna. Join up and leave. There was nothing left for him here.

He took the glass globe off his kerosene lamp, held the flame of his Zippo to the wick, then put the globe back on. It was sooty at the top, and he should wash it so the light could shine clear, but he didn't care. It was good enough. It would take the edge off the darkness inside the log walls, and perhaps tonight he would read again, Hemingway maybe, and maybe forget for a moment or two. Maybe.

A knock on the rough wood door nearly startled him out of his chair. He rose slowly, crossed the small distance, lifted the latch, and pulled the door open.

"Wade! Jesus! You look like hell!" It was Jake, still in his snowshoes and his face both frosted and rosy from the cold.

"Jake," Wade said. "What are you doing here?"

"It's Christmas, for God's sake, Wade, and no one's seen you in weeks!"

"Christmas?"

"Yes sir. And I've brought some moose steaks and some potatoes and even an onion. Damn it's cold out here!" Jake quickly unfastened the leather bindings on his snowshoes and kicked them aside. "Come on. Let me in, and let's get that door closed."

Wade stepped aside and his cousin entered, bringing in below zero air with him. Wade looked at the sky above the snow-shrouded trees, stared for a moment at the blue-gray of the disappearing day.

"For God's sake, Wade, close the damn door," Jake said, and Wade slowly and silently obeyed, his eyes lingering on the sky.

Later, after Jake fried up the moose steaks and the potatoes and the onion and they sat at the small table Wade had
partially cleared, Jake said, "I got the claim adjacent to the
Harker mine. How's that for a Christmas surprise?"

The lump of meat, which was sliding down Wade's throat,
stuck. He didn't know what to give his attention to: what his
cousin just said, or the bit of moose that could exact the creature's revenge posthumously. He coughed, grabbed the jelly jar
of whiskey Jake had poured for him, and took a burning drink.
"What?" he said when he could talk again.

"I filed on the claim downstream from the Harker mine. It
wasn't any good to anyone while Henry was working his, you
know, with the run-off and such. John Capp knows all about
that, and the person who staked it must have figured that out
because he never proved up and let it go. It was just sitting
there. And now it's golden—it should yield, you know—get
a water cannon like Henry had. I can't believe no one else
thought of it and snatched it up before I did 'cause it will be a
while, you know, before they sort out the Harker mine."

Wade felt his mouth moving, but he couldn't find words.
He felt like a fish thrown onto the shore, gasping. Did it matter
if Jake filed on an adjacent claim? Someone would have, sooner
or later—John Capp most likely, whose absence from the state
is probably the only reason Jake beat him to it. But Wade would
never work it, if he ever decided he could return to that life.
No, he would have to mine a claim somewhere far away. Then
there was that other thing Jake said. "Why will it be a while?"
Wade finally asked.

"To sort out the Harker mine?" Jake shrugged and cut
through the chunk of meat on his plate. Bloody. He liked it
rare, Wade remembered, even when he was a boy. "First of all,

they have to find Anna Harker," he said. "And sometimes here in Alaska, as I learned up at Lawry, people just disappear." He lifted his fork to his mouth, lips glistening. "Then—after when and if they find her—they have to figure out who died first, to see which family can lay claim to it."

Wade stared at his cousin, at the thick waves of coppery hair that went back from his forehead, the red-gold whiskers sprouting on his round face, at his mouth moving as he clewed on the meat, his tongue licking the juices off his lips. Then abruptly Jake stopped eating and looked across the table at Wade. "Hey," he said. "Say something."

There were words lining up on Wade's tongue, he felt them there, but his thoughts were cloudy and jumbled. He felt uneasy and he didn't know why. "Someone will have to prove up on the Harker claim," he finally managed to say. "You'll have to deal with those tailings."

"I thought about that. We could make them an offer to put in the hours on the claim. Be worth somebody's time."

"Jesus. You weren't there, Jake. If you'd been, you wouldn't want to set foot on that property." Wade's eyes wandered around his small cabin, every inch of which he had painstakingly built, and which suddenly seemed foreign to him, strange, the walls dark and looming and ragged and rough, the light from the lamp yellow and sickly. He thought about Jake filing on that claim. It made sense, of course it did. It's not like he filed on Henry and Anna's operation, but on an unwanted and forgotten section between Harkers' and Capp's. There was nothing wrong with that.

"I imagine they'll sell it—whichever family gets it," Jake added, and Wade wanted him to shut up, to just shut up. But Jake continued, "It would be a good one to grab, if the price is right."

Wade's eyes refocused on Jake's face. The lamp cast dark shadows on his features, transforming them, and for a moment

Wade wondered who he was looking at. He quickly lifted his whiskey and his hands were shaking, like they did on the day it all started, the liquid in the jar moving like a lake during an earthquake.

"Wade? Are you okay, buddy?"

Wade took a long drink. The whiskey burned down his throat. What was he thinking?

"Wade? Hey, little cousin, you're looking a tad green around the gills there. You feeling okay?"

"I don't know." His head hurt. He told himself, you go through this with everyone, everyone becomes a suspect. You just hadn't gotten around to Jake yet. Ja-kee. Your cousin.

"Wade, maybe you should go home, you know, like for the rest of the winter. See Aunt Jean and my mom. You're looking a little bush-wacky."

Wade shook his head. *For God's sake, stop. This is Jake.* "No . . . I'm all right. Forget it."

Jake kept looking at him. "You still thinking about joining up?"

"How could we not?"

"I don't know. I'm thinking I might wait it out a bit, see if my number comes up."

"Hmm." Wade looked down at the half-eaten steak on his plate and shoved it aside. "I don't think I can wait."

"Sure you can. I'll need you next summer, at the new place."

Wade smiled a little, but didn't reply. The world in which that could happen no longer existed. He looked at his cousin's face, washed yellow from the kerosene lamp, the shadows shifting as he moved, then he let his eyes wander to a dark corner of the cabin where everything was vague and shadowy, indistinct.

Billie Sutherland

SOMEHOW TIME KEPT GOING BY, with visitors coming and going at the roadhouse and boxes of bread and other baked goods heading north on the train, and one afternoon Billie was visiting the Finn and looked out the window and saw snow swirling down.

"Here it comes," the Finn had said, and Billie turned toward him and smiled. She had made little progress in solving the murders, but she met Montana down at the river on a fairly regular basis and he talked about his old horses, remembering their names and breeds and how long they lived and how they died, and told her countless stories of his days on the trail.

"One day I was approaching the cabin owned by Mr. Jacobs," he told her one cold, clear but windy day, "and the horses stopped short of the place and would not go any farther. I thought there must be a bear, and I pulled my rifle out of the scabbard. But it wasn't no bear. As I got closer to the cabin I saw old Jacobs lying on the ground by his woodpile, white as a ghost and still as stone and looking at the sky with vacant eyes. His heart must have given out, or something, and it looked like he'd been layin' there for several days. I went back to the horses to go fetch the neighbors, and those horses were only too happy to turn around and get out of there. Somehow they knew that Death was there on the trail in front of them.

"We buried the old man near his cabin, like he would have wanted. He'd spent thirty years or so out there in the wild by himself, listening to the rain in the summer and watching the northern lights dance across the sky in the winter, hearing the odd wolf howling a distant hello. A good life. Anyone can have a good life in Alaska, if all they need is what the land has to offer and a roof over their head and wood for the stove."

Billie liked the stories and thought that maybe she could do that, too: just live. But then she would remember and feel the twisting in her gut.

One morning she woke up late to find Maddie putting on her thick wool coat and heading for the door.

"What is it?" Billie asked.

"What is it?" Maddie echoed. "Nothing to worry about, Billie. It's Veterans Day. There's a ceremony at the cemetery. Wouldn't you like to come?"

Billie froze for an odd moment, trying to collect her thoughts. Maddie cocked her head, staring at her. "It's just a small ceremony, Billie," she said. "Then we have lunch at the schoolhouse. Attendance is not required."

"No—I'd like to go," Billie said.

"Then get some warm clothes on. It's a good ten below out there. I'll see you at the cemetery."

Billie hurried back to her room and pulled on her winter gear. She looked quickly at herself in the old mirror, and her eyes glinted back at her from one of the clearer sections of glass. How plain she looked now, she realized, with no makeup and hair in need of a proper cut. She stepped closer and stared for a moment, then brushed at her hair with her hand. The ruff on the hood of her tan parka lay on her shoulders and she remembered how smart she used to feel in this coat, how sharp. Deep down in one of the pockets was an old tube of lipstick and she pulled it out and put a light coat on her lips. Then she pulled a wool headband over her ears and used it to arrange her hair into some semblance of prettiness and orderliness and allowed herself a small smile. Then she hurried out the door.

The air was sharp with cold. The clouds that had dumped the last foot of snow lay in a bank on the horizon, but most of the sky was a soft, pastel blue. Billie pulled on her mittens as she walked, wishing she had her cigarettes and her lighter, but at the same time realizing she didn't seem to have room for them anymore, in this quiet life that was busier than she remembered her former one to be.

She went through the village proper without seeing a soul, walked across the tracks and took a shortcut through the woods on a trail that led to the cemetery and passed Nellie's place on the way. The cabin was small and tucked back in among the trees; a cottony stream of smoke twirled up out of the chimney. But, like the village, the place was deserted, and Billie picked up her pace.

The entire village was gathered on the grounds of the small shadowy graveyard—everyone from Jim Davies, the businessman who now owned the Clearwater Inn, to Grandma Millie, the old widow and former schoolteacher everyone said ran the village. Billie spotted the Finn and her heart skipped a beat: he was wearing the uniform of the US Air Force. He was dashing and older and younger at once, a cluster of medals on the left side of his chest. He had been gone for the last week or so, flying for a company up north. She had missed him— missed their tea, missed the sight of him walking down the street. She hoped to catch his eye, but he stood somberly with the other uniformed men—the other veterans in the community—so Billie slipped in among the villagers and found a spot beside Maddie.

"Glad you could make it," Maddie said.

Grandma Millie, wearing the vest of the ladies' auxiliary over her army green parka, stood in front of the gathering. She blinked, coughed, stomped her feet, and began. "It's always cold on Veterans Day, isn't it?" she said. "And we have to come out of our warm houses and cabins and shacks and whatever to come all the way over here to this cold plot of land to hear me say just about the same words I said last year."

Billie looked around. Was she supposed to laugh?

"And probably the year before that and the year before that," Millie continued. "But we come because we're here, and because we can, to pay homage to those members of our community who left their own warm houses and cabins and shacks and took a much longer walk into a much colder world not knowing if they would ever return, and some of them didn't. So it's up to all of us to come out here in the cold so we can remember to be grateful for our lives and our houses and our cabins and our shacks. Because even though this day marks the anniversary of the end of the war that was supposed to end all wars, that didn't happen, as we too well know. And if that war couldn't do it, you'd think the one that followed could, but here we are, two wars down in the twentieth century and on the brink of another one. Bloody hell. That's all I got to say, and the Finn here is going to pick up where I left off and read us a poem," here she looked at a tiny piece of paper in her hand, "written by Wilfrid Wilson Gibson, a veteran of World War I, then we can say a prayer and go get warm and eat."

The villagers nodded their approval, then the Finn stepped forward, removed his hat, and held it in his hand.

His thick hair fell across one side of his forehead, and he kept his eyes on the snowy ground until he spoke, then as he did he looked somewhere past the gathering in the little circle of cleared land with its tombstones and crooked crosses and spirit houses of the dead.

> They ask me where I've been,
> And what I've done and seen.
> But what can I reply
> Who know it wasn't I,
> But someone just like me,
> Who went across the sea
> And with my head and hands
> Killed men in foreign lands . . .
> Though I must bear the blame
> Because he bore my name.

As she listened Billie felt her throat tighten, and she became suddenly aware of how ensconced she had been in her own world, both before and after the event that changed her life. She felt, too, how the people in the village were bonded in a way she had only begun to understand. She watched their faces as they watched their friend, who was young once and went off to a war she was too young to remember. The Finn finished the poem and looked back down at the ground as he stepped back to where he had been, and a visiting priest stepped forward and said a prayer, after which a moment of understood silence washed over the group before they began to move and head back toward the schoolhouse. Billie walked quietly along with all the others, and after a short time she realized the Finn had come up beside her, and she slipped off her mitten and let her hand hold on to his.

Anna Harker

WHO KNOWS WHEN A MARRIAGE GOES BAD? When it starts to turn, like potatoes in a root cellar, thought safe in the dark but whose true condition lay unseen. I had not known that Wade Daniels was Jake Timmers's cousin and was working that mine only three miles from ours; we had revealed little to each other the day we met by the lake, as if any other world we belonged to did not exist there at that time. My memories of the day took on a dreamlike feel with sharp, clearly defined moments combined with others that were fading, faint, fuzzy, and confused. After I had my clothes back on, he lent me his wool shirt for extra warmth, and I sat on the shore for a brief time watching him fish. We chatted a little about fishing techniques and fly-fishing versus lure fishing, and he asked me numerous questions about the salmon runs. Whenever he looked away, I studied him. He wasn't much more than a medium height, and he was slimly built, not unlike Henry, and he had a slightly curved nose and dark blue eyes that sparkled like the lake in the sun. I realized soon that I should go, that I was too comfortable there, in the presence of this stranger, the sound of his fishing line whispering softly in my ear.

My days at the mining camp were mired in endless drudgery and routine: cooking breakfast, cleaning up after, fixing lunch and delivering it to the operation by the stream where Henry and Nate worked the "little giants"—the two small water cannons Henry had shipped up from California that blasted the sides of Ramshackle and made its waters run thick with muddy tailings. Sometimes Henry would smile; sometimes he would look at what I fixed and sigh sharply as his mother often did, leaving me to wonder what it was I had done or not done that failed his expectations of the meal. Then I would return to camp, either happy or saddened, and begin preparations for the next meal, or worse, try to bake bread that didn't look and feel like a pale (or perhaps black) brick, the wood cookstove spewing smoke and the oven either too hot or too cool. There was laundry to do, which required water not equally as dirty as the clothes themselves, and there was the drinking water to be hauled. However, since these last two chores got me out of the kitchen and away from the camp, they swiftly became my favorite afternoon duties. So one day, toward the middle of the season, I carried a bucket of laundry to leave soaking, a second bucket to carry back for drinking, and instead of a bear gun strapped across my chest I opted to stick my fishing pole down the back of my shirt and put my tackle box into the empty bucket.

The small, untainted stream was northwest of the camp over several hills. Soon I put the world of mines and miners behind me—the roar of the cannons and the devastation to the landscape they wrought and the occasional bark from Henry to fetch him this or that—and felt myself again in the wild country, smelling the tundra and feeling the spring of it beneath my feet, hearing the wind come down from the mountain glacier so cold and fresh, like an emissary of the purity of that massive and pristine not-so-distant place rising up before me. The Alaska Range. White and glorious, wrapped in wind and wonder.

After several ups and downs of hills, the stream came into view, a swift silver slice through the terrain. My delight at seeing it, however, was jolted by the unexpected sight of a figure fishing from the spot I had come to think of as my own. My heart fell and jumped at once; while I was disappointed to be intruded upon, I soon recognized him, Wade Daniels, somehow far from the shores of my favorite little lake.

He turned his head mid-cast and saw me, and to hide my surprise I tromped forward, placed my buckets down on a thin strip of rocks between the water and the tundra, and pulled my pole out from the back of my shirt as if it were the most natural thing in the world, all the while aware of his wide-eyed stare.

"Fancy meeting you here," I said and fixed my line.

He tipped his head, delight beginning to dance across his face. "So the mermaid is a miner," he said.

I laughed and cast out into the stream. "Not so much a miner as a miner's maid," I said.

He glanced back the way I had come. "You must be at the Harker mine."

"Yes," I said. I could see a question on his face, one he opted not to ask. I felt this strange desire not to say anything, to pretend, for a moment, that I was once again Anna Lee, and I could flirt with this interesting new face that I found so rewarding to look at, as if something in it replenished something in me that I had not noticed was waning. But the temptation was quickly squashed by a sliver of shame cutting through me, and I said, "I'm Anna Harker. Henry is my husband."

If he was disappointed, he did not show it, and only said, "Well, it's nice to see you again, Anna Harker."

I gave him a nod and cast my line. "And where in these hills are you?"

"Timmers's. Jake's my cousin."

Of course. Henry had said Jake's cousin had arrived to help, adding how all the relatives in the world wouldn't pull gold out of that claim. Henry's father once owned it and sold it long ago, starting a chain of unhappy prospectors.

Now Wade Daniels said, "I think something must be wrong with me."

"Why?" It seemed an odd thing to say.

"I'd so much rather pull fish from these streams than gold. I can't seem to catch the fever."

I laughed at that. "Oh, me neither. Take me back to the valley and the rivers there."

"And the lakes," he added.

"And the lakes. Though someone has gone and bought mine." I watched his line sing through the air, a sound like a quiet *shhhh*.

"You can swim there any time."

"Well, thank you." I knew I was blushing, and the image of swimming without my clothes reminded me of the chore I was neglecting. I cranked my reel. "Though I'll have to get a proper bathing suit," I added.

Like before, I could see him wanting to say something then thinking better of it. I poured some water over the bucket of clothes, rubbed them down with my bar of brown soap, then left them to soak. I picked up my pole and Wade nodded his approval. "Best to let them soak," he said.

"Yes," I agreed.

"Might as well fish while you wait."

"Absolutely."

"I'll try not to let my line get tangled with yours."

"And I shall try to do the same," I said, and so we stood there fishing in the mountain stream as the afternoon passed and the laundry soaked and the water ran clear and bright shiny fish flashed and glinted at the ends of our lines. And despite my best intentions, I remembered Anna Lee.

Wade Daniels

"SO CAN YOU TAKE ME UP THERE?" Wade stood at the side door of the airplane hangar, his boots wet from the mud and slush of breakup. The Finn had answered the door in his dirty-white union suit and stood there blinking at Wade.

"Where exactly?"

"The hills. The Harris Hills."

He rubbed his eye and scratched his head, his dark blond hair messy and thick. "I think there'd be a good chance we'd get the plane stuck."

Wade shook his head. "Montana came down from the road-house yesterday. He said the airstrip's still solid from when it was packed down for John Capp's freight that you took up there."

The Finn looked at the sky. It was overcast, but Wade knew the ceiling was high enough for flying. "Why do you need to go up there?" the Finn asked.

Wade swallowed against the tightness in his throat. "The bears will be out soon."

"You going hunting?"

"No."

The Finn stood there, his sleepy blue eyes searching Wade's face, and Wade wondered how a kid could be so damned good at flying an airplane. "Hey," the Finn said suddenly. "You joining up?"

It took Wade a moment, but he nodded grimly.

"Yeah—me too. I'd rather keep flying over the woods than fly and get shot at and drop a bunch of bombs on people, but I guess it's all got to be done."

"You're a bit young," Wade said, "to be doing stuff like that."

The Finn shrugged, shook his head, and looked at the sky. "I don't see how anybody could be old enough for that, really. But I gotta go. I can help. I think I can help. We're all gonna get called up anyway, sooner or later."

Wade fought an impulse to tell him to stay, to stay and be young and alive while he could. He took a deep breath. "So, I need to get up there, though, first. The bears will be out soon."

"And? If you're not hunting them—"

He gritted his teeth, then said, "She's still out there. Someone's got to find her before the bears do." He could feel the Finn looking at him. He clenched his jaw and waited.

"Anna Harker." The Finn looked at the sky again. "All right," he said. "Let me get some coffee and something in my gut. Go get your gear."

"I've got it with me," Wade said.

The Finn's eyes looked past Wade to the backpack on the snowy gravel behind him. "All right," he said again. "At least let a fella get dressed." The Finn disappeared inside the hangar, and Wade closed his eyes for a moment and pulled a deep breath of watery spring air into his lungs. He had almost hoped the Finn would say no. Almost. Though he knew Anna was never going to walk out of those hills, he didn't want to see her how she would be. There was a twisting in his gut that pushed bile up to the back of his throat. But he knew he had to go.

A short time later they were in the plane taxiing down the runway; the young pilot in his goggles and sheepskin flight hat, and Wade silent beside him with his backpack and snowshoes in the back. Out the window Wade could see some kids—a small group of boys—stop and watch the plane. The Finn gave his engine a little extra hit of gasoline so the engine revved and roared and the plane leapt forward a little and the kids started waving. Wade could see how they liked the Finn, and he felt a shadow pass over his heart, like a raven passing through a beam of sunlight, when he thought of a young fellow like the Finn—not much more than a kid himself—joining the war effort. Let the fellows like him do it instead, he thought; those of us who won't quite see the sun the same again.

The Finn tipped a wing to the village after they lifted off the airstrip and headed toward the Harris Hills, following the path the rivers carved out of the country centuries ago. Wade could see beneath him the easing of winter on the land, the pencil-sharp edges melted into a soft charcoal blur, with sections of open water in the river below and the deep snow pulling away from the trees. Then the landscape shifted as the plane left the river valley and flew cross-country over the hills, which rolled lonely and white until evidence of the mines of men peeked out here and there from beneath the winter wrappings: a roofline, a dredge, which some of the bigger operations had, the latter like a prehistoric creature frozen in place. Then the winter trail, winding along on top of the buried road, and then the Harrisville Roadhouse, shuttered and still, and the runway that Wade hoped was truly safe enough to land on.

The Finn came in fast, touched the surface lightly with the airplane's skis, and used a good half of the runway before he slowed. Wade hadn't realized he was holding his breath until he started breathing again. But the Finn, he noticed, never flinched.

Soon Wade's backpack and snowshoes lay on the frozen ground, and the Finn stood beside the plane, hesitant now to leave him behind.

"How will I know when to come back for you?" he asked, his tinted goggles hanging around his neck, and his hands shoved into the deep pockets of his coveralls.

"I don't know." Wade hadn't really thought about it. It was spring, but the wind still blew cold and he shivered as it swept past him on its way. "It'll be slow going," he said. "Could you fly over, say, in three days or so, weather permitting? I'll stomp out a message in the snow, if I need you to land."

"All right. Will do," the Finn said. He kicked at the snow with his boots for a minute then said, "Do you really think she's out here?"

"Don't you?"

"Yeah, I guess, given the alternatives. I just, you know." He scrunched his face up a bit, as if pushing a nail into his skin, and his eyes grazed Wade's before he looked up at the sky. "There wasn't ever gonna be a good answer to the question of where she ended up, was there?"

Wade lowered his gaze and shook his head. "No."

"Well then find her." He lifted his goggles back up onto his face. "I guess that's all we can do for her now."

"I will try."

"All right. I'll give you a flyover in a few days."

Wade watched the plane slide across the snow and lift into the air, and a few minutes later, as the sound faded and disappeared, he found himself alone with the wilderness and the cold, lonesome wind that came down from the ancient glaciers in the range.

Billie Sutherland

IT HAPPENED ONE DAY, when she was over at the Finn's for tea. She wanted him to help her develop a new configuration for a murder suspect, one that eliminated Montana. They were going down a list of everyone the Finn could remember as living in the village at the time, and if they were interviewed by Ben Fairfield and/or the FBI, and if their activities were accounted for on the day in question. For the time being, they were ignoring the big question of travel time to the hills.

"Grandma Millie," the Finn said.

"What?"

"Look—she was indisposed for some mysterious reason right after school got out until the next morning. She's one fierce woman. She could have run up there and back. My money's on her."

She realized he was joking and started laughing, a real laugh like she hadn't felt in what seemed a long, long time. Then suddenly he leaned forward across the tiny table, placed his hands on the sides of her face, and kissed her.

"Sorry," he whispered, pressing his forehead against hers.

"Don't be," she said, and let him kiss her again, and lips together they maneuvered around the table and Billie forgot about everything except the feel of him close to her and the touch of his hands.

Later they lay in his bed, hearts still pounding, the blanket pulled carelessly across their mostly naked bodies. They both looked at the ceiling and she wondered what he thought. Then he looked at her with a smile and brushed away the hair that had fallen across her face.

"So," he said.

"So."

"That's a surprise."

"Indeed."

"Good surprise."

She smiled a little but kept quiet. She hadn't thought of the ramifications. She hadn't thought.

"What is it?" he asked.

She shook her head. "Nothing."

"Billie, I like you."

"Aren't you afraid?" she asked, unable to keep the words from spilling out.

"Afraid? I was in the war, Billie. Not a lot scares me."

"Have you ever been in love?" she asked quietly, instantly regretting the words.

"Once."

"Once?"

"I fell in love once. It was when I was real young, and when I was in the war."

"Oh." She found herself strangely jealous. A war romance. She couldn't imagine anything more romantic.

"A nurse."

Of course.

"A young English girl named Eva."

"Pretty."

"She was."

"I meant the name."

"That, too."

"What happened?"

He looked at her a moment, then turned his gaze toward the window. "The war ended. I came home."

She wondered what really happened, but didn't ask. He sighed and shifted on the bed to face her. "I don't like talking about it," he said. "The war. It's all I can do to get through Veterans Day and Memorial Day where it's all in the forefront of everyone's mind. But Eva was—she was like hope amid so much death and destruction. She was like a memory of a sunny day or a field of flowers or a quiet night beneath the stars. We met in London when I was on furlough, and somehow held steady in all that chaos. But at the end of the war I couldn't . . . I couldn't simply be happy. I felt hollowed out inside."

The soft light of the overcast winter day outside gathered in the room, and they lay in silence for a time, and Billie fought the urge to speak or get up and turn on the lights to break the thick, gray feel that had settled over them. Then the sound of yelling in the street outside broke through the hush. The Finn fastened his pants and rushed to the window. Billie grabbed the nearest shirt—his soft flannel, full of the scent of his skin—put it on and followed.

Outside several people were running down Main Street, yelling something, and doors were opening and people emerging. Fire, Billie thought, and looked over the rooftops for smoke but didn't see anything. Down below Grandma Millie came running past and the Finn yanked open the window.

"Millie! What's going on?" he yelled out into the cold air.

Millie looked up toward them, her face taking note of Billie standing there behind him. "The president! The president's been shot, Goddamn it!" she yelled. Billie and the Finn exchanged a quick glance. "Which president?" he yelled.

"The only one we've got, Goddamn it! Kennedy!" she yelled back and continued on her way to the growing congregation in the cold street.

"Oh my God," Billie said, and the Finn rushed over to his radio and turned it on. She crossed the room and stood beside him. Soon he found a signal, faint and full of static, and they leaned close to hear.

Anna Harker

IT WAS NEW YEAR'S EVE. New Year's Eve 1938. Then 1939, then 1940, the last one for me, it seems. But on New Year's Eve 1938, I still had nearly three blessed years stretching out before me. It was cold, thirty-five below and counting, but the roadhouse was crowded and warm and cheery, and we were all drinking too much: rhubarb wine and home brew, nicely aged and foamy. Henry had wanted me to wear a dress, but I pretended not to hear him, that I was too busy helping my mother pull loaves of bread from the oven and sweep the ashes away from the fireplace, and stayed in my wool pants with the suspenders I was so fond of and a thick flannel shirt. A party! We didn't have many of those. Usually everyone went to the Clearwater, but since my marriage to Henry, my mother was trying to be more sociable, hoping, I imagined, to become someone Henry's mother saw as fitting to be related to. And that Merkle would be accepted as well. Once again the rumblings in Europe hung over us, and the occasional little knife-like jab, stabbing Merkle in the back, could be heard. *Those Germans, you know* . . . But Merkle did know, and his unspoken reply to the remarks he heard: *Isn't that the country and the people I left behind?*

New Year's Eve 1938 and the open house at the roadhouse. Along with all the baked goods we could fit, we had big pots of moose stew filled with onions, potatoes, and carrots from the root cellar. A pot of hot cocoa for any children who might come. Root beer we made ourselves. The Ricola jukebox Merkle had given my mother for Christmas, and a cup full of nickels for people to plunk into it and choose a song.

I was talking to Nellie, herself so quietly grown in the shadow of her family's many losses. She wouldn't drink, but I had a jelly jar full of rhubarb wine that made my cheeks flush red. It's lost to me now, what we were talking about (Henry's sisters, most likely), but my head tipped back as I laughed to nearly the point of tears, and as I recovered I felt two pairs of eyes upon me: Henry, who of course wanted me to be more ladylike, and Wade Daniels, whose entrance into the room I had not noticed. But his eyes glittered as he looked my way, his lips turned up in a chuckling smile, and there I stood, between that smile and Henry's frown, frozen in a moment of indecision: do I keep laughing, or make myself stop? But Nellie leaned forward, saving me, and whispered, "What would George think of us now, eh?" and we slipped into a subdued remembrance of her brother and my friend. But later, after the clock struck twelve and the room was a collage of hugs and kisses and toasts, there was the clink of a jelly jar against mine and I turned to see Wade Daniels. "Hello, friend," he said.

"Hello."

"Happy New Year to you."

"And to you."

"Here's to a year of fabulous fishing."

"Ha! Yes! I'll drink to that!" I said and raised my glass while Henry pulled me away by my arm. And into that space of floor I had occupied, Nellie slipped quietly, a soft smile on her face as she watched Wade watch me go, herself not seeing the fire in his eyes.

New Year's Eve 1939. Again my mother's attempt at a party, and this time I wore a dress for Henry, wool and gray and so boring I couldn't hardly stand it, but it fit nicely and went well with my wedding shoes, which still pinched my toes and left them vulnerable to the cold drafts that drifted across the floor. Henry wore a tartan dress shirt and wool trousers and a tweed jacket with lapels on the shoulders. All new, like my dress. He wore his wedding shoes, too, but shoes were on his list of things to buy: saddle shoes for him, and sling back shoes for me. We needed nice things, he said, to match the bank account, but his mother warned: Don't go looking like you have too much.

He had bottles of champagne sent up on the train from Anchorage, and special glasses to drink it from. There weren't enough glasses for everyone, so only some of us had them while those that did not had jelly jars. After a round of toasts, I quietly set mine down.

Wade and Nellie were there, drinking from the jelly jars, and at one point Henry and I stood face to face with the two of them.

Well, Happy New Year.

And Happy New Year to the both of you.

We were polite. I let my eyes glaze over slightly so I could not really see them, see him. Nellie, who rarely if ever drank, was drunk and hung on Wade's arm. Wade himself was a little wobbly and raised his jelly jar to my face. *Happy New Year, Mrs. Harker,* and Nellie laughed and nearly slid to the floor.

Later Henry asked, *What was that about?* He was not stupid. But I said, *I've no idea.*

New Year's Eve 1940. The party again, but no dress for me. *It's forty below for God's sake,* I'd said. Last year I froze. I tried to please Henry by wearing the sweater he gave me for Christmas, deep green with a band of white snowflakes across the chest, but I wore wool pants and my old suspenders and the mukluks Merkle gave me. I wasn't happy, but at least I was warm. Wade was there, across the crowded room leaning against a wall, drinking somberly and quietly and steadily. When Henry was deep in conversion with several fellow miners over new mining equipment, I wove my way through the cluster of bodies until I was against the same wall as Wade. He tipped his glass in my direction. I held his gaze. Nellie came through the door in her long wool coat, saw us there, and left. *Happy New Year!* someone yelled and I saw Henry trying to reach me through the cheering crowd.

But I am getting ahead of myself. There was New Year's Eve 1938. Then there was the summer the Flying Finn came to town and flew me out of the hills and home for my birthday.

Wade Daniels

HE HATED TO THINK IT, what he was looking for. Some sign in the soggy melting snow, some indication animals had been in an area, searching and digging. He took one weary step in front of the other, the sticky wet snow clinging to the leather webbing and the wooden frames of his snowshoes, the pull of which he felt in the muscles of his thighs. The warmth of the sun broke through the cold wind that ripped across the hills. A year ago he would have reveled in such a day and not minded the hard slog of the travel: it was still easier than in summer, to go cross-country, with enough of winter left on the ground to keep you above the low-lying tangles of brush, no mosquitoes to be found, and the sun breaking the back of winter's cold. A day like today he would have been out checking his beaver sets, stopping midway on the trail to build a small fire to boil water for tea. A year ago, before the world became a different place. Now his life was death and war, thoughts of Anna out here, somewhere, under the snow.

It was his second day. Reluctantly, after a day of wandering the hills, he had gone to Jake's mining camp as the light began to fade and spent the night there. He had wanted to camp, but the wind grew colder as the sun sank in the sky. It might be spring, but in the hills winter still lurked in the shadows. He felt it chasing him as he changed course and headed for shelter. He dug out the doorway of Jake's crude and tiny shack, crawled into his sleeping bag, and slept fitfully, waking up every few hours to the black of the night.

Tonight, he would rather sleep out in the hills if he could find a spot where he would be protected from the wind. Jake's had felt like a tomb, the dirt floor beneath the bunk hard and frozen but still smelling like a grave. Today, back out in the open, the appearance of the sun and the feel of the wind breathed life back into him, and he experienced a moment, the first since last fall, where he felt that maybe he could live again. There was still the wilderness, and it still called to him. He would have to see, if he survived the war.

Hours passed. Every so often he would stop, lift his binoculars, and scan the white hills speckled with the tips of alders poking through the white, like stubble on a chin. He was sweating, his wool coat now tied around his waist. You had to watch yourself, he knew, on days like this, the warmth of the sun luring you into complacency. He knew that more men died from hypothermia in the woods on the warmer days of winter and fall than colder ones where the weather issued steady warnings you couldn't argue with or ignore.

As he finished another scan, sometime well into afternoon, he could feel how the wind was quickly licking away the sweat on his brow. Time to keep moving, and time soon to decide whether or not to camp, though the lingering light made it tempting to push into the evening. He felt his throat tighten and lifted his binoculars yet again. On a distant hill to his left he saw three caribou, sticklike figures on the horizon. He looked around for the rest of the herd—on the other side of the hill, most likely, anywhere from a dozen to a hundred. He watched them for a moment, then lowered the binoculars and rubbed his eyes. Think, he told himself, think. There must be some logic to wherever Anna had been. Far enough away from the camp that they missed her on those first, crucial days, yet she couldn't have been too far out or the killer would not have found her. And like with Henry and Nate, she either knew him or was surprised by him, in order for him to get close. Of course it was possible the killer had a gun, saw Anna out on the tundra somewhere, and shot her from a distance, but a clean death would have robbed the killer of whatever it was he had fed on as he swung his bloody ax. Wade realized he had to come in closer to the Harkers' camp, but this time he would approach it from the opposite direction of the past searches: from the outside, heading in, as opposed to from the inside, fanning out. So he went farther from the camp, as if rolling down toward lower elevations, until he came to where the Harkers' stream sliced through the frozen landscape in front of him. He turned then and cut upward diagonally toward the camp.

After a while Wade could see, up ahead and to his right, the rise of a buried boulder mounding up through the snow, and then suddenly there was a magpie, white and blue-black iridescent, cutting crisply through the air, its shadow falling on the snow. Anna's favorite. He lifted his binoculars and looked in the direction it was heading, toward the boulder. It was a big boulder, bits of gray now showing through. He turned on his snowshoes and walked toward it, knowing he would pay for this extra distance.

He felt himself pushing on, pushing forward, as if he had fallen off the world and had no choice but this, this direction, this now, this moment. As he drew closer he noticed tiny shrew tracks in the snow, like delicate crocheting he remembered his mother doing. And there were indications of old tracks from bigger animals, soft little lines of nondescript dents fading away. His heart began pounding, thundering, and his whole body began to shake. The boulder was before him, large and looming. Something small and black moved—a glimpse of the magpie, he thought; he couldn't tell. He was running now, pulling the heavy snow-caked snowshoes along, the burning in his thighs long forgotten. He veered to the left to skirt the obstruction, leaned forward as he looked.

A lock of black hair stuck out from the snow, waving in the cold silent wind.

He fell, one snowshoe crossing the front of the other, down into the snow, and he lay there unable to move for what seemed an eternity, watching the lock of Anna's dark hair dance.

Billie Sutherland

"I STOLE IT OFF THE DEAD WALL," Nellie said. She handed
the picture to Billie. The "Dead Wall" was in the Clearwater,
a place to hang pictures of those who have gone "farther up
the creek," as the old people were fond of saying. The picture
was of a somber-faced young man in military dress, his eyes
wincing as if he was in pain.

"Who is he?" Billie asked. She was visiting Nellie in her
small but tidy cabin on the other side of the railroad tracks.
They sat at a small rectangular table covered with a flowered
tablecloth. Outside the window winter was progressing; both
the snow and the cold deepening by the week but Nellie's
assortment of hanging bird feeders turned her front yard into
a menagerie of winged creatures: magpies, chickadees, gray
jays. They swooped and squawked—movement and sound in
the stillness of the cold.

"Wade Daniels," Nellie said. "I loved him."

"Oh." The man who found Anna. Billie could tell that
there was a sad story here, between him and Nellie, even without the war taking him away. She thought about how, while
she was growing up in Anchorage reveling in the magic of an
Alaska childhood, one hundred miles to the north a host of
dramas were unfolding. "What happened?"

"He died, in the war. He did good, though. He jumped out
of airplanes. He became a captain and he had lots of medals."
She ran her finger along the once-white border of the photo.

"He came here with his cousin, Jake. Jake Timmers. He lived here too. He came here first. Wade came here to be with him, and that's how come I met him."

Nellie sighed. Billie felt a flood of compassion for her, this strange, gentle person who seemed more girl than aging woman. "I'm sorry, Nellie."

"So handsome, eh? Better with his beard. The army must have made him shave it. His family sent the picture to the village after he was killed. They wanted us to remember him. I wanted to tell them I would never forget, but they would say, 'Who are you?' and I would have to say, 'No one,' though we spent some time, eh, he would let me go with him when he went fishing, and he took me once to the big New Year's Eve party at the roadhouse like on a date. So we spent some time together, yah. But then he said, maybe I was too young and we should wait before getting too serious. And I said okay, and we kept going for awhile, but then it was like how the night comes back in the summer, at first you don't notice it, then all of a sudden you see that the darkness has come back and the midnight sun has slipped away. That's what it was like for me. I thought we were waiting together. But I was waiting alone."

"He didn't love you?"

Nellie shook her head. "No. I don't think so. Maybe a little. There was someone else."

"I see," Billie said, a rush of shame pulsing through her. She had caused pain, and worse.

Nellie nodded. "She was my friend, the person he loved. But they were a secret, because she had a husband."

Billie averted her eyes to the tabletop. Nellie continued, "She died. Then he got sad and went to the war. And I lost them both, yah."

"Anna," Billie said. She lifted her gaze. "Anna?"

Nellie nodded.

"Oh, Nellie. Do people know about this?"

"Mr. Fairfield talked to me."

"But that's not in any of the reporting." She reminded herself that some of the records were lost when Fairfield's building burned.

Nellie shook her head. "He told me he wouldn't tell anybody. He said he knew Wade didn't do it and what happened between him and Anna was a separate thing. But it would hurt everybody, if it was told. So you won't tell nobody, eh?"

"No," Billie said. She could feel her hands beginning to shake.

Billie, don't say anything. Jimmy Johnson had said this, her own secret.

I have to say something!

Listen, listen to me, sweetheart. This is your neighbor. You don't know how she got in here or why she did this. You obviously don't know who she is.

Was. *Was!* she'd screamed.

Nellie got up and took the blue enameled coffee pot off the stove and refilled Billie's cup, sliding the can of evaporated milk across the table toward her.

"I'm going to tell you something bad," Nellie said.

Billie's heart thumped in her chest. "The Tell-Tale Heart," a story she liked when she was young. A story she now feared.

"When Anna died, I was sad, but then I was glad too," Nellie said quietly. "I was sure he could love me. So I was glad that she was out of the way."

Nellie waited for Billie to say something. Billie lifted her cup to her lips, trying hard to steady her hand. The coffee burned on its way down, and Billie swallowed fast and hard.

"You probably really didn't feel that way," she said. "It's very confusing, I imagine, when you lose someone."

"No, I was glad. I had it all planned out. I would let him be sad, and I would be sad too. Then little by little we would be un-sad. And little by little he would remember that we would have some fun times, eh, fishing and talking and kissing. Then we would be back to where we were."

Billie looked at the walls of the old cabin, at the lonely narrow bed along the far wall.

"Then the war took him away. If he had just waited, then maybe he would not have wanted to go. But he did, and he never came back, and slowly I realized how foolish I had been, not because I loved him, but to be angry at Anna for loving him too. It wasn't her fault. Everyone wanted her to marry Henry. And maybe she didn't want it so much, you know?"

There were words that rose up into Billie's throat, and she felt the aching hold of them there. But her story was not for sharing. She thought of her Seattle apartment. Was the telltale heart there, beating?

"And you can't tell anyone, yah, about what I said," Nellie added. "I was angry at her but I never told anybody. The last time I saw her, I was mad and I told her I knew about what she was doing." Nellie's dark eyes glanced at Billie. "But I could never tell. It was not only for her sake but for his too. I don't think they wanted it to happen. It just did. I got pulled into it because I liked him so much, and for a little while, he let me be with him." She smiled sadly across the table at Billie, her still-smooth face creasing gently around the eyes. "She told me she was sorry if it messed things up. But I didn't tell her it was okay." Nellie picked at a worn spot on her mug, blue enamel like the coffee pot. "So that's my story," she said, not looking up. "My bad thing."

"We all have bad things," Billie said. She looked out the window, at the way the day was slipping away. She stayed long enough to finish her coffee, then made her excuses and went out into the cold afternoon, walking swiftly back into the village to beat the darkness, thinking of Wade Daniels and Anna Harker. She thought of Jimmy Johnson, all the things she knew about him: the ripple of muscles across his abdomen, the fine dark hairs on his forearm, the little patch of black curls in the center of his smooth and otherwise hairless chest. The scar on his knee from a childhood tumble off a bike. Banker's son, middle child, proud adoring parents and sister with a lisp, track star in high school. He loved lasagna and he loved French toast, and they ate lasagna in Italy and French toast in France. She knew everything about him, except his life with his wife. Billie didn't even know her name.

Anna Harker

IT WAS MY BIRTHDAY, JUNE. Henry had said, "I have a special surprise for you." It was a gray day, still, the mosquitoes fierce. "Go down to Harrisville," Henry said. "It will be waiting." I did not know what he could mean. And I did not know the sky had a ceiling that could fall.

I laced up my boots, put on my hat, and grabbed the shotgun I carried on longer walks in case of bears. I was disgruntled at having to walk all the way to Harrisville. It was well over four miles. And then I would have to walk back. If Henry wanted to give me a present, I thought, he could give me a day of rest.

I saw a grizzly bear on a distant hill as I made my way down the trail. It was far enough away that I didn't worry, but still I looked back over my shoulder now and again lest it find its way onto the trail behind me.

As I neared Harrisville and the roofline of the roadhouse came into view, I could see something shiny and large, white and green, gleaming quietly in the gray of the day like a fish down in the water. A plane. I wondered where it had come from and why someone would fly out to this lonely place. As I drew closer, my thoughts intent on entering the roadhouse and getting myself a drink of water and perhaps a cup of tea, I saw a young man with a boyish face and a flop of sandy-colored hair falling across one side of his forehead. He was sitting in a chair outside swatting at the bugs. I nodded to him and kept walking toward the door when he said, "Are you Mrs. Harker?"

I stopped. "Yes," I said, my mind working as I wondered what it was Henry had planned for me.

The young man stood—a boy, really, in so many ways, but tall—and reached out his hand. "I'm Atlee Virtanen, the Flying Finn, and I'm here at your husband's request to take you into town for your birthday."

"The flying what?" I said.

"Finn. The Flying Finn."

"And you're a pilot?"

"Yes ma'am."

"And Finnish?"

"Well, back in the day. That's where part of my family comes from. Ever fly before?"

"No. Never."

"Ready to give it a try?"

"And your first name is Atlee?" I wasn't sure I heard him right. The name wasn't familiar to me.

"Yes, ma'am, but everyone calls me the Finn."

"Everyone?"

"Well, everyone down there in your little town."

"Village," I corrected, and almost laughed as I imagined how the nickname got started. "So are you one of us now?"

"Yes, ma'am, I suppose I am. The flying's good and I somehow managed to beat the other pilots here. I like it fine in your little village. Ready to go?"

He didn't look old enough to fly, but I figured he got up here in one piece, so I said, Yes! and soon we were up in the sky, looking down at all the hills, my hands shaking and my stomach flopping as my heart pounded with excitement. We spotted the grizzly bear I had seen earlier, now just a little miniature of itself, and the Finn flew over our camp and then swooped low over the operation where Henry and Nate Peterson labored among the mosquitoes. I waved from the window, imagining my face looking like a small photo in a locket. Henry waved back, and we flew away.

I had never imagined such beauty, and my eyes filled with tears. Alaska, Alaska. These hills, endless and serene, the mining operations tiny and inconsequential. And then the land flooded green beneath us as trees appeared and clustered and thickened, sprouting from the earth like blades of bright spring grass. I let a small cry of joy escape my lips, barely heard even by me over the noise of the plane, as the first glimpse of the first river came into view, rushing and winding through the trees. Then up ahead the larger, mightier Susitna, and I knew I was almost home, and when the village appeared it touched my heart at how tiny it was, a little toy set I would have liked to play with when I was small.

The Finn looked at me, and I smiled.

I had lunch with my mother at the roadhouse, and she had baked a chocolate cake and decorated the top with wild roses. That was one of many summer things missed while at the mines: the blooming of the roses, whose soft pink petals turn the lush green woods into a fairy kingdom for a few glorious but swiftly passing weeks between the last of June and the beginning of July.

"My goodness, Anna, so much?" my mother said as she sat across the table from me. I had put a rather large slice of the cake onto my plate. "Doesn't Henry feed you up there?"

"Oh, yes, Henry feeds me," I said. "But my own cooking, and no chocolate cake."

"Your stepfather was going to walk over and surprise you."

"Oh no!"

"It's all right. The Flying Finn dropped him a message."

"He did?"

"Right out of the plane," my mother said. "We put it in a flour sack with a few loaves of bread and two pounds of sugar." And then she told me about the Finn, who arrived shortly after the last of us left for the mines and who had a delivery route from Anchorage, meaning we could get mail and supplies now, on days when there was no train.

"This cake is wonderful," I said.

"My old sour-milk cake. You may take the rest back to Henry and Mr. Peterson."

The memory echoes through me now, like ripples over water. It is far away and close at once; I can hear my mother's laughter tinkling in my ears, taste again the dark, moist chocolate of her grand sour-milk cake, the sticky frosting smearing across my lips. It was in these moments the Finn walked in the door and said, "I'm sorry, Anna, but the ceiling dropped and I can't take you back just now," and I shrugged and smiled because that meant more time with my mother, more time at home. More time away from Henry and the drudgery of the camp: he and Nate would have to find their own dinner tonight. And how was it, then, that all the rest began? Another announcement from the Finn that we would have to wait until morning. There were cards and tea with my mother before she tired and went off to bed, and then the night was mine. The feeling of freedom was delicious, and I looked out the window and saw the sky was clearing. I grabbed a fishing pole from the shed and walked down to the river.

Wade Daniels

"I HAVE TO ASK, Wade, you understand, it's just procedure and I have to follow protocol."

Wade nodded. He was back in Fairfield's office, sitting in a chair across the desk from the commissioner, his boots making a puddle on the floor.

"How did you know to look where you did?" Fairfield winced at the sound of his own words, then started coughing. The commissioner had been sick on and off all winter, ever since that cold walk out from the mines.

"I didn't know anything," Wade said, "except that she couldn't be too far, but far enough, and that we never deliberately came at the search from the outside moving in toward the camp; we never actively looked at it from the other direction."

Fairfield held a handkerchief over his mouth and coughed and nodded, his eyes watering slightly. He cleared his throat. "The FBI, you know, those fellows got called away. Everything's all about the war. There's not much I can do besides file the report."

"The war doesn't mean this didn't happen," Wade said, his voice trembling. "We can't forget about it."

"No, of course not. But it does mean I'm on my own here." He coughed again and leaned back in his chair, staring past Wade to the window that faced Main Street. "Tell me your thoughts. I'm at a loss."

Wade licked his dry, chapped lips. He was wind burned, a little sunburned, and a little frostbit all at once. After he found Anna, he wouldn't leave her and waited two days at the spot after snowshoeing a message in the snow for the Finn. Once he was spotted, and the Finn flew low enough to gather that Wade had found something, it was another day before the Finn, Fairfield, and Thomas Merkle appeared on the horizon. Then slowly they removed Anna's pale frozen remains from her cold grave of snow, Fairfield documenting the procedure with photographs while the Finn sat in the snow nearby trying not to look, and likely trying not to cry, while Wade and Merkle had to summon the strength to pull back the snow, a little bit at a time.

"Oh my darling, my darling, we'll get you home now, we'll get you home," Merkle muttered again and again. "Perhaps you're there already, and we haven't seen you, sitting at the counter or running down the hall, or watching the snow spill down on the street outside the window. Anna, Anna, you come home now, little one."

Gradually, Wade's sorrow was swallowed by a rage that rose up from deep within him as if that, like Anna, had lain frozen these long, sad months. Someone had done this to her, cut off her ear and put an ax in her back and left her there to die. Her eyes, frozen and open and dull like pebbles removed from a stream, looked up toward the sky as she lay with half her face on a pillow of tundra, and as Wade watched Merkle brush the snow from her and gently smooth back what hair wasn't stiff with frozen blood, he saw the expression there, across her features, somehow peaceful and content. That nearly broke him, and he stepped back, and the Finn rose and stood by him and put his arm around his shoulder, Wade noting the cold tears on the young man's cheeks. He took several deep breaths and went back to work. When she was free, they rolled her in a canvas tarp, secured her to a sled, and made the long trek back to the airfield. Anna was brought home first, so her mother could see her, a scene Wade had thankfully missed, and then flown to Anchorage for autopsy.

That was four days ago. Wade had stayed home until Jake showed up to tell him Fairfield needed to see him.

"I don't know what's going to happen now," Fairfield said. "My only suspects are you and Montana, and neither one of you did it. I've spent every waking minute of this goddamned winter going over it again and again. I keep looking for a motive, since nothing was missing and Anna, apparently was—unmolested, so I have to figure someone simply didn't like the three of them, that's all I can think of."

He knew he should tell Fairfield that Jake filed on the claim downstream from the Harker mine. That haunted Wade, and he tried not to think about it. But Jake was an opportunist, and being an opportunist does not make one a murderer. And then there was Nellie, and how hurt she was. But how would she even get up there, let alone leave enough of her humanity behind to do what was done? It kept coming back to Montana. He was there, not far, and he had reason to be angry at the Harkers.

"Everyone who was up there's got an alibi, except Montana," Fairfield said. "And I suppose there's a chance someone showed up out of the blue, but that's a rare sort of thing given nothing was stolen. And whoever it was went out of his way to track Anna, only to kill her and leave her." He started coughing again, and Wade's chest hurt listening to him. When he finished, he took some deep breaths and cleared his throat. "Anna," he said, "she was a once-in-a-lifetime kind of gal, don't you think?"

Wade felt his neck prickle, as if an unseen hand hovered near the back of it. "Yes."

"Love or money—it seems these things come down to that in one way or another."

Wade nodded. But he'd been over this and over this and over this: if it was about love, then he or Nellie would be the killers because Henry obviously wasn't. Had something happened he'd forgotten? He ran his hand through his thick, dirty hair. He felt light-headed and weak and knew he was pale and trembling.

"Did you like her, Wade? Anna?"

Here was the moment, he thought, the one he'd been expecting for so long. "Yes."

"How much?"

He couldn't answer. He was in the avalanche now, he knew, and was crashing toward the bottom.

"How much, Wade?" Fairfield's voice was even and calm.

"More than I had a right to," Wade said, looking at the edge of Fairfield's desk, too tired to face the older man's eyes.

Fairfield nodded. "I kind of thought so."

"I would never have hurt her."

"I kind of thought that too." He put a clenched hand to his mouth, as if he was going to cough again, then cleared his throat and drew in a long breath. "Anybody out there, besides Henry, have reason to be upset about that?"

Wade knew what he should say. But how could he betray Nellie?

"Wade, I need you to answer that. Not answering only makes it look worse."

"I was seeing Nellie for awhile."

"She knows how you felt about Anna?"

"She confronted Anna about it last spring." *Nellie knows,* Anna had said, and Wade had flushed with shame.

"She pretty upset?"

"She was a little angry, but come on—you saw what was done. I don't see Nellie doing that."

"Could she have had some help maybe?"

"I meant she doesn't have it in her to do something like that or anything close to it."

Fairfield stabbed the end of his pen against the paper on his desk. "I do agree, but I'll have to find out where she was on the days in question. I'll be discreet about it."

"Thank you."

"What am I missing?"

"Same thing all the rest of us are."

"Someone out there knows what happened."

"I know."

"So that's—that's all for now, Wade. I appreciate you being straight with me."

Wade rose and put on his hat and coat. He nodded to Fairfield, who started coughing again, then went out the door and pulled it closed behind him.

Billie Sutherland

"SO WHERE ARE WE, BILLIE?" the Finn asked. She looked around. She and the Finn had snowshoed along the frozen river on a day when the sun struggled to rise high enough into the sky to linger briefly before slowly sinking down. But the mountains were brilliant and beautiful, pastel blues and whites now touched with a soft pink on the tops of the assorted peaks.

"You know what I mean," he said. She did, but didn't know how to answer. She had returned to the hangar a few times, for tea and casual conversation, but she kept the visits short and the tone light, like a stop sign floating in the air between them.

"Is it that hard to talk to me?" he asked, moving again, his long legs steady and giraffe-like as he strode along beside her. She looked up at his face and was struck at how fitting he looked, in the surrounding landscape, as if he emerged from the land itself. Rugged. Beautiful. Honest.

"Can I ask you something?" she asked. They stopped again, though each time they did they could feel the clutch of the cold.

"Of course."

"Do you think it's possible Anna Harker and Wade Daniels loved each other?"

He took a deep breath that crystalized into a cloud of frost when he exhaled. She could see the disappointment on his face. "Changing the subject, are we? All right. That's a loaded question. What—or I should say who—gave you that idea?"

"I can't say. But someone told me something, and now I'm wondering."

He looked past her, his brow furrowed, his eyes narrowed against the sting of below-zero air. "I don't know. I'd hate to think that they would do something like that to Henry. Neither seemed the type."

"The type?" she asked, though she knew what type he meant. She was that type. Billie Sutherland. Red-lipped stewardess. She didn't care, did she, that Jimmy Johnson had a wife, and that a wife was a person who lived, laughed, and cried.

"Billie, what is it?" he asked. "If it's what happened between us, well, don't let it worry you, all right? I'm a big boy. But I won't lie and say it didn't matter. To me I mean. It mattered to me."

She looked down at the smooth layer of snow, a white-blue in the slipping daylight, fresh and undisturbed save for the trail of their tracks that led from the village. "Timing has a lot to do with things like this," she said, not looking at him. "Timing and lack of other options."

She could feel his eyes searching her face. "It's not a timing thing, Billie," he said. "And it's not a somebody or anybody thing. It's a you thing."

"You don't know me."

She continued not to look at him as they stood and breathed in the cold, white clouds leaving their mouths and dispersing into the blue-gray of the fading light.

He shook his head, looking up at the sky. In just a few rapid moments the blue above them had darkened several shades, and here and there a faint star appeared. "They're always there, aren't they?" he said.

"What?"

"The stars. All day long we don't see them, and we think of them as not being there, that they appear—come out—when night comes, as if arriving from someplace else. But it's the daylight that comes and goes and hides the night, which is always there, waiting, like there's a curtain pulled across it." He looked down at her, and she felt her heart quicken as she let his eyes meet hers. "You know what the best part of the night is?"

She gave a small shrug, not wanting to say the wrong thing.

"It makes the day all the brighter. You figure it out, Billie, and when you do, you let me know, okay?" He kissed her forehead and walked off and left her there. She watched him blend into the landscape—the frozen river and the distant mountains and all the shades of pastel blue and white. Part of her wanted to call out to him; part of her felt the ease of relief. Billie breathed in the sharp, cold air—so clean, she thought; there was something so clean about the below-zero world. She tried to imagine Anna here, years ago, meeting Wade perhaps, and watching the setting sun bathe the mountains pink. But her eyes kept going to the fading figure of the Finn, and as the distance between them grew she realized she'd better strike off in the same direction before it got too dark. Still, she continued to stand there, for a few moments unable to move, while one by one stars filled the sky above her.

Anna Harker

HE WAS THERE, by the river in the soft June midsummer
light, that day that was my twenty-fourth birthday, a silhouette
against the backdrop of silver water and white mountains now
washed with gold as the sun came through the clouds before
it settled lower on the horizon. I stood and watched him, his
wrist flicking and the rod spinning, the soft hiss of line cutting
through the air. But it wasn't long before he felt me there and
looked over his shoulder and smiled. "It's you," he said.

"And it's you," I replied. I walked up to the bank, slightly
downstream from where he fished, and tossed in my line.

"Came down, I see," he said.

"And you as well."

"Errands for my cousin. Our equipment is best at breaking, it seems. What's your excuse?"

"It's my birthday."

He smiled at me, dimples appearing in the sides of his
face beneath the short growth of his beard. "Well then, a very
happy birthday to you, Miss Anna."

"Thank you, Mr. Wade."

And we laughed and fished, him with his flies and me
with my lures, and I felt so content, right then, in a way I
hadn't in years. Well, since marrying Henry, when I became
the object of great expectations. It was my birthday. I'd had
my first flight in an airplane, followed by my mother's chocolate cake for lunch, and now I was fishing in the soft light of

a summer night, the roar of the river in my ears and the gulls squawking and flapping overhead. I felt his eyes on me, and I realized I was smiling to myself as the breeze blew in all the green smells of the surrounding woodlands.

"What's your story, Anna Harker?" he asked, looking at me sideways with a small, mischievous smile on his mouth and in his eyes.

"My story?"

"The story of you, Anna Harker."

"My story," I said again, thinking as I reeled in my line and cast it back out. Where would I begin, I wondered then as I wonder now. On that day I began my story at the literal beginning of me, my very early childhood on a Washington State farm with my mother and grandparents, then the journey north to Uncle Mike, then his death and the entrance of Merkle all in the same day, until marrying Henry on that very beach four years ago. He watched me as I talked, his eyes flitting back and forth between my face and his flying line, until I felt I had adequately summarized my life, after which I shrugged and tossed out my line again.

"That's an amazing story," he said. "It must have been pretty special to be here before the proper onset of civilization."

"Are we properly civilized?" I asked. "Heaven help us." We shared a laugh, then I said, "So now it's your turn."

"My turn?"

"To tell your story. The story of you."

"Aw—my story pales in comparison to yours."

"I doubt it. So tell me."

He shook his head. "There's not much to it. I hadn't really been anywhere until now. I was busy keeping my family's farm going, and there wasn't much time or opportunity for much else." He smiled a little, then tossed his line. "My mom finally sold part of it. I guess she either realized I was never going to be much of a farmer in my life, or that I was never going to have much of a life if I kept being a farmer." He looked at me and shrugged. "I followed my cousin north and left my mom and what remained of the farm behind. I kind of feel like it's all—my story, I mean—starting here."

"She forgave you for it—your mother?"

"Oh yeah. It got to the point she wanted me to go. I think it was the war, you know. She thinks we're bound to get caught up in it sooner or later. She figured I'd better get going while I could."

"I don't think my grandparents ever forgave my uncle Mike for leaving the family farm," I said, "or my mother for having me. It's nice your mother gave you her blessing."

He looked over the water toward the distant trees on the other side. "I always felt I was living someone else's life. Or that I had no story. But Alaska—I feel that it's my story. This place."

"Well, I know that feeling," I said. "I don't need too much more than this."

It would have been all right if we had left it there, a pleasant evening by the river with harmless conversation. But as we talked and fished, a bridge was being knitted between us, built out of words and looks and whatever it is that draws one person to another. When we left the river, where the fish weren't biting, we left together and walked into the village, tethered together by those unseen strings. We walked past the roadhouse and found ourselves at the inn, which was like a magnet that pulled us to it. "A birthday drink," he said and we set our fishing poles by the door and walked inside and sat at the bar. It was quiet and oddly somber at first, but once it got out it was my birthday the toasts kept coming. "I only knew you since you were a little curly haired rascal," old Carlson, one of the old-timers now retired from his mine, said. "Always running around all covered in dirt. Now look at you. You growed up, Anna."

"I think so," I said, laughing. "But I seem to still manage to get all covered in dirt."

"Now that I'd like to see," Wade said.

"Well, she is a miner's wife," Carlson said. "Where is young Henry anyway?"

"Out in the dirt," I said, and we all laughed some more.

Then somehow it was past midnight, and we were again by the river, Wade and I, and somehow I was on his back, getting a piggyback ride, my fist full of wild roses, and he was twirling me around above the silty sand, and then we tumbled down onto it, still laughing, and as I caught my breath my eyes went from the pearly gray sky above to his face now beside me, his eyes looking into mine.

"You are the most beautiful human I have ever known," he said, and I tried to laugh but I kissed him instead, and it wasn't the whiskey, and it wasn't the freedom, it was only him, and only me, at home with each other like fish in a stream, our breath in each other's lungs, our arms and legs and fingers entwined.

We awoke still on that gray sand, where once I played with George and once I married Henry, wrapped in the soft mist of morning, clinging together for warmth. We lay there looking at each other, our eyes close together, words lost to us, moments of time rushing by like the river water beside us. Slowly I pulled myself away, and my eyes kept contact with his, and I stood, covered with silt and bits of roses, grabbed my fishing pole and walked away.

When I turned back to look at him, he was standing by the water, and I saw a rose fall from his hand. I could see that rose in my mind, swirling away in the current, untethered, going wherever it would go, on its way.

I told myself: The ceiling dropped. It was my birthday. I was drunk. But nothing helped. The ceiling had dropped, and the sky was tumbling down.

Wade Daniels

THE SPRING FOREST was sparse and silent, the trees gray and dim in the sinking snow. Night fell slowly now, like a cloudy dream of endless twilight, and Wade felt a twinge of the usual discontent a night like this would bring: too warm to be cold, too cold to be warm, the snow so soft and mushy even snowshoes weren't of much use. But the familiar feeling was swiftly fleeting, and he returned to the hollowness that had haunted him since finding Anna. Sorrow and anger had wrought their way through him, like rot through the center of a piece of wood.

He sat on his little slab of porch, legs hanging down and feet resting in the snow, staring at the endless trees unable to imagine the world turning green again. A month from now the snow would be gone. Two months from now the frantic growing season would be underway, with leaves popping open and life sprouting up from the soggy ground. He would make sure he was gone before the snow was. He couldn't bear to see the other side of spring.

Something moved, now, among the trees, tall and featureless in the dim light, like a long, thin shadow-colored ghost. He watched the figure approach and recognized Montana, recognized, too, the haunted, hunted look on a face grown thin and haggard, like the one that stared back at him from the surface of his window glass.

Montana came up, eyes on the slushy ground in front of him, walked past Wade, then sat not far from him on the porch slab.

For a while they didn't speak. Then Montana asked, "So where was she?"

"On the downward side of the hill to the northeast of the camp. On a flat spot, near a boulder."

Montana blew air through his teeth, a lonely whistling sound. "How'd we miss that?"

"Snow came. Snow came too dammed soon." Wade couldn't see the man beside him, but he could feel the shaking of his head. Long moments passed without speaking. How did they lose their lives, he thought, referring to himself and Montana, when no ax came anywhere near?

"There's no way out of this," Montana said.

"I know."

"It's always gonna be here."

"Yep."

"But at least Anna's been found. At least no one can blame her now."

Wade nodded and felt the sting of tears in his eyes. He had cleared her. It was the only thing that anyone could do for her, and he had done it.

Montana sucked at the tobacco wad in the side of his cheek and spit brown juice onto the remains of the snow. "But you know, there's talk about you, now."

"I'd heard."

"Here's the thing," Montana said. "Somebody's done it. It wasn't you, it wasn't me, and it wasn't Anna, God bless her."

Wade said nothing and felt Montana's watery eyes on him.

"We can agree on that, can't we?" Montana said. "That you and I had nothin' to do with it."

Finally, Wade nodded. "I never really thought you did," he said.

"Thank you," Montana said. "What do you think, then?"

Wade shook his head and looked up at the pale gray sky. "I've been over it and over it. I don't know." He took a deep breath. "Why did you go over there that day?"

"I'd like to say I was checking on them, checking on the place in light of John Cobb's men lurking around. But the truth is I always went over there. When they were there, I wanted them to see me and remember it was my gold they were pulling out of the ground and my cabin that supplied the roof over their heads at night. When they were gone, I wanted to sit for awhile and pretend it was still mine."

"You shouldn't have done that."

"I know. I can see how this makes me look. Crazy old man. Crazy old angry man. But I went over there that morning because I thought they'd be gone."

Wade nodded and bit at his bottom lip. "And you didn't go over the day before?"

"No. Wish I had. But that was the day I thought they were leaving, and I didn't want them to catch me on the trail."

"What do you remember about that day? Anything?"

"No. I mean, nothing out of the ordinary. It was a windy day, but it seemed quiet in the hills. I worked my claim. I forgot to take any lunch with me, so I walked back to my cabin in the early afternoon. That's when I thought I heard a plane. Just a tiny, little buzzing sound drifting on the wind."

"A buzzing?"

"Yeah. Like a giant mosquito. Somewhere in the hills. I didn't hear it for long. Them FBI guys figured it was a chainsaw somewhere, or maybe a distant plane. Or that I'd made it up, I don't know."

Wade felt a sense of uneasiness wash through him. "What do you think it was?" Wade asked.

"I don't know. Maybe nothing—anything I could think of didn't seem to fit and didn't make sense. Not that any part of this makes any sense. There was no reason for anyone to kill those young folks. Nobody could know what the families would end up doing with the claim. Nobody stole anything. It was like someone just wanted them dead. Or someone wanted anybody dead, and those three were handy."

The motive was always the snag, Wade knew. Who would do that for nothing? He thought of Jake and that new claim. That's not worth it, either. But the idea of it bothered him, like the sound of a whisper he couldn't quite hear.

As if knowing his thoughts, Montana said, "There are people in this world who are beyond understanding, who do things that make no sense. Look at that war over there in that other part of the world. All because one kind of people can't stand another kind. Ain't the world big enough for everyone? Ain't there enough gold and enough open claims in those hills for everyone? I came to Alaska, all those years ago, because it seemed like the land of plenty with room for all. I never expected something like this. But I also never expected Emmitt Harker to not give me one more year to make good on my debt. So maybe it just goes to show ya. We take ourselves with us no matter where. Whoever did that, brought his demons with him. And likely left a trail—something not quite right, you know, they did or were connected to, somewhere along the line."

The words were like a cold hand on Wade's soul. A trail. A trail of deeds, a trail that linked into other trails, like those that riddled the hills. Little things that accumulate in a life.

Oh, he would never do anything like that! He remembered his Aunt Dorothy, standing outside their farmhouse, his mother beside her, fending off a farmer who said Jake and another boy took his old collie and bludgeoned it to death with baseball bats. Jake said he didn't do it, so did the other boy.

But Wade also remembered being out with Jake and some of Jake's friends, older boys, and there was a big bonfire in the woods. Somehow they'd captured a groundhog, which squirmed around in a green canvas duffle. Then they picked up the bag and emptied it out into the middle of the blaze. The creature screamed, Jake laughed, and Wade got sick and ran home alone through the trees.

Then there was Lawry, the thought like a heavy curtain with something moving behind it. Or maybe nothing. Or maybe something. Jake was there. Jake was here. Should that have been enough for Wade to put it together?

"What are you thinking?" Montana asked.

Wade shook his head, tried to swallow. "Just something. Nothing really. Just how a person gets started down a trail like that." He hoped that would be enough to satisfy Montana.

Montana spit again on the aging snow. "If you take away the logical reasons for killing someone: love, greed, anger, well—you're left with an empty hole. Some people are like an empty hole." He stood to leave.

My boy would never. His aunt's voice again. Then an image of Jake, in his cabin last winter, licking the blood from his steak off his lips. *And sometimes here in Alaska, as I learned up at Lawry, people just disappear.*

Wade tried to swallow again but his mouth went dry. He could be wrong, all wrong about the thought that was growing in his brain. Please, he thought. *Please.*

Billie Sutherland

"MERRY CHRISTMAS."

"That time already?"

"No—it's in a few days. But I wanted to come by before I left." Billie stood in the cold outside the door of Montana's dark, rough cabin. The cabin was on the edge of the village in a patch of woods near the river. She'd followed a small trail through the woods after arriving at the end of the road. Behind the cabin an old horse barn still stood, one half of the roof caving in from the snow.

"Come in," he said, and stepped aside to let her enter.

The cabin was low-roofed and gray; the windows small. It was still light out, but he had a kerosene lantern lit on the cluttered table. A fire burned in the old potbellied woodstove in the corner, and the place, like its owner, smelled of smoke. Montana lifted a stack of old magazines from a chair. "Have a seat," he said. "I don't get much company."

Billie placed a bag of baked goods on the table: cranberry bread, blueberry muffins, and gingerbread cake. She'd been careful not to let Maddie know she was coming here, and she took the baked goods out from those she had set aside to take to her family.

He looked at the bag.

"For you," she said. "Some things I baked." She had given some to the Finn as well, the feel of the encounter still sharp in her heart. He'd opened the door, and she'd said, "I wasn't sure if it would be okay to stop by, but I—"

He'd smiled. "It's fine, Billie. Of course it is. I didn't mean to get all dramatic on you."

She almost laughed. "Thank you. I brought you some things. Merry Christmas."

He took the bag she held out to him. "Hmm. Feels like something good. Here, wait a minute." He'd stepped back by his coat rack and produced a book tied with a red ribbon. On a simple white tag he'd written *Billie*.

"It's blank," he'd said. "I thought you might like to write about some things."

"Thank you."

"Friends?"

"Friends."

And she left him at that. Now, at this other stop, the old man carefully opened the bag and looked inside. Billie saw his eyes blinking rapidly, and her heart twisted at the idea that he might cry.

"Thank you," he said. "I don't have nothing for you."

"That's all right. I wasn't—"

"But that's the fun of it, if I remember. Wait a minute." He went to a rough wooden bookshelf not far from the small cot where he slept, pulled something from behind a cluster of dusty books and wiped it off with the edge of his flannel shirt.

"Here," he said, walking slowly back to the table.

"Really, I—"

"No, go on—take it. It's not much."

It was an old picture, in a small silver frame. A young Montana standing by one of his horses, a big smile on his face, the river in the background. "Thank you," Billie said. "I love it."

"I had it taken for my mother, then picked up the frame one time when I went in to Anchorage. It took me so long to get it ready that she died before I got it in the mail to her."

"Oh. I'm so sorry."

"I wanted to show her I was okay here. And I wanted to show her my beautiful horse."

Billie put the photograph into the big pocket of her winter coat and felt it there, along with the little blank book, as she made her way back into the village in the fading light.

Grandma Millie was sitting at the front room table with Maddie when Billie entered, a rush of cold following her in through the door. The two women were planning the yearly roadhouse Christmas dinner, which Billie would miss, and they sat with the list of guests they knew were coming so they could make sure they would have something everyone would like. The Finn would be on the list. Montana would not.

"Cup of cocoa before your train, Billie?" Maddie asked, and Billie nodded and joined the women while she waited for the next hour to pass before grabbing her bag and heading for the depot. Against her protests the two women joined her for the short walk in the dark and the cold to the depot, Maddie more jovial than Billie could recall ever having seen her, and Millie her usual boisterous self. "Now don't go running off with any smart fellows down there," Millie said. "We've decided we like you, and we want to keep you."

"We'll enjoy eating all the fruits of your labors, Billie," Maddie said. "And do have a wonderful time with your family." When they heard the train whistle in the distance Maddie gave Billie an unexpected hug, and the two older women lingered in the cold and waved the train away after Billie climbed aboard and found a seat. She waved back and watched until every last light from the village disappeared from view and the train moved forward through the miles of dark woods.

Anna Harker

I REMEMBER THE NIGHT, the winter after the summer Wade and I broke my promises to Henry on the river silt. There was an owl somewhere in the woods around the village, which were as silent as the surface of the frozen rivers save for the occasional whine from a dog on its line. I lay in my bed, in the modest cabin Henry and I lived in that bordered the stretch of the village airstrip. The woodstove breathed—a soft, living sound that spoke of warmth and comfort in a world snuggled tight against the thirty-below-zero air beyond the door, the windows, and the walls.

The cabin was dark except for the moonlight that spilled in across the table in the kitchen area where a kerosene lamp sat in the center, its duties done for the night when Henry, a few hours earlier, turned it down and blew it out even though I was not yet ready to put down my reading, a new book called *The Grapes of Wrath* lent to me by Mrs. Wilson—Millie—who was my teacher when we were both much younger. Henry's eyes caught mine as his breath traveled down the glass globe and extinguished the light-giving flame. My lips parted to speak, but Henry said, "It's late, Anna, nearly 9:30. We should sleep." His face in darkness now, the moon not yet risen, and I felt—why, I now wonder, as it seems so silly and unnecessary—that I had no choice but to go along, though inside my blood quietly boiled. I made Henry pay for it by lying still as he moved on top of me, hating myself for being so complicit, so ordinary, so unlike the me I had always known. It was after he fell asleep, and I lay there awake watching the moonlight come slipping in, that I heard the owl.

Who-h'WHOO, who, who. A voice so deep and clear. Somewhere, I knew, another owl would hear the call and answer. I slipped out of bed, pulled a pair of long johns on beneath my flannel nightgown and tiptoed to the door, where I put on my winter coat, a thick hat, and the mukluks Merkle gave me when I was a teen, still my favorites. Then I went out into the night, where the big round moon cast blue shadows on the snow and did nothing to dim the thick splattering of stars that filled the sky. "Star soup," Uncle Mike used to say, looking up at night. "Ummm . . . Yum." And he would stretch his arm up, as if his hand were a giant spoon, and pretend to take a big scoop of the sky and slurp it into his mouth. In my child's mind I would picture a river of stars pouring into him.

In the quiet of this night I stood still outside the door and listened until I heard it again, *who-h'WHOO, who, who,* then tread softly toward the sound. I cut across the village airstrip, toward the woods that fringed the river. There were few lights to be seen in any of the cabins and houses, and the sharp, freezing air was lightly scented with wood smoke. I felt free, the way I had felt most of my life, the way I felt the previous summer with Wade Daniels on the riverbank, though I recognized in that case freedom crossed many lines. Nothing of that sort could happen again, and hadn't, and we both seemed to be avoiding the stream in the hills where our paths used to cross on occasion. Once, though, when I came down my little trail and saw him there, I turned and started back the way I came, a quick glance over my shoulder confirming that he had seen my almost arrival. The unspoken questions on his face pulled on my heart. I didn't know what to do, about any of it, except stay away from what my heart yearned for most. But I could steal as many moments like this—alone in the night following the cry of the owl—as I chose.

I followed the airstrip down toward the river, walking on top of the packed and hardened snow, and when I heard the next *who-h'WHOO, who, who*, I knew I was getting closer. I continued on to the edge of the frozen river so I could see the moonlight glaze the landscape with a shimmering light. I took it all in: the stars, the sparkling snow, the white ribbon of river leading north and south, the dark mystery of the trees on either side. *Who-h'WHOO, who, who!* The owl again, and I looked upriver in the direction the call had come from, and to my surprise I saw a figure there, standing like I was, on the edge of the woods, so still and shadowy that had not the head moved slightly I would have felt my imagination was getting the best of me. Like me, the figure seemed to be listening and appeared to look toward the trees on the other side. And then I heard it, the answering call, *who-h'WHOO, who, who*, from those distant woods. Then the nearer call, so clear and close and brilliant: *Who-h'WHOO, who, who!* I could not see the shadowed face of the person who shared this moment with me, but I felt the distant companionship in this time and this place, on this planet hurtling through space.

Perhaps I did know who it was, knew the size and shape of him, but in the silence of the night it was as if we made an unspoken pact to leave it be.

The night that followed was similar—Henry sticking to his strict bedtime routine, myself waiting for him to fall asleep then slipping out the door and into that cold and glittering moonlit world to follow the call of the owl. And again, once at the river, I saw the shadowed form of a fellow human being. The owl cried out: *who-h'WHOO, who, who!* And moments later the answering call from the woods on the other side of the river found its way into my ears. *Who-h'WHOO, who, who, who-h'WHOO, who, who.* I heard, now, footsteps on the hard snow and saw the figure approaching, gaining the shape and definition that had somehow become so dear to me.

"Wade," I said, and could see in the moonlight his welcoming smile.

"Anna."

He stopped short of touching me, and bathed in the moonlight we looked like silver ghosts.

"I haven't seen you since—"

"New Year's Eve," I said.

"Yes. I've been trapping."

"Oh," I said, as if that explained why he was a scarce sight in the village the past months. His trapline, I guessed, would not stretch the distance of a line like Merkle's. Wade was choosing to stay away, and I knew why, or thought I knew. He was seeing Nellie. And he did not want to see me. Why was he here now?

"Some of the miners have been meeting," he said. "We're—I mean Jake, actually, and the rest—are thinking of joining in on some new equipment."

If my face flushed, the cold quickly chastened it, but the fact that Henry had not been invited to these meetings was not lost on me, nor the reason why he was excluded. My heart twisted for him suddenly, that man who was my husband, whose crime here it seemed was doing well at what he did. He had made it on his own, and even though our mine—the one that had been Montana's, lest we forget—was purchased from his father, Henry had paid a fair price for it, or at least a fair price for a mine that was not producing. It was a gamble. That it paid off was held against Henry, something I found hard to understand.

"Well, I'd best head home," Wade said. "Moonlight's bright enough." He smiled, and our eyes met, but he made no motion to walk away. A long quiet moment would pass before I would listen to the sound of his boots on the snow until it faded into the silence.

There would be another night when we would meet like this, and everything would break lose between us with our bodies, oblivious to the cold, finding each other through layers of clothes. But this night, this night that I can feel again as if I am there, we stood separate yet together in a magical winter world.

Wade Daniels

THE TRAIN BLEW ITS WHISTLE, long and loud, as it pulled away from the depot and headed south. Wade sat alone in the near-empty train, shaking with cold though the car was warm. Maybe it wasn't the cold that made him shiver. Maybe it was knowing where he was going and what he was doing and why.

He tried to shift his thoughts, and invented a fantasy: Anna here, beside him, his loving wife, holding his hand as they watch the miles pass by.

This will be fun, she says. *We haven't been to Anchorage in so long.*

I know, he says. *Why do we stay away?*

Because we love the rivers, she says, *and the mountains, and the trees.*

Yes, yes we do.

"Your ticket, sir."

Wade opened his eyes. The conductor loomed above him, his body rocking with the movement of the train, his black suit crisp and sharp. "Going on holiday?" he asked as Wade pulled the ticket out from his jacket pocket.

No," Wade said. "Business." What else could he call it? That seemed an accurate assessment. But he felt as if he were traveling to a funeral. Whose, he wondered. His own? The funeral of part of him, of life as he had known it.

He wondered if there would be a funeral now, for Anna. She was still at the medical examiner's office in Anchorage.

Could he go there? Should he go there? It was likely he couldn't. But maybe he could walk past, maybe he could touch the outside wall.

He had come to think, though, of Anna's body as not really her. It saved him somewhat, to think of her as removed from what she had become.

He leaned his head against the cool window and watched the landscape slide by. Spruce trees, birch trees, snow, and spots of ground, sometimes the river, sometimes the remains of a moose carcass from a winter collision with a train. Alaska. Beautiful and harsh at once. April and the days were already stretching long, and soon the rivers would open and there would be fishing to be had. He tried to remember the feel of it, the feel of a happy day, the sun on his face and his reel spinning in his hand. But he wasn't that person anymore. He caught his own eyes in the reflection on the glass. Who was he, then?

He let himself doze a little before the train arrived in Anchorage. He got himself to sleep by imagining another life: one where he loved Nellie, not Anna. Where Nellie was waiting for him in the little cabin by the lake, making her fry bread and mixing up some pemmican, dreaming of that big family she wanted so badly. It would have been easy, that life, and maybe it would have happened, but something else happened on the way, an intersection. A beautiful woman with wet wild hair, shivering in the water. The cold silt by the river and the warm place of her, the beautiful place, that took him in and felt like home. The simple pleasure of standing beside her by the streambed as they each cast their lines, her shoulder close, her dark hair spilling down across the blue and white check of her flannel shirt.

The whistle blew and he opened his eyes, unable for a moment to distinguish between what he dreamt and what he thought. The train was pulling into the small frontier city now, and Wade watched as roads and houses appeared. "Here we are, folks," the conductor said. "Anchor-town!" The whistle blew a few times more, and soon he heard the hissing and squealing of the brakes as the train slowed and rolled into the station. He could just leave, he realized. Get off the train and get to the airport and wait for a plane that was headed east. Walk away and be done with it all. Let his Alaska story end before it got any worse, if that was even possible, and spend a little more time with his mom than he had allotted before joining up. She would like that. But even as he envisioned his mother's happy face, he knew he couldn't go. Not yet. Slowly and reluctantly, he rose and walked off the train.

It was raining in Anchorage, an early, spring rain, and the smell of it mixed with the smells of the city: wet asphalt, car exhaust. He carried a small duffle and wandered slowly into town, making his way to the Inlet View Inn, where he entered and inquired about a room.

"How long are you here for?" the proprietress, a thin redhead with her hair piled on top of her head, asked.

"A few days," he said, pulling out the worn leather wallet his mother had given him when he was sixteen. "Tonight and tomorrow night." He had made arrangements to fly back up with the Finn, who was making a mail run, so he wouldn't have to wait for the next train.

"And where are you from, handsome?" She smiled, handed him the guest book, and watched as he wrote, *Susitna Station*.

"Oh," she said. "Where those awful murders happened. Thank God they found the Mrs. I mean, to keep the men from talking. 'It had to be the woman,' they were all saying and imagined she'd run off to Cuba with some mysterious stranger or something like that. But no woman would do that, what was done there, Lizzie Borden aside. Don't cha think?"

Wade nodded, put his wallet back in his pocket, and took the key from the counter. His room was on the ground floor and had a window that gave him, like the name of the inn promised, a view of the inlet. He wanted to sit there, on the small single bed, and stare out at the gray moving water. Sit there and watch the dark eventually come, merging with the remains of the day, the dusk growing and spreading and deepening and darkening. He could do that, just sit there. But he had to go, see if there was anything anywhere for him to find.

Billie Sutherland

"DID YOU SHOW HER?" Aunt Sam burst into Howard's office where Billie stood near the window looking out at the lights on the street below as her uncle finished proofing a story for the evening's paper.

"Sam!" he said. "It's Christmas Eve for God's sake!"

"Show me what?" Billie said, a slow, sinking feeling forming in her stomach.

"It can wait," Howard said.

"No, it can't," Sam said.

"No, it can't," Billie agreed. "Show me what?" She knew she didn't want to know but had quickly determined that not knowing would be worse.

"Sit down, Billie," Howard said. She took a seat across from him, and he pulled an envelope from his desk. Sam stood beside him, eyes round.

"Morty Roberts," Howard said.

"What?"

"Remember him? He was one of my editors."

"One of *our* editors," Sam corrected.

"Yes. Of course. He's in Seattle now, at the *Times*."

"Oh." Her hands were beginning to shake. She held them in her lap.

"Billie, why didn't you say something?" Sam asked as Howard pulled a clipping from the envelope. Billie snatched it from his hand.

"Woman Found Dead in Apartment; Suicide Suspected"

She read the headline and closed her eyes. She knew all that came next. She'd read the story, and she'd lived the story, that different story that only she and Jimmy knew.

A woman was found dead in the apartment of Seattle resident Billie Sutherland, formerly of Alaska, who told investigators the woman was a neighbor in the building.

Their flights got in an hour apart. Jimmy had lost the set of keys she had given him and so waited for her at the airport. They took a taxi and had drinks in a bar where no one knew them, then tumbled into the apartment, already pulling at their clothes.

Aren't you afraid?

You don't scare me, Alaska.

He pressed her against the bathroom door. She reached behind her back and turned the knob.

Sutherland, a stewardess, found the woman dead in her bathtub after returning home from a late flight. Investigators say the woman appeared to have slit her wrists and at this time no foul play is suspected.

Billie screamed. Jimmy said, *Amy!*

No—that's my neighbor—Amelia! Oh God! Skin as white as the porcelain tub. Water the color of the wine they'd drunk together.

Billie that's my wife—that's Amy!

There was a letter on the vanity. It was written with Billie's lipstick. *Liars,* it said. *You're both a couple of liars!* She could lie, too, it said. Amy Johnson gets the last laugh. Amy Johnson will haunt their dreams.

Billie held the letter. Jimmy said, *Get rid of it. Now! Here—tear it up and flush it down the toilet.*

No! We can't—

Billie, get ahold of yourself.

That's where your keys went, Jimmy! That's where your keys went!

I know that! Don't you think I realize that?

The news story read, "Sutherland said she had given the woman her spare set of keys so the woman could water her houseplants in her absences." A lie, the first of many little tiny lies, like needles in her heart.

I'm calling the police.

Let me get out of here first.

You can't leave!

Billie I can't be here. That's my wife for God's sake! It'll kill my career to be caught here with you!

"Billie?" Aunt Sam said, pulling up a chair beside her.

"It's Christmas Eve, Sam," Howard repeated. "I said we should wait."

Billie lifted one hand, as if she could freeze the room, then with the other handed the clipping back to Howard.

"He called a week or so ago and said, wasn't that our niece?" Howard said. "I told him to mail the clipping and I'd get back to him. He's doing a follow-up."

"A follow-up?"

"It seems the woman in your tub was married to a United co-pilot," Sam said. "Did you know that?"

"Yes—I mean no. No. I didn't know who she was. She was my neighbor. Amelia."

"So did you know this woman's husband?"

"I did. But I didn't know she was the wife."

"The wife," Sam said. "Oh, Billie, what have you done?"

"I knew he was married," Billie said quietly. "And I just didn't think."

"Don't tell us anything else," Howard said. "That way we don't have to lie to Morty."

"My wife was obviously not well," Jimmy Johnson told Morty Roberts. It was January, and Billie was back in Susitna Station, and Uncle Howard sent her the follow-up clipping in the mail.

Of course I knew Billie Sutherland. We were colleagues. Sure, we'd bump into each other now and then at airports. Nice girl. My wife must have picked her out of a hat, hoping to ruin my career or feed her delusions or something. I don't know. I didn't know she was in so much trouble. Really. I would have helped her if I had. I was gone a lot, and left her alone a lot. She'd had several miscarriages, and maybe that was a factor—I don't know. Then she got a job—or said she got a job— with a travel magazine in Seattle and seemed busier, happier, and had to stay over in Seattle now and then. But I know now that wasn't true—the job part. I blame myself. And I'm sorry, too, about Billie Sutherland, that Amy drug her into all this. I hope she'll recover.

Billie read the story over and over, two columns, half a page long. A face shot of Jimmy. "Months Later, Pilot Still Mourns Wife's Strange Suicide."

"What kind of news story could hold your attention like that, Billie?" Maddie asked, coming up behind her with her broom in hand. Billie handed her the clipping, and Maddie leaned her broom against the wall and sat down at one of the dining room tables. Her eyes scanned over the words. "I never thought you came here for the scenery, Billie," Maddie said quietly, handing the clipping back to her. "Don't hang on to it real hard, whatever the rest of that story is."

Billie took the clipping back to her room, folded it neatly, and taped it into the back of the book the Finn had given her. Then she picked up a pen and opened the book to those first fresh empty pages. *Dear Amy*, she wrote.

I knew you as Amelia, and I met you during the last year of your life. We drank a lot of wine together, laughed a lot, ate together sometimes, and went to the movies once.

I had no idea who you were. I should have cared. I should have cared about Jimmy Johnson's wife, should have wondered about her, should have . . .

I'm sorry, I'm sorry, I'm sorry.

She didn't know what to write beyond that. But she had hope that she would find the words.

Anna Harker

MY LIFE IS BURSTING through the seams. Reality, apparently, is loosely stitched, and one moment I am here, dying on the tundra, the blood pulsing out of me in waves with every beat of my failing heart, and the next I am in the garden with my mother, digging potatoes all of a fall evening.

Can't we play seeks? I say. The tiny shovel I wield is cold in my hands. I look toward the river and see the autumn sunset, salmon-raspberry pink, and I want to go hide behind the giant cottonwood trees that the river washed up last spring when it was high.

The river smells bad, my mother says. *All those dead fish on the shore, remember? You might step on one if we go down there now.*

George will come with me, I say. *Can't I?* I could picture George running deftly across the cold silt, magically avoiding the smelling carcasses of the rotting salmon, their lives on a timer, river to ocean to river again, be born, live awhile, swim unimaginable distances, spawn, then die.

George should be a good boy and be home in bed.

But I'm not home in bed. Am I bad?

My mother's foot on the shovel, her skirt hitched above the knee. I see her thick dark stockings above her tall leather boots. *You're home in your garden,* she says, *with your mother, harvesting the potatoes before the ground freezes.*

Should I be in bed?

Yes, probably.

Then why ain't I?

Then why aren't I, she says. *You're not, because your mother is bad.*

You're a bad mommy?

I'm bad for not getting you in bed sooner. I'm bad because I forgot to do all of my chores today. She laughs, the sound like crystals falling through the sky.

So am I bad, or you?

She stops smiling. *We're not bad, Anna. We're disorganized.*

Is that bad?

No, heavens no.

Then the back door of the roadhouse opens, and Uncle Mike comes out. *What's going on out here?* he bellows.

Oh no! says my mother. *It's the boss-man! We're done for.*

Oh no! I say and start to run, but Uncle Mike catches me and lifts me toward the beautiful pink and indigo sky.

I gotcha now! he says. And I laugh and squeal and laugh and squeal. The evening air is cold and rich and filled with the smell of dirt and dead leaves and cranberries. The river is a baritone, low and steady, and above it my mother's tinkling laugh and Uncle Mike's fierce fake commands and my happy squeaks dance and dance and continue on and on until they find me here, in this now. Until they find me, back in the garden again, with George kicking the dirt with his new shoes while he says, *So, you want to go fishing tomorrow?* And there I am again, sneaking in the back door after sleeping in the river sand with Wade Daniels the night of my birthday, hungover and damp and cold and ashamed, yet more awake than I had ever felt, and here I am now, in the garden, and my mother is coming out the back door. She is getting older, getting old. How had I not noticed? She lifts her small, pointed shovel from where it leans against the wall, walks out to the garden, and begins to dig. The potatoes, I see, have come in good this year, but when did they ever come in bad beneath the rich river soil and the tender care of my mother's touch? She digs and pulls, shakes the dirt loose, lays them in a pile. The day is starting to fade, and I look with her toward the river for that first kiss of twilight on the edge of the sky. The day like a goodbye, fading and passing. I expect her to start digging again but she drops the shovel and starts walking. She walks out of the garden and skirts along the side of the roadhouse, finds the street. She moves fast, then faster, a jog, then a run.

Mama, I want to say, *I'm here—wait!* But if I say it or don't, she keeps moving. She goes down to the river, where the remains of the spawned-out salmon lay like booby traps among the gray river silt and the clumps of washed-out driftwood. She stops at the water, bends, and puts her hand down into it, her brow furrowed. Does she know? Can she know? Can she feel me when I am oh so many miles away? She rises and looks toward the mountains, at the smaller hills that loom beneath. All at once I can see her life: the young sparkling dark-eyed girl who loved the farmer's son. My father. She never told me but I know this now, somehow. The friend she talked about, Johnny Ferris, with the bouncing curling hair and with whom she ran through the fields unafraid of garter snakes or anything else hidden in the golden blades. Then a night under a bright full moon, wrapped in a blanket and hidden away in those same fields, their bodies young and untouched but touching now in a world that seemed endless and in front of them with promises spilling easily from both their lips. He would go to the city and get them started, get them a life away from farms and fields and endless work, and so he does, after the harvest comes and goes, and Madeline is left in an empty field.

Oh, Mama, a girl alone, save the brother who brought her north and the little girl who hands her the pieces of potatoes with the eyes in the spring, which they place in the soil and dig up again in the fall, the little piece becoming many, whole once more.

She looks toward the mountains. The wind blows through. She tugs her wool shirt tight around and pulls inward against the cold.

Wade Daniels

HE WALKED BACK OUT into the streets of the small but ever-growing city, bathed now in the soft light of a spring night, the rain turning into sparse, scattered soggy flakes, as if the heavens were tired of it all and shook the remainder of winter from the clouds. Wade watched the flakes hit the sidewalk and disappear. He took a deep breath and could almost taste the nearby ocean in the air. He loved everything Alaska, including this city. He grieved for it, as if it were already gone from him, cut down in the hills like his very soul. He would be leaving soon, perhaps never to return, Alaska taken from him by murder and war.

Up ahead the lights of Fourth Avenue, Anchorage's main street, glowed faintly in the lingering daylight. In the distance he could see the Chugach Mountains, softer and gentler than the massive range farther north. He walked over to the Cheechako Tavern, hating to leave the clean, fresh outside behind, and slipped into the darker shades of shadows beyond the door.

There were several men at the bar sitting in a swirl of smoke. A couple sat at a table, looking rough and weary, as if the newly deceased winter had turned them to stone. But he must look similar, he knew; he was, on occasion, startled by his own reflection, as if a stranger had worked his way into his home and took his place in the glass.

Time and again over the passing months Nellie would appear, place her soft hand on his cheek, and say, "So what's happened to you, eh?"

He sat at the far end of the bar and ordered a glass of beer. He would have preferred a whiskey, but he hadn't eaten since breakfast, and a beer would help fill the emptiness in his stomach. He watched the window by the door, the occasional figure walking past, and the gradual descent of a dusky dark. He drank slowly, but the glass was soon empty. He was about to order another when the door swung open and a thin, wiry man with big round eyes and a tangle of corkscrew-like hair came in and sat in the unoccupied stretch between Wade and the smoking men.

"Mike Mullins," Wade said, and when the man turned to him Wade could tell he was about to say "No," but stopped himself and said instead, "Hey—you're Jake Timmers's cousin, aren't you?" He scooted himself along the barstools until he was beside Wade.

"Wade Daniels," Wade said.

"Yeah—I remember. You were in here with Jake at Fur Rondy last year."

Wade nodded. It seemed a long time ago.

"Tough times for you people up north," Mullins said. "Those murders—talk of the town around here all winter long."

Wade winced inside but tried to hold steady. The bartender placed a frothy beer and a short glass of whiskey in front of Mullins, and Wade indicated he would like the same.

He felt he knew what was coming. There was an edge to Mullins, some vibration in the way his eyes kept darting around.

"Were you friends with those folks?" Mullins asked.

"Yeah."

"And you're the one that found the wife. It was in the papers."

"Yes."

"Hmm."

Wade looked at him. "I wouldn't hurt those people."

"It's just strange, that's all. I didn't really put it together until now."

"And what's that?"

"You and your cousin. You know before he started mining in the Harrisville area, he was up in Lawry when a miner disappeared."

"I know."

"Martin Bell—Marty. He was a nice fellow. Walked out of there and never showed up anywhere. But Jake was questioned—well, along with most of the other fellas up there. It never came to anything. But it's a little strange. He was investigated, now you're being investigated, or if you're not, you likely will be. It's right to say that, isn't it? Though if you killed her, why would you go back out there and find her? But you and your cousin have a way of being in the wrong place at the wrong time—or something."

Or something. "What do you think happened to Martin Bell?"

Mullins shrugged. "He's not the first person to walk off into the wilderness and disappear, and he won't be the last. We might have paved streets and automobiles here in Anchorage, but this state is big and it's wild. It'll eat you up if you don't watch it." He lifted his whiskey in a toast, then downed most of what was in the glass. "He was a nice fellow, Marty Bell. No offense, but he was a cut above your cousin. Educated, quiet, polite, and all that. Maybe if he hadn't met your cousin he never would have gone up to Lawry, and he'd still be alive today. If he's dead now, that is, which is likely the case."

Wade's mind churned. What had Jake said, about Bell, exactly? Or hadn't said. Wade had never thought that Jake and the missing miner went up to Lawry together. They would have passed through Susitna Station as they rode the train north. Would that have been Jake's first glimpse of the village where Anna was living her life, not knowing that fate rode through on the rails?

"I think they met here, in this very bar. Bell was looking for summer work, and Jake had just gotten on with that big company working up at Lawry."

Wade downed his whiskey and felt the warmth of it slide through him. He didn't know, he reminded himself. He kept thinking of Jake, at his table at Christmas, the moose blood dripping from his mouth. But he could be wrong. God, he hoped he was wrong. The opposing thoughts continued to ping-pong through Wade's mind as he and Mullins passed the time drinking and talking, and Wade let his new friend solve the murders in the Harris Hills for him: "Not that Montana fellow, too obvious. But one of the other miners there, sick to death of Harker's success and young snottiness, that's what I think. Couldn't even take the sight of him anymore." The analysis comforted Wade somewhat. It made it all seem so crazy, so unreal, as they sat there in a bar in Anchorage talking about it as if it were something someone made up in a book. Wade could almost feel what it might be like to have a life again. But as they stumbled into the street in the after-midnight hours and parted ways, Mullins, walking backward down the sidewalk as he continued to chat, said, "Your cousin, though, he's one strange one. You wouldn't catch me out there in the woods with him!" And he laughed and smiled and went on his way, leaving Wade to crash back into reality and its heavy hold on his heart.

Billie Sutherland

"SO THE HARKER MINE was eventually bought by someone named John Cobb."

"Where'd you hear that?" Uncle Howard said.

"Your story." Billie set the old newspaper onto her uncle's desk. "This one wasn't in your folder." Somehow the last long months of winter had passed, and now spring was on the horizon. Another holiday, another journey to Anchorage.

Howard leaned across his desk and studied the headline. "I remember. That was years after the murders, though, wasn't it?"

"Yes." It was a small story, buried on the third page. "Was John Cobb ever a suspect?"

"Yes and no," Howard said. "He was a bully of a businessman who didn't like Henry. He was already back in Washington when the murders happened, and all his minions were similarly accounted for."

"Maybe he hired some unknown assailant."

"It could have happened," Howard said. "Gold does strange things to people."

And love, Billie thought. Her mind went to Nellie and the secret she'd told her. Like Nellie, Billie had become a shadowed person, a person with secrets. Of all the people in her life, Uncle Howard and Aunt Sam were the two who now knew the most about her, and with them she had held back as much as she could. Jimmy Johnson knew her, yes—but she obviously didn't know him. While Billie had opened up a little to Maddie, there was so much she *wasn't* telling her, including her friendship with Montana and what Nellie told her about Anna. It all left Billie feeling lonely and disconnected.

"Maybe we can talk more about that later," Howard said. "Don't forget to put that back in the archives."

"Yes, sir." Billie stood and walked out of the office. She took a few steps and turned, looked back at Uncle Howard, and she could tell by the look on his face that he was hearing the same thing she was: a noise like a freight train, or like the bottom of a jet airliner passing right above your head. Then everything was moving everywhere, as if the newspaper office were a sailing ship smashing upon rocks.

Billie grabbed onto the doorframe as the newsroom turned into chaos. Howard tried to shout above the sounds of things crashing and people screaming. "Under your desks! Under your desks! Billie, get under something. Now!"

Billie stumbled into her uncle's office and dove with him under his large old oak desk.

"Damn! You like history, Billie, we're living it now!" he yelled.

The building creaked and moaned, and there was the sound of shattering glass. Pictures flew off the walls. It felt like a wild bull had lifted the land upon its back and was trying to shake it off. Four and a half long minutes later it began to subside and finally stopped. Billie and Howard looked at each other. "Stay here," he told his niece as he pulled himself out from under the desk. "Everyone okay?" he yelled, and as the affirmative answers came from the newsroom, Billie left the cover of the desk and went to the window that overlooked the street.

Her hand went to her mouth. The city—her city, the city she had grown up with—was in ruins. Buildings were sideways to each other and a section of the street had sunk down into the earth, cars and all. People moved slowly, as if in a dream, amid the broken glass and fallen signs and all the things that were strewn about where they were not supposed to be.

"Can we go out there?" she asked.

"I don't know," Howard said. "But I'm going to gather a news team and give it a try."

"We need to see if we can help."

"I need you to stay put and stay safe."

"Not a chance," she said. "Do you have a first-aid kit here? Go on and give it to me, and I'll go with your team."

"All right," he said, shaking his head. "After my own heart, always. Come on—let's head out and see how things are."

As they walked through the snowy, shattered streets, Billie couldn't help but think of a broken toy, as if the city were a model smashed by an angry child. Amid the visual chaos there was a strange quiet in this new, electric-free world. She walked with her uncle, a young photographer, and an equally young reporter, both of whom were white with shock. "Mom and Aunt Sam," Billie said as she walked beside her uncle.

"Phone lines are down and my car, well, it's in that new made ditch," Howard said, looking at the collapsed street. "But we'll get out that way soon. Or we'll find someone to drive you."

"All right." Her father would be at the airfield, she knew; she couldn't imagine the damage there. To keep focused, though, and for now, she searched the streets for people who needed help. She'd had basic first-aid training, years ago when she'd dreamed of becoming a nurse, and it stuck with her. They came upon a woman whose leg had been cut when she fell on some broken glass; Billie bandaged her wound, then helped a young man with a gash on the side of his face. When they rounded a corner to where the big department store stood, its walls looking as if damaged by war, Billie knew whatever injuries happened in there would be over her head. She felt her uncle's hand on her shoulder and heard the steady clicking of the photographer's camera. The reporter had walked forward and stood talking to several men. After a few minutes he came back and said to Billie's uncle, "Sounds like your neighborhood's been hard hit. Some houses have slid into the bay." Before Howard could reply the reporter fished his keys out of his pocket. "Take my car. We'll hold the fort until you get back," then Billie and her uncle went running toward the newsroom.

The short drive seemed to take ages. There were gaping cracks in the roads when they least expected them, and as they neared their neighborhood they began to fear the worst of everything. It was true; houses had slid down to the sea, as if the neighborhood were a cake and God took a slice, leaving what was left to tumble and slide. But their houses were still there—Billie's parents', and the one down the street that belonged to Howard and Sam. They were both somewhat crooked, but both still there. As they pulled closer to the former, Billie's mother and Aunt Sam ran out to greet them. Billie emerged from the passenger side, dazed at the scene not far from where she stood, where whole houses had vanished from view.

The following hours were sharp and defined yet slow moving, as if all time was submerged in a pool of thick, liquid glass. Howard returned to the paper, and Billie and her mother combed the neighborhood in search of anyone who might need help. Sam had grabbed a camera from the arctic entry of her home, traded her shoes for a pair of rubber boots, and set off toward where the street had collapsed and the houses had slid into the inlet.

"Don't go too far, Sam," Billie's mother, Clara, warned. "There might be a tidal wave!" Sam nodded, cheeks flushed, and ran down the street, her sweater sliding off her shoulders and her hair hanging loose from her careless bun.

"Your father had better be all right," her mother said as they watched Sam run. "I will never, ever forgive him if he's not." They guessed Billie's brother was safe at his girlfriend's house in midtown; word had filtered down that the area was not badly hit. But they had not heard a word from Billie's father, and knew only that the airfield had been destroyed.

Billie's breath stuck in her throat for a moment. There was something in her mother's grim face and strained tone that cracked open something Billie had long failed to see: love. Love for her father. "He'll be okay, Mom," she said.

Her mother nodded and put an arm around her shoulders. "Yes. He wouldn't dare leave us in this mess. Now come on, Birdie, let's check on the Thompsons." She clucked her tongue and shook her head. "Birdie, for once I wish you were still up north."

"We don't know what's happened there," Billie said.

"No, I suppose we don't. I suppose we don't know what's happened to the rest of Alaska, either."

Over the next few days they would learn, as news trickled in and messages were exchanged over shortwave radios, that while Anchorage was spared the fury of the ocean, tsunamis hit seaside towns across Alaska and slammed shores in Oregon and California. In Alaska 115 were killed, and 16 in those other states. The quake would measure a magnitude 9.2.

But on that first day, as they waited for news, Billie and Clara took a sled load of wood up to the home of an elderly couple, the Thompsons, and helped them get a fire going in the stove and put some kerosene in the old oil lamps for when it got dark. As the light began to slip away Sam returned, muddy and cold, and went straight to what was left of Hal and Clara's liquor supply while Billie and Clara swept broken glass and started a fire in the fireplace, Clara continually looking out a broken window and up the darkening street.

"He'll show up," Sam said. "Now Howard, we're likely not to see him again for the next month or two!"

"I should go help him," Billie said.

"You stay here," Clara said. "God knows what's going on downtown." The words had barely left her lips when they heard a rumble and felt a shake that was soon passing.

"Aftershock," Billie said.

"Like it really makes a difference what you call it," Sam noted.

Billie went to the window and looked outside, trying to see in the last of the light. There was a figure in the street, featureless but familiar. "Mom," Billie said. "Dad's coming." She watched as her mother dropped a broom and ran out the door and became a moving shape in the dark that found and merged with the other there on the street, making one dark shape as they stood for a long while, as still as the street beneath them, all blending together into the night.

Several days later Billie found herself downtown again, joining the cleanup efforts. As she looked down the mangled street near the newspaper office, she couldn't imagine it ever being put right again, just as she couldn't imagine that where she stood at the moment was where she had stood countless times during her life, growing up in this northern city, watching the dog teams whiz past during one Fur Rondy race after another. Or where she volunteered, when she was seventeen, to be thrown about in a blanket toss at the mercy of a circle of young Native men, far from their villages and in town for that same annual celebration. She'd yelled with delight as she went up into the air and back down again, over and over in her fur-trimmed parka and mukluks. Afterward she kissed each and every young man on the cheek, leaving her red lipstick on their smooth olive skin.

"Oh, Billie," her mother had said, and Aunt Sam had clapped with her big mittens on and quickly volunteered to take Billie's place on the blanket. Now Billie wondered how the street would ever be the same.

She picked up some shards of lumber from a shattered building and carried them over to a growing pile. She looked around for Sam, who had been working with her, but then saw a familiar figure walking toward her down the wounded street. She was seeing things, she thought, but no—the man approaching her was real and unmistakably the Finn, and he walked straight up to her, dropped his bag, and put his arms around her.

"It's a lot easier to find someone in a village than in a city," he said, his mouth near her ear as he pressed her to him and stroked her hair.

"Why are you here?" she managed to say.

"I had to see if you were okay," he said. "And because I've been missing you for months."

She could feel him looking around the street in front of him. "Jesus Christ," he said. Billie nodded but kept herself there, pressed against him, where she could hear the steady rhythm inside his chest.

SEPTEMBER 29, 1941
Anna Harker

I DON'T KNOW WHERE I AM RIGHT NOW, but it is very
bright, like springtime when the sun hits the snow and yes,
that is where I am now, somehow, struggling to see against
the glare of the sun on the snow and smelling the fresh cool
clean of it. I close my eyes against it, and for a moment I
smell the tundra and the bitter scent of blood, but I will
myself back to where I had been and find myself again in a
spring day by the frozen river, somewhere it is impossible
for me to be.

Or is it? Hope fills my heart. Has the horror of the day
been nothing but a dream, and am I now awake? I look, squint-
ing against the brightness, and see that I am not alone. Wade
is here, kneeling in the snow mere yards from where I stand,
his fist against his mouth and his brow furrowed in thought.
I try to speak but I make no sound. He looks toward me, and
I try again, but then I see that he looks past me, as if I am not
even here, and I look behind me and I see Nellie, in a flowered kuspuk and her old leather mukluks, coming toward us.
She passes so close to me I can see the gentle rose color in her
cheeks and the beating of the thick dark lashes on her blinking
eyes, smell the apple smell of her breath.

Nellie!

But she doesn't hear me. I cry out again as she walks
farther from me, and slowly I realize that I am somewhere
where I no longer belong. I am, somehow, in the world that
has gone on without me.

She walks up to my darling, my Wade, her mukluks leaving slushy tracks in the warming snow, and she sits down on her knees beside him. I am now in front of them, facing them, and see the expression of sorrow and love across Nellie's face. I want to say, *Nellie, I didn't realize*, but I did. I knew. The very first time I saw them in the same space together, that forever ago New Year's Eve, her face spoke the words her mouth could not.

"You don't have to go, eh?" she says now. "There are other people who can do that, you know. Fight that war. You can stay here."

"No," he says. "I can't stay, Nell."

I feel a sting in my heart at the way he says her name, Nell. I can feel the familiarity of it on his tongue, and in his tone I can hear what his words fail to express: remorse, regret. I feel a strange, selfish fear sweep over me, but then he looks at me without seeing me, and I can feel his heart, and we are lying on a blanket beside the lake, my head against his chest. Then Wade looks down at the snow in front of him and Nellie stares across the frozen river at the distant trees. The wind blows her hair across one side of her soft round face and she pushes it away with a mittened hand.

"I don't think you are right," she says. "You can stay."

"Nellie—"

"This river, it always runs." She speaks quickly, and I think it is to keep him from saying something that she does not want to hear. "Things happen to it. Trees block it. Water floods it. It goes one way, then goes another and cuts a new channel. It never stays the same, but it's always there." She turns to him and my soul weeps at the sadness in her eyes. "You don't have to go. The fish will still jump for you. And someday, it will make you happy again."

"What's this river got to do with a war thousands of miles away?"

"What's the war got to do with you going?"

"It's what I'm going to, isn't it?"

"It's not what you're going to. It's what you're leaving." She looks back to the river.

Wade shakes his head. "What I'm leaving is already gone."

"Not all of it." She looks at him again now, eyes round and wet. "Not all of it, eh?"

"Oh, Nellie," he says, and she doesn't wait, she pulls herself up out of the snow and goes back the way she came, tears streaking across her soft, round cheeks. He watches her, picks up a chunk of ice from the snow, and makes to throw it at the river in front of him but instead lets it drop from his hand. He hangs his head, eyes closed, and I see how he shakes.

"Six months," he says aloud. "Six months, Anna."

I start at the sound of my name. Am I here? Does he know I am?

"Six months is too goddamned long to be here. Too long! I can't take another day, I'm done. I'm done. But I will find you first. I promise you, I will find you first." Now he tips his face up to the blue blue sky. "Nellie, I'm sorry. It's over for me. And I never should have let you be my girl. I never should have, because I was always hers, and I will find her and then I'm gone, I'm gone."

If I had breath, I would be holding it, and I still cannot determine what is the dream and what is not. But I know this: we hurt more than just ourselves, he and I, as if behind us we left a trail covered in thorns and flanked by wolves. I reach for him, where he sits, in this day, in a world from which I have vanished. I reach for him but feel myself being pulled away, pulled back to the tundra and the chill air of the dying day, where I lay alone in my broken body, wondering where it is I had just gone, wondering where it is I am soon to go.

APRIL 1942
Wade Daniels

HE AWOKE TO SOFT GRAY-YELLOW LIGHT sifting in
through the blinds of his room. His head hurt; he had drunk
too much, and that drunken state had taken him home in his
dreams. Home to his mother and the farm, to his unhappy
father who worked in an office in the nearest town, selling
insurance, while Wade and his mother did all they could to
feed the animals and milk the cows and gather the eggs and
plant the crops so his father wouldn't lose the dream that he'd
had: to run a farm like his father had, and his father before him.
It was a lot of work, but Wade didn't mind. He liked being
outside, he liked the animals, he liked watching the forest
beyond the fields where the wind blew through the trees and
the sun kissed on its slide down into the horizon. Any girl he
dated was sure to end up helping him haul a bucket of slop or
two—he didn't date often. To the town girls he wasn't slick
enough and to the farm girls he was more of the same.

Then his father died, on a winter day, the light leaving
the sky, as he was returning to his office from a late lunch with
a client. He dropped dead on the sidewalk, just like that, and
the phone in their neighbor's house rang, and their neighbor,
Mr. Jones, had the sad duty of driving over to inform Wade
and his mother of what had occurred, Mrs. Jones beside him
to help with the shock. It took Wade a long time to feel like
he could leave his mother. "Wade," she finally said, "there's a
world out there waiting for you. Get off of this farm for God's
sake—go live." And so he did. Until last fall.

He stared at the plain white walls of the room. He would go home for a visit soon, as soon as he felt he could leave this behind. Then join up and hand his life over to the war. He hoped he'd make it home one more time after basic training, before being shipped overseas, because that's where he would go. That's where they were all going, all the young men. He told himself he would be going anyway, would be stepping forward to do what had to be done, even if a madman with an ax hadn't taken the world from him.

He breathed, got up, got dressed, and went back out into the streets of Anchorage.

The day was warm and slushy, the snow from last night mixing with water on the sidewalks and the street. He ate a quick breakfast at a small diner then tried to decide what to do next. He needed more information on Martin Bell's disappearance. He could go to the police; maybe he should go to the police. But he felt that would somehow betray Fairfield, who fretted about the murders day in and day out, frustrated and disappointed in his own inability to catch the killer in their community. He thought of the newspaper here and wondered if that event was covered with as much fervor as the murders of the Harkers and Nate Peterson. He set off in the right direction, and let the fresh air fill his lungs and clear his mind.

When he reached the *Anchorage Telegraph* he hesitated before opening the door. Maybe he should leave it all alone. He shouldn't be thinking these thoughts about his own cousin. The thought, or the breakfast, or all he drank last night sent a wave of nausea through him. It was one of those things, he knew. Once you think it you can't unthink it, and it eats you alive until you get to the bottom of it. It wasn't going to go away. There was nothing he could do about that. So he pushed open the door and found himself in a world buzzing with activity: phones ringing, the clacking of multiple typewriters, people working at desks or, with stacks of papers in their hands, walking from one to the other. He stood there a moment, then it seemed everyone saw him at once, and a dozen sets of eyes zeroed in on him. Then a woman in a dark wool dress, glasses, and hair twisted up on the back of her head walked over to where he stood.

"Can I help you?" she asked. "Are you here to see someone?"

"I was wondering—" He wasn't sure for a moment how to say what he wanted, and he felt his mouth go dry as a strange panic swept through him. "I was wondering if you had any back issues from eight years ago. Like August and September, something like that."

"Oh," she said briskly. "You want to go to the morgue."

"No," he said before he realized what she meant. "I mean yes."

"Gotcha. Let me find someone to take you down there. Dave?" she called, and a young man at one of the desks looked up. But then another man, older, wearing a white shirt and a loose tie, stopped on his journey across the room, looked at Wade, and said, "I've got it, Mary."

"Are you sure, Mr. Wells?" the woman asked.

The man nodded, pointed at Wade, and said, "Be right with you." He then walked over to a desk where another young man sat, handed him the pile of papers, said something, then walked back over to Wade.

"Howard Wells," he said, holding out his hand, and Wade realized why his mouth was dry. He was in the papers—this paper—after he found Anna.

"Artie," he said. "Artie Melville." It was his grandfather's name.

"Nice to meet you." The two men shook hands. "Now just follow me."

They went to the back of the main room and through a door where a set of narrow stairs led down to a basement, lit by several bare bulbs scattered across the ceiling. It was cold and musty with deep shelves along the walls covered with stacks of old papers.

"We use the honor system here," Wells said. "Don't take anything, and put everything back where you got it. And sign the guest book on the table before you leave."

Wade nodded and thanked the man, who then left him alone in the stark uncomfortable room. The papers were arranged by years, with the oldest ones on the highest shelves, and with each stack containing a month's worth. He would start with August, eight years ago.

Billie Sutherland

THE FINN'S VISIT WAS SHORT, as he had volunteered to fly loads of supplies to hard hit areas around the state, and several days later Billie found herself back at the newspaper morgue. She had offered to put it back together while she remained stuck in Anchorage waiting for either the Finn or her father to have the time to fly her back to Susitna Station. Large sections of the rail line had been destroyed in the quake, but otherwise the village had survived intact.

On their brief afternoon together, the Finn had taken her to the cemetery to show her where Anna and Henry Harker were buried. "So why are they buried here?" Billie had asked. He had taken her down a line of graves until they came to two at the end of a row and near a birch tree whose bare branches swayed over them.

"We didn't have a cemetery yet," he said, squatting down and brushing the dirt away from the old green-gray tombstones that sat crookedly in the weary remains of the snow. "That didn't happen until '51 I think, or somewhere in there. Until then everyone came down here, except the Natives. They had their own burial spots."

As Billie looked at the graves, she'd thought of Amelia Johnson, buried somewhere in some cemetery Billie would likely never see. She would have to tell the Finn, she realized, about that grievous error she'd made but couldn't and didn't do it on that particular day. The thought of confessing was an additional shadow now on her shoulder as she looked around the ruined morgue. This was where she had been minutes before the quake hit. The shelves were put back upright for her, but everything that had been on them was strewn in a deep layer across the floor. Billie tied a kerchief around her hair and got to work.

Here it was, the life of her city and much of the state spread out in black and white across the concrete. She kept her eyes on the dates and page numbers, focusing first on putting together the issues that had separated, then sorting by years. "WE'RE IN!" was a headline that leapt off the page from a mere five years ago, statehood at last for the territory, whose former status already seemed well into the past. Billie liked being able to say she was here when, but she was learning that, in a place like Susitna Station, real residency requires more years than she has lived. It didn't matter that she was a lifelong Alaskan, born here, a rarity among the non-Native population of the state. What matters was how many winters you'd survived, how many trails you walked down.

As she finished a preliminary organization of one area of the morgue and shifted her attention to the next, a row of books that lay like fallen dominoes beneath some papers caught her eye. She lifted one of the logbooks, or "guest" books for the morgue and flipped through the entries—not many; in fact, the book was half empty. She picked up another and found it to be full; the third was completely empty. She thought about her recent visits to the morgue and how she never noticed the guest books, which might explain the lack of entries. Or it could be that old news is old news, and those who seek the specified past are few and far between. She took a pen from her shirt pocket and reopened the half-full book. There, at number

59 (lucky, she thought, 59 being the year of statehood), she scrawled her oversized, looping signature: Billie Sutherland. She flipped backward through the pages to see if she recognized any old Anchorage names on the lines or perhaps that of a former classmate on a research outing. And indeed she saw more than a few names she recognized, and an awful lot she didn't. After finishing the half-full book, she picked up the full one to take a quick look, starting in the back again, and here she saw fewer and fewer familiar names, names from deeper in the past. She was about to close the cover when she saw, in the middle of a page, a name she did recognize and her lips parted and her heart gave a jolt: Wade Daniels.

"Oh," she said out loud and ran the tip of her long thin finger over the signature, which was strong but not showy, a man who knew who he was, she thought, without knowing why. She looked toward the stairs and thought she should run up immediately to tell Uncle Howard, but another part of her wanted to hoard the information, to give herself a chance to see what she thought about it without the interference of others.

"What were you looking for?" she whispered to the signature of a man long dead. Perhaps it was the obvious: stories about the murders. But maybe it was something else, something less obvious. If it were true he loved Anna Harker, then wouldn't he want to find out who killed her? Wouldn't that be the one single thing burning away in his heart and in his mind? She looked around at the heaps of papers yet to be organized. *Pretend, Billie; pretend,* she thought. Pretend someone you love has been brutally murdered, and no one seems to know why or by whom. Why would you come to a newspaper morgue? You would come, she realized, to see if the event that ruined your life had ever happened before, or to get information on a particular individual that had caught your attention in the matter.

It took her two days of sorting and organizing and scanning. At first, when she saw the "Missing Miner" headlines she did nothing but simply set the papers aside and continued on. But after reading a few sordid but unrelated stories about love gone wrong with violent endings in various territory towns, she returned to the pile where she put the papers that had run stories about a young man from California, "highly educated," who, along with a man he met in an Anchorage bar, set off to the interior of Alaska to work in the gold-bearing hills. The name of the man he went with caught her attention. Suddenly she saw herself back at Nellie's cabin, listening to Nellie's story of love, war, and loss, and the mention of Wade Daniels's cousin, Jake Timmers.

Billie took several deep breaths. It could mean nothing; it could mean something. There was a picture of Timmers and Martin Bell, standing beside a motorcycle on an Anchorage street. She read the stories over carefully, paying close attention to the quotes of Jake Timmers. It truly could be what it seems, she thought, but something kept scratching at the back of her mind. How many people are out there, she wondered, who were on hand at two different places where people died or disappeared under mysterious circumstances? Because even though no one says the disappearance of Martin Bell was suspicious, to Billie it was obviously so: anyone at the Lawry mining operation could have done anything to him and no one would have been the wiser. Jake Timmers had been there, just as he had been a miner in the Harris Hills when the murders happened.

Billie looked again at the photograph and read the cutline: *Martin Bell (left) and Jake Timmers stand beside Timmers's motorcycle shortly before venturing to the Lawry Mine.*

Billie stared at the photo. Did Timmers take the motorcycle with him to Susitna Station? Could someone have ridden a motorcycle—that motorcycle—into the Harris Hills? She felt the cold of the morgue like a clammy hand on her back. When they were at the cemetery she'd asked the Finn if Ben Fairfield was buried there too, and to her surprise the Finn told her Fairfield was still alive and living with a niece in Washington State. She could write to him. She would write to him, whenever she retuned to Susitna Station. Billie grabbed the pile of papers and the old guest book, then looked behind her to where the stairs led upward toward daylight and Uncle Howard.

Anna Harker

NELLIE HAD ASKED ME TO MEET HER by the river. Why am I thinking this? Why do I feel like I must—but no, I know why. Because Nellie knows, and I can feel now how much it hurt her. But Nellie does not know that it isn't because of me she doesn't have Wade. It is because of him, because he is fond of her but not in love with her, as kind and gentle and pretty as she is. Yet that is a thing that could change; I feel that too, but it would take an older man, and a wiser man than he is now to learn that sometimes love is a quiet, gentle thing. And who am I to know this? I simply feel, somehow, as if all of life is spread out before me, like the view of this country I was enjoying when the ax struck. A knowing I have never experienced before, all tangled up in the muddle of the life that I had lived. It is like the river, everything—moving and timeless, and we ride it for a while before our journey ends.

The river. That's where Nellie told me, the night before I left for the hills.

"I know what you're doing, eh," she said, and tears filled her eyes. "Isn't Henry enough for you? You always need so much, you always take so much—George, Henry, now him— now Wade. He would have liked me if not for you, you know, things happened between us, eh? Those things, they were love things, loving things. But you won't let him go."

Her words filled me with shame. She was right, so right— what I was doing was so terribly, terribly wrong. I wanted to tell her how I tried to stop, I wanted to tell her about my great fight against it, against the pain and the longing of wanting to be by his side so badly it was like drowning again, the water pressing all around me and my lungs wanting me to breathe, just breathe, which I did, even though I knew the breathing would kill me.

"George loved you, you know, but once Henry came to town he wasn't good enough for you anymore—you walked away from him and left him without his good friend so he found those boys to hang out with, those no good boys and then he died, he died because of those stupid friends he got because he knew you didn't love him anymore. He was a stupid Native, that's all he was to you!"

Was that what happened? Her words burned me with shame. But George left me first—left both of us—to be with those boys. But still—. I will forever wish that I had stopped him that night, that I had said, *Stay, George. Stay with me awhile,* and let him kiss me again, and that I had stood up to my mother and all the others and let it take me where it would. But instead I watched him walk away into the land of shadows.

"I don't have anyone, Anna! Your people brought the flu that killed my parents and left me and George alone except for Aunt Ruby. Then George drank your white people alcohol, and he got killed by your white people train. Then Wade Daniels comes to town, and he takes from me something I can only give once, and I think it's because he loves me, and then I see it's because he loves you and can't stand to think of you with Henry and not with him! You take everything, Anna! You've taken everything from me!"

This last crushed me with the truth of it, and I looked at the river, longing to run into it and drown. "Nellie I am so sorry," was all I could say, and my sweet friend sobbed like the child she once was, the little girl who was always running after me and George, wanting to play. "Nellie—" I reached for her but she rushed away, stumbling across the river silt as she ran and wove among the driftwood that had gathered on the shore. "I'm sorry," I said, and stood alone with the sound of the rivers and the squawking terns and gulls. I sat down on the cold silt and stayed there for a long time, then when I could no longer deny the chill of the evening, I rose and rambled my way along the shore, thinking about Nellie and thinking about George and wishing I could go back and do things over and make everything right. But so much was gone and out of my hands, like fallen trees swept down the river. There was, however, one thing that I could fix, that I could make right, and maybe by doing so I could at least have Nellie back. The summer would offer some separation, as it wasn't often Wade and I both found ourselves at our stream (and listen to me, now as I did then, calling it "our" stream) at the same time. Maybe in the between-times, resolve could build within me, until one day I could simply say, *Enough*. I could hope for that. But that was something we had both tried, many times before, and sometimes months—even half a year, once—would pass. But always we ended up back to where we had been.

Maybe it was Nellie's harsh words, or the thought of releasing Wade Daniels as if I could really do that, as if he were a fish on my line that I would send back to the water, but I felt a chill run through me that had nothing to do with the cooling temperature. I looked around, almost expecting someone to appear, to pop out from behind a piece of driftwood or emerge from a dense cluster of leafy alders that sprouted up from the silt. But all was quiet, save for the cries of the gulls and the deep steady pulse of the river.

I cut across the river shore toward the trees, and after working my way through a patch of alders, I found myself facing a slough that was too deep to cross now in the spring run-off. And there I saw something, so very odd: an old raft that George and I had built, in our childhood long ago, that my stepfather helped us with and that could actually float. Of course we were forbidden to take it out onto the river itself, but this slough—which I realized had previously been dry for years—provided a safe, sheltered place for us to imagine our river adventures. It sat now, unfortunately for me, on the other side of the water, and I saw that it had been reworked to some extent, and that a fresh length of rope tied it to a tree. I couldn't imagine who could have found and resurrected the old thing, and I took it as a sign that my life could be salvaged and fixed, redeemed.

Wade Daniels

HE WAS DREAMING, AND KNEW IT, somehow, even as he was in the thick of it. He and Jake were going to the stream that ran through the family farm in the woods beyond the fields. Well, Jake was going, and Wade was following, running, trying to catch him, trying to keep up.

"Ja-kee! Ja-kee!" he yelled, and his foot caught on a tree root and he fell into the old leaves and pine needles. His knee began to bleed and he began to cry, looking up at the tops of the trees that seemed to be looking down at him angrily, as if he'd done something wrong, as if he shouldn't be there, in the woods. They were so big, and he was so small, and everything else seemed so far away: the farm, the fields, the sun in the sky, and Ja-kee, who he couldn't find.

I've got you. Come on, quit your blubbering, Ja-kee wouldn't leave his little buddy behind. Come on, Wade, the fish are a-waitin'.

And that was where Wade told himself to wake up, to just wake up, because a strange sorrow was swelling in his heart and he knew he would cry, and not only in the dream. He opened his eyes once more to the soft gray-white of the rented room. He wanted to hang on to the dream, to the good part, going fishing with his cousin, but all too soon his mind flooded with everything he had filled it with yesterday, and he wished beyond hope that he could rewrite it, that he could bend the pieces to fit a different puzzle than the one they matched up with now. Ja-kee. Oh, Ja-kee.

The ruined lives of a senseless act. But there his hope lay: this made no sense, except in light of Montana's "empty hole" theory. But is an empty hole that big and that deep, and could it exist for so long right under his nose?

He thought about the newspaper articles he'd read in the newspaper morgue the day before. It took a good while to find anything, his eyes scanning page after black and white page, until finally a headline on the bottom of the front page read "Anchorage Man Missing in Interior."

Friends and family of Martin Bell have expressed concern since the new Anchorage resident failed to turn up after leaving the Lawry gold mine and striking out on his own to leave the wilderness. According to John Owens, supervisor of the Lawry operation, Bell said he would hike out to the railroad and flag down a train to either Anchorage or Fairbanks, whichever came first, then fly home to California where he was to return to his college studies. However, Bell has neither been seen nor heard from again. Jake Timmers, who traveled with Bell to Lawry and who worked with him there, said he and the other men at the mine tried to discourage Bell from setting out on the six-mile hike on his own. "I had concerns right from the start that he wouldn't make it," Timmers said. "He had a lot of education, but that don't do you much good when up against the wilds of Alaska."

Then, several weeks later, another: "Miner Still Missing." But all the stories were the same, smart man makes a not-so-smart choice and heads off into the wild.

What's the matter, tadpole—you think you're smarter than me?

The words leapt into his mind, some long-lost memory. Jake pressing the book Wade was reading hard against his face. Why? Because he'd said, *You never heard of Charles Dickens?*

Dickens smickens, Jake had said. *What, you think you're all English-y now? How about an American writer? How about Jack London?*

And Wade replied, *You never read him, either.*

Then the book was smashed against his face, so hard that Wade would not have been able to breathe except for the crack of the spine. The more Wade struggled, the harder Jake pressed. Then Wade quit struggling and pretended to be dead, like he had read you should do with bears. Jake lifted the book and stared at Wade's frozen face, and long seconds passed before he said Wade's name.

But what does that mean, Wade wondered—Jake didn't like smart people so every now and then he killed a few of them off? Wade pictured Henry Harker and Nate Peterson in the Clearwater together, sitting aloofly at a table with scotch in their glasses, their hair combed, and their clothes clean. But what does that mean, Wade wondered again. Nothing or everything. There were so many missing pieces.

After he left the paper yesterday he went to the Cheechako again and sat and drank. Mullins failed to reappear, and sometime during the night Bert the bartender—broad shouldered and square faced—said, "I never cared for your cousin." Wade couldn't clearly recall how he'd responded, but there was a faint memory somewhere in the jumble of the evening of laughing, and then not.

He washed up, gathered his things, and left the room. Tilly, the proprietress, was in the lounge near the front desk drinking coffee, smoking a cigarette, and filing her nails. She looked coolly up at Wade. "I did know your cousin," she said, "and no, I did not like him."

Wade placed his duffle on the floor, trying to grasp what Tilly said. Then he remembered, faint and fuzzy, how Tilly was sitting in this room when he got in last night. What had he said?

"You asked me last night," Tilly volunteered, her voice warming a little. "I didn't answer you then because I didn't realize who your cousin was. But I know now. Anchorage hasn't totally lost its small-town ways." She smiled at him, then blew the dust off the nail she was filing.

"Why didn't you like him?"

"Sit down," she said, standing up. "Let me get you some coffee first."

Wade obeyed and watched her walk to the front of the counter and return with a cup of coffee.

"I forgot to ask if you took anything in it," she said as she handed it to him.

"This is fine," Wade said. "Thank you."

She sat in a chair across from him. "He's a bit of a looker, your cousin."

"I suppose."

"But I seem to have disappointed him one night, after he followed me back here from the Cheechako. He seemed to have the wrong impression of me." She took a drag from her cigarette, her lipstick leaving a red ring on the filter.

"I'm sorry," Wade said.

"I asked him to leave. There was a moment when he just stood there, like he was thinking about whether or not to walk out the door. Then he looked at me in a way I'll never forget—

it made my blood run cold. I always wondered what he was thinking about doing, what the option was if he didn't leave like I asked. I'd heard he'd gone north, and when I heard about those poor people up there, I thought: *It could've been me.*"

"What?"

"It was just a thought. But I knew about poor Marty Bell, and I saw how Jake looked at me that night. Cousin or no, I'd stay away from him if I were you." She stubbed out her cigarette, rose, and walked over to the counter. "Please don't tell him you stayed here," she said. "And no offense, but please find someplace else yourself next time you come to town."

Wade swallowed hard against her words. Then he thanked her and settled up his bill.

He walked through town for a while, feeling low and carrying his duffle, and he found himself standing in front of a funeral home. Was this where Anna was? He realized likely not, not yet, maybe not for quite awhile. She was somewhere in the city, wherever it was the medical examiner did his dark work, and Wade pictured a room like the newspaper morgue, damp and cold and musty, bare light bulbs hanging from the ceiling.

She's not there, he told himself. *She's in the hills, or by the river, or in the woods somewhere, riding the wind.* He was never sure he believed in an afterlife, but he found now that it was necessary for him to think of Anna as still existing somewhere, somehow. He walked away from the low-roofed, nondescript building that seemed to be making an effort not to stand out too much, not to call attention to its necessity in this world of the living.

Later in the day he made his way over to the airfield where he met up with the Finn, and he experienced a moment of comfort at the sight of the Finn's familiar, earnest face. They loaded his duffle and he climbed in, longing to be flying home to a place that still felt like one. "Have a good trip?" the Finn asked as he pulled his goggles down over his eyes.

"Good enough," Wade replied. As the plane began its taxi down the runway, he realized something he did. In the morgue of the newspaper, in the guest log, the name he'd signed. Wade Daniels. His own.

LATE APRIL 1964
Billie Sutherland

IN THE WOODS the earth still clung to its shrinking shroud
of snow, with some patches of dark, muddy ground spotting
the dirty white. The sun shone through the leafless branches
of the trees, dappling the light and giving a strange brightness and clarity to the landscape, like a window that had been
freshly washed. The air smelled like water. "Breakup," Billie
said as she pulled her sunken snowshoe out from the snow.

"Almost over," the Finn said, walking in front of her.

"Breakup," she said, "is one of those things. It's not over
until it's over. You're forgetting I grew up in Alaska. I know
breakup."

"I don't forget anything about you, Billie." He looked over
his shoulder at her, his thick tawny hair falling across one of his
eyes before he pushed it back behind his ear. They exchanged
a smile, then went back to the business of making their way
across the soggy sinking landscape. The Finn was taking her
to Wade Daniels's cabin. "I've been looking after it for the
family," he'd said. "Wade filed for it under the Homestead Act,
and now it's gone back to the state, and the state is thinking
it wants to sell. I've been thinking maybe I might like to have
it." But they had a different reason for going there today. Jake
Timmers's motorcycle was stored near the back of the cabin,
under a rotting canvas tarp tucked beneath the eaves.

The Finn said, "Almost there," and Billie could see the
shape of something taking form beyond the trees, and soon they

were shuffling up to the lonely quiet of a home long deserted, the sun warm on the gray and fading log walls. Beyond the cabin was the lake, gray and white and dangerous in this in-between state, neither frozen nor thawed. Billie could easily imagine it in the summer sun, the light glinting off the blue water. "This is lovely," she said. "It must be a great swimming hole."

"Oh yeah," the Finn said. "The local kids have always come out here. It's also full of trout."

"Is it big enough to land a float plane on?"

"Maybe for the brave and the not-so-smart," he said. "I prefer a little more room than this allows."

She turned her attention to the cabin.

"Small, but efficient," the Finn noted.

"You could always build onto it if you bought it."

"I could, and I would. Especially if I had a reason to."

Billie smiled, but kept her eyes from meeting his. "So where's that motorcycle?" she asked, and he led to where the old machine, rusted and weary, leaned up against a wall, the tarp nothing more than a ragged cloak barely clinging on. The Finn leaned forward and pulled the useless cloth away. Billie got as close to it as her snowshoes would allow and squatted down to look at the old machine.

"No one knew what to do with it," the Finn said. "Most of his and Wade's belongings were shipped back to their family, but it was a bit impractical to ship this."

Billie touched the rotting seat, which appeared to have been gnawed at by shrews. "What do you think of that idea, that he could have used this to go up to the mines?" she asked.

"You know what I think. If we could get him and that bike across that river and then back over it again, then it's a possibility."

"Someone did it, Atlee."

"Oh, I know." He knelt beside her. "And it's a hard fact that we might never know for sure who that was. Sometimes things are the way they are, and there's not a lot you can do. I felt that way about the war." He sighed and looked up at a spruce tree as a magpie squawked from one of its branches. "Nature makes sense, though, don't you think? Everything has its place, and it all harmonizes somehow, like a long, complicated song. But as far as the murders go, unless someone comes forward with something in regard to Jake Timmers, we're waiting for Martin Bell's story to come out from the underbrush, and the wilderness can keep a secret for a long, long time."

Billie thought of the hills and the wind blowing through them, and the silence that must exist up there three-quarters of the year. Farther north sat the other gold-bearing hills where Martin Bell walked out of camp and never emerged, both hills shrouded in the silence of their secrets.

"Maybe Ben Fairfield can add something," she said. She had sent him a letter a week ago.

"Maybe." He was close enough that she could feel the warmth coming off his body in the cool spring air. His green-checked flannel was rolled to his elbows, and his face was open and easy, his blue eyes sparking with interest and at the same time not pressing her. She was safe with him, and she would never have to say a thing. But the words were climbing up her throat. She stared at the motorcycle and said, "I was in a bit of trouble before I came here."

She felt his eyes on her face. "What sort of trouble?"

"I was in a relationship with a married man. I—wasn't thinking." She took a deep breath, felt it go in, felt it go out.

"His wife found out, and she befriended me. I didn't know who she really was; I didn't have any idea. Then she killed herself. In my bathtub. And I lied about it." Her hands began to shake. "I lied, but I had been lying all along, inside. Lying and cheating. It's my fault she died." She stayed still, waiting, listening for a change in his breathing, for a shift in the beating of his heart.

"You don't need to go that far, Billie," he said quietly. "You can put a whole lot of that elsewhere. Nobody made her do what she did. You were only one part of that equation."

"A big part."

"Maybe, maybe not. But he was the one cheating on her, not you."

"I was part of it."

"Agreed."

She let her eyes meet his for a quick moment. She could feel the relief of things breaking and cracking, even though the cost for that could be high.

"People do things they regret," he said. "Things they wish they could undo. It's part of learning. It's part of life."

"But surely it makes you think less of me."

He put his steady hand on her shaking one. "Not less, just a bit differently. But I've lived long enough to know it takes a while to get to know another human being. So not less, though, Billie. Not less."

She swallowed against the tightness in her throat. "Thank you," she said.

"No thanks needed. Come on. It should be a bit easier going back, seeing as how we broke trail on the way in."

He straightened and held out his hand. She took it in hers, and he helped her stand.

Anna Harker

CAN WE PRETEND—can we please just pretend? Only for a few minutes. Please.

It's easier for you than it is for me, Anna.

I don't think it could possibly be.

You leave me to go back to him. I leave you to think about you being with him.

But you don't have the weight, I said. *You don't have the weight.*

The memory is a jagged flash charging through me, the two of us by our fishing stream, pressed up against the bank where the tall grasses bowed over us.

So you see how we must stop.

I have never disagreed.

If this day ends the way I predict it will, with the life leaving my body and my existence here coming to an end, that would have been the second to last time I saw Wade Daniels. The last time, then, would be the evening before he and Jake Timmers left the mines for the season, when they showed up unexpectedly at our camp. I was outside starting a fire to cook our dinner over; a long hike had yielded some fall ptarmigan, which I killed with my shotgun as they flew up toward the blue sky. The sound of the gun rang out through the hills. As the birds tumbled back to the ground I was overcome with a feeling of grief and regret. I had hunted all my life, always eating what I killed, and understood this to be part of all that was, but that day I felt something had been marred, some perfect beauty had been altered by my loud gun and the quiet death of the birds, whose wings felt wind for the final time. I lifted them from the tundra—three—and tried to cheer myself with thoughts of the fine dinner I would make, cooking them over an open fire.

As I cut across the tundra and toward the trail back to camp, I saw a figure atop a hill that overlooked our camp. I stopped, and several long moments crept by before the figure turned his gaze in my direction and I could feel, across the distance, his registration of the sight of me. In the silhouette I recognized the wide-brimmed hat and the straight, bearded form: Montana. He was impatient for us to leave, I could feel that, and I wondered why. Was he planning on panning in the stream on his old claim in our absence? Or was there something he had left behind there, which he longed for but was afraid to ask us for. And maybe—and this I felt might be truest—he wanted simply to remind us the place was once his and that he had lost it in a way he never felt was fair. But I had known Montana nearly my entire life, and though not the friendliest of persons, beneath his gruff exterior there was, I was sure, a kind and perhaps a wounded soul. Whatever he had felt for my mother would not have turned rancid inside of him. I watched him turn and walk away, disappearing down the side of the hill, and then continued on my way.

Later, I was building my cook fire, with the flames barely biting into wood, when I felt something behind me and turned to see first Jake then Wade. The sight startled and shook me, and my reaction must have been visible as Jake took off his hat and said, "Didn't mean to frighten you, Anna."

"Well, if you were a bear I suppose you would have got me," I said.

"I suppose I would have. Is Henry about?"

"He and Nate are at the creek. You can go down."

"Thank you, ma'am," he said, and he and Wade walked past, Wade meeting my eyes only briefly. Yes, we must stop, I thought as I saw the hint of unhappiness in his eyes. *Enough.* I watched him walk away, following his cousin, then turned back to my struggling fire.

Some time later, when I was burning the last of the feathers off the plucked birds and getting ready to string them across a bed of coals to roast, Henry and Nate came up the trail with Jake and Wade following behind. I did not expect them to return this way and felt my heart leap with a joy I promptly beat back into the ground.

"Anna," Henry said, "I've invited Jake and Wade to join us for supper and share your fine birds." Henry looked at the two men. "My wife is quite the huntress," he said.

"Yes," Jake said. "So it would seem."

At other times extra people at dinner would have sent me into a frazzle, but I had potatoes and some jarred greens sent up with the Finn from my mother's garden, and cooking outdoors over an open fire was something I understood a bit better than laboring over a hot cookstove. We watched the sun go down over the hills as the birds sizzled away and the potatoes baked in a Dutch oven buried in the coals. The men talked of the mining season, Henry and Nate puffing on their pipes, discussing wish lists of equipment. It was all very amiable, and I found I could relax and even enjoy it as the sky began to darken, and I no longer worried my face would betray me. There was a cool nip in the air and as I pulled my wool shirt tight, I felt Wade's eyes and let mine meet his briefly across the fire. But then as I looked to the side of him I saw Jake Timmers looking at me as well, and there was something about the slight smile on his face that filled me with worry. Did he know? But then he told a funny joke, at Montana's expense, and as we laughed in the glow of the firelight the moment passed.

Then the talk turned to the war, that distant shadow creeping across the sky, and Jake turned to Nate and Henry and said, "Don't you feel as if you should go over there and help?" There was a flurry of glances around our little fire circle.

"If the country joins the war effort I will, naturally," Nate said, and Henry concurred. Nate knocked his pipe against the stump he sat on to release the ashes. "Won't you?" he countered, looking at Jake.

"Sure," Jake said. "I'd love to kill a few Germans." And there was something about the way he said it that made me uneasy, almost as if he were thinking about my beloved stepfather and not those other Germans in the war.

"Any one of us could be called up at anytime, given the fact that we all had to register last year," Nate reminded. "So until then, gentlemen, I suggest we mine for gold and enjoy what little time there may be left before we're all sent somewhere we'd rather not be." He relit his pipe, his words falling ominously in my memory now. That night we were fearful of the war. But something else was lurking in the shadows.

Henry said, "So, Jake, will you be filing on any new claims anytime soon?" And the talk went back to mining, but I felt the cold of the night clinging to my back.

Shortly after dinner Wade and Jake took their leave of us, the men shaking hands and saying, "See you back in town." I stood apart somewhat, on the other side of the fire, and they both thanked me for the dinner as they turned to leave, Wade letting his eyes touch mine one last time as he lifted his hand in a small little wave before they disappeared down the trail and into the dark. I sat back down by the faint fire and reached my hands out to the last of the heat as the quiet night deepened around me.

Wade Daniels

THE NARROW DIRT ROAD was wet and slick with mud from recent rain. Wade walked along, passing a few houses with whining dogs straining on the ends of chains until he came to the small shack that Jake rented from one of John Cobb's men who, like his boss, decided to live elsewhere when not mining in the hills. The motorcycle was tipped against a tarpaper-covered wall, and an ax lay wet on the ground beside a chopping block. Wade walked up to this and knelt down, his thoughts going where he did not want them to go as he imagined the ax striking the side of Anna's head.

"Wade?"

He heard Jake's voice but for a moment couldn't move.

"Hey. You okay?"

Wade stood, slowly, and looked at Jake, framed now in the open doorway of the shack. Wade looked at him.

"You okay, cuz? What's the matter? Your number get called, too? I was getting ready to come see you. I don't know what to do."

Wade's brain started working again, and he connected the words and the picture in front of him, Jake in the doorway, in his long johns and drab wool pants, suspenders dangling, and a piece of paper in his hand. For a moment the man was his cousin again, Jake, the brother he never had, the boy he could count on to stick up for him on the playground at school, to talk to him on dark nights in the farmhouse when the wind blew scary outside, and they huddled together under a sleeping bag. And now Jake was the one who looked pale and scared, holding the white piece of ominous paper in his shaking hand. "Damn it to hell," he said, his voice trembling.

Wade stepped forward and took the paper from his cousin. "Greetings:" it read. "Having submitted yourself to a local board for the purpose of determining your availability for training and service in the armed forces of the United States, you are hereby notified that you have now been selected for training and service in the Land or Naval Forces—"

"It came to my mom's because that's the address I put down. Then my mom went to the local draft board and told them where I was." Jake's voice trembled, and Wade realized he was afraid. Again his two sets of feelings for his cousin battled inside of him. He wanted to comfort him. He wanted to kill him.

"You were gonna get called, Jake—sooner or later. We all are." He managed to keep his voice steady and gave his cousin back the order. "They don't give you much time." He had noticed the date. Jake had less than ten days to get back to Vermont. Wade's thoughts spun. He had meant to go straight to Fairfield's office and tell him everything. But what did he know, really? What had felt so solid and real, just hours ago as he flew above the clouds with the Finn, now seemed like vapor in his hand. It was all speculation and suspicion. He turned his head slightly and let his eyes slide back to the ax on the ground. An ax like they all had, sold at Harker's, identical to the one at Jake's mining camp that had been found and checked during the searches last fall. Still, Wade found he could not look away from it, an ax like any other, but it called to him, somehow, and he felt his heart begin to race, and he imagined picking it up out of the wet dirt and burying it squarely into his cousin's head.

"I'm losing my mind," he said out loud and looked back at his cousin, whose eyes flitted between his face and the ax.

"What's going on with you, Wade?"

"Tell me, Jake."

"Tell you what?"

"Tell me you didn't do that to Anna and Henry and Nate Peterson." It was all he could do to say the words, all he could do to hold his cousin's eye.

"I don't know what you're talking about."

Wade held his eyes for a few moments longer, then he had to look away. Wade felt his lips trembling and fought against it.

"Christ, you're a mess, Wade—look at you. You need to get out of here. Come back with me, okay? Let's surprise our moms. Let's go have some family time before I have to go, okay? And maybe I can get out of it, somehow. Maybe my mom had no right to tell them where I was. Or maybe I could just say I'm needed here in the territory—what are they gonna do—send someone all the way up here for me?"

Something surged inside of him, and Wade lunged forward and grabbed Jake by the neck of the shirt, pushing him into the shack and across the narrow span of it, pressing him up against the wall. "I know it was you," Wade said, his voice rough and cracking. "I know it was you but what choice do I have? I can't prove it and if I kill you I'm the one going to jail, not you. Martin Bell. How could it be coincidence that you were in Lawry when that happened, and now you're here!"

"I wasn't in the hills, Wade—remember? People saw me. Fairfield's already cleared me!"

"You rode the motorbike, Jake—I know what you did! You could go up and back in a day if you could get it across the river, and I don't know yet how you did that but you did somehow. Montana heard it. He doesn't realize what he heard, but I know—I know!"

"Wade, stop! If it was me then prove it! I dare you! And then when you can't you'll be sorry you accused me like this!" Jake's eyes were wide and his voice trembled.

"I don't have to prove it to know it, Jake!"

"Listen, little cousin," Jake said through gritted teeth. "You and Mrs. Harker—that wasn't too hard to figure out. You had more reason than me to want them dead. But I didn't tell anyone about that, and I'm not going to because you're my family. You're my *family*, Wade, and I'm yours!"

Wade's insides fell to his feet and he released his hold on his cousin with a final shove against the rough wooden wall. "Pack your stuff and get out of here," he said. "You go report to that board and do your duty because if you don't I will find you, and if I have to I will kill you if the war doesn't get you first. And as long as I know you're still walking this earth I'm going to make sure I'm still walking it too, war or no war, and I will always be there, Jake, one step behind you." Wade stepped backward, then turned and walked out the door. He would go ahead and see Fairfield, for whatever good it would do, then get on with his own business of farewell.

Billie Sutherland

A WEEK AFTER VISITING Wade Daniels's cabin, Billie read
her letter from Ben Fairfield as she walked down the melting,
muddy street.

> *Dear Miss Sutherland,*
> *It was with great interest I received your letter*
> *and read the inquiry within. Needless to say, your*
> *interest came as quite a surprise to this old man, though*
> *nevertheless the event of which you wrote is one never*
> *forgotten. In truth, what happened to those fine young*
> *folks and the fact that I proved helpless in solving that*
> *most heinous crime is something I live with every day of*
> *my own unnecessarily long existence.*
> *Let me address the first concern, regarding a*
> *possible romance between Anna Harker and Wade*
> *Daniels. Daniels was, at the time, overly eager to*
> *participate in the search for Mrs. Harker, which initially*
> *aroused my suspicion only because it's a classic syndrome*
> *affecting the guilty. But in those early days I sensed*
> *nothing from Daniels except earnestness and sincerity,*
> *though I admit I began to wonder if he possessed some*
> *affection for Mrs. Harker that was above the level*
> *expected in a small town (village) where many people*
> *interact as a large extended family. And of course when*

he discovered Mrs. Harker's remains I had to treat
him as an official suspect, but his reasoning rang true
to both the territory and the initial search efforts as
to why the body had not been discovered during our
earlier attempts. It was quite obvious Mrs. Harker's
remains had been in place for the entirety of the winter,
and we concluded at the time that she lay where she
had fallen. Still, I continued to suspect there was some
deep affection for Mrs. Harker motivating Daniels, and
when questioned on that matter he admitted that it was
indeed so. However, further investigation and analysis
convinced me that this inconvenient romance had
nothing whatsoever to do with the murders themselves.
In addition, Daniels, being an avid fisherman and the
fall rivers being good for fishing, was seen by a number
of residents on a near daily basis walking through the
village to the rivers with his fishing pole during the time
the murders would have been committed.

Now on to your second line of questioning,
regarding your discovery of Jake Timmers's connection
to the disappearance of young Martin Bell. I became
aware of this situation by Daniels himself, who was, as
you are aware, the younger cousin of Timmers. Wade—
if I may call him by his first name—came to my office
(which was, incidentally, located next door to the
Clearwater Inn, handy in the case of a ruckus at the bar,
but which was accidentally burnt to the ground in the
course of one such ruckus shortly after my departure)
in a very grim mood some time after his discovery of
Mrs. Harker's remains. He pointed out this factor of his
cousin's past and his concern that perhaps his cousin

played a part in the awful crime. But there was an issue of motive, and while Wade also pointed out that his cousin had recently filed on a claim downstream from the Harkers, which would have been difficult to mine in the wash of the tailings from their operation while that was on-going, it seemed, for lack of better wording, a scant motivation for killing three people. But I brought Timmers in for questioning, and while I found something unexplainably odd about the young man, with no solid proof and no magic ball through which to see, I was helpless to do anything. Timmers at the time was already drafted, and Daniels enlisted shortly thereafter, and they both, sadly, never returned.

It is my opinion, for whatever it's worth, that whoever committed this crime had reasons that go beyond what we can comprehend, perhaps linked to a deep psychological wound or, in contrast, a deep psychological lacking. I tend to think the latter, and that the crimes were committed primarily out of an irritation for those killed and a lack of empathy for their lives. Someone who thinks he is—or was, if the case may be—so very different from the rest of us mere humans, who are all in this boat of living until we die. For this person, making the final decision for his victims is more the motive than any earthly goods; however, if the deaths could have come to some convenience for him, I'm sure he would have taken full advantage. I have had many long years to ponder this and have concluded that Mr. Timmers was indeed the most likely suspect, if for no other reason than a feeling of emptiness that pervaded from his person, but with no solid proof, there was very little I could do. Now, if the remains of our Martin Bell should be found and show evidence of a murder, that would tip the scales for me in this river of uncertainty. However, the question still remains as to how Timmers would have stolen himself back to the mines and returned to the village unseen in a short time frame as he, like Daniels, was seen about the village. Now to your third point. Daniels and I discussed the possibility that Timmers used his motorcycle, but he would have had to get it and himself across the river, and he did not own his own boat and no one ferried him.

I greatly appreciate your interest in this case and in one old man with a few regrets. Please convey my best to the good citizens of your community, or to those who remember me at least, and note that I have never forgotten the fine quality of most of the people there nor the beauty of that magnificent, wild landscape in which the village resides.

With best wishes,
Ben Fairfield

After she finished Billie reread the letter, which was typed save for the shaky scrawl of the old man's signature. The mail sack dangled down her arm and banged against her leg as she walked. When she neared the roadhouse, she put the letter back into the envelope and shoved it deep into the pocket of her canvas coat before opening the door. She hung the bag on a nail and walked swiftly to her room. But here the door was open, and Maddie stood inside, and Billie's heart sank when she saw that the little framed photograph of Montana was in her hands.

Maddie glanced at Billie and said, "He didn't do it," as she looked back at the picture. "I've known that. For years I've known that. I knew him, and I knew he couldn't. But I needed someone to blame." She put the picture back on Billie's dresser and turned to her. "I'm sorry. I wasn't snooping. Millie is going to town and I wanted her to pick up a proper curtain rod for this room. I'm having Nellie make some new curtains." She walked past Billie, then paused and squeezed Billie's hand. "Don't waste as many years hating yourself as I did hating someone who didn't deserve it."

Maddie left the room and Billie felt the letter in her pocket. She could show it to Maddie, and maybe it would give her some relief. Or not. Anna's secret might be a new wound, fresh and sharp upon the old.

SEPTEMBER 29, 1941
Anna Harker

THINK, ANNA, THINK. Who would do this to you?

One would imagine that this would be foremost in my dying thoughts, but I realize I have spent all this time, these precious minutes ticking out like drops of blood, thinking of the life I have lived, not the reason I am leaving it. What good would it do, anyway? Who would I tell? If only I had been able to turn my head and see my murderer walk away with his bloody ax. There—now I feel it, anger intruding into this peaceful eddy I have landed in. Who sneaks up on a woman— on anybody—and hacks on her with an ax? No one I know. And the truth of that phrase rings through me: *No one I know.* No one I really know.

That settled, I can dismiss Montana and his skulking presence in the hills around the camp. Montana I know. Untidy and unruly and often rude, especially when drunk, beneath those frowning brows are eyes that spark with the light from his soul, and hidden there beneath the untrimmed mustache and unkempt beard I know was a smile spread often for me. John Cobb—jealous of Henry, I know, resentful that someone so young could be doing so well. But he should long be back at his other life, far away in warmer climes, and would need a magic wand to travel here and do this. And no—his way of getting to Henry was made quite clear: the courts would be his weapon of choice. And Cobb, too, I know; he is much too refined to have done this, despite the fact he would have liked to see us gone.

Nate Peterson. What do I really know of Nate? Nothing really, only that he is smart and educated and polite, that his mother and father and siblings dote on him and send him packages with goodies that he shares with me and Henry. No. My fear of Nate is fear for him, that he and Henry were felled the same as I.

And Henry, who I so completely betrayed. I felt it in his touch last night, his love for me. He told me with his hands and with his lips, that story of imperfect but steady devotion that took to heart the role of husband and provider and protector but sometimes forgot lover and friend. He would be disappointed in me, and greatly saddened, but he would not be enraged.

Wade would never, I am sure. And if he had then I am happy to die and leave a world where I could be so entirely wrong about a human being. But every cell in my body knows it was not him.

Nellie. I saw it there, in her eyes: hate, hurt, and anger. But I have watched those eyes nearly my entire life, and I know there is nothing that would drive her to this. But there was something that evening, as we met down by the river, that made the hair on my arms stand on end, and I see now that whatever it was had nothing to do with her angry words toward me. There was some feeling in the air, drifting on the wind like a scent, and while we talked on the open beach by the water, I found myself constantly turning my head and looking toward the brush and woods beyond. And the raft by the slough—I keep going back to that, tied there by the tree, bobbing ever so slightly on the slow-moving water. I see it now, again, just as it has popped in my mind over and over during the course of the summer. What is it? There was something there, wasn't there, in the brush on the other side. I let myself go back, feel

myself standing on the shore, looking at the raft. I feel something, and I look in the woods, my eyes skimming across the
bushes and the leaves.

I look deeper. I look deeper into the woods, past the new
green of the alder leaves. I had seen it—him—hadn't I, that
night? Saw but didn't see, because why would this face, framed
by leaves and shrouded by brush, be there, watching me in
silence as if I were an innocent animal come down to this sweet
slow slough and he like the tiger in the jungle. Jake Timmers,
who I knew but did not know, who was watching me through
the leaves on the trees. Back in town. And oh yes—yes, the
buzzing sound, floating in and out on the wind. Mosquito, I
had thought, then thought, maybe not, and now I know. I see
Wade on the dusty trail out of town. *Come on Anna, it's Jake's.
Let me give you a ride.* But it was not Wade who rode it today.

How did he do it? Did he cross the river on the poor little
raft George and I had built, the motorcycle placed carefully in
the center? A fall river, running low and gentle—he could do
it. He could make it across on a raft with some care and with
some skill. The rest would be fairly easy, the road being dry,
and he would likely have made it a little ways down the rough
trails toward camp.

Why me? Or why us should that be the case, me and
Henry and poor Nate Peterson, whose elegant, fragile mother
might perhaps never see him again? Because we were here, I
suppose, the last save Montana in this part of the hills. We
were here, like three caribou separated from the herd, busy and
distracted with our packing up the operation, easy—but not
overly easy—prey for the hunter. There seems no other reason
for it, and I would laugh if I could at the absurdity. Though
he served as best man at our wedding, it was only because

there was no else to stand beside Henry, his college friends thousands of miles away. There was no real liking between them, but I never felt any real dislike, either—just a blankness. Still, I could sense some irritation on his part regarding Henry and Nate and their important pipes and expensive woodsman boots. I remember that last night, by the fire, Jake looking down at Henry's boots in the firelight.

Those are nice boots.

Henry twisting his foot and glancing down a moment, and—what did he do? Shrugged a little. And Jake Timmers, his eyes reflecting the flames, looking then at Henry's face, his lips curled at the corner in a smile.

We'll tie the sticks together, then we'll float down the river, all the way to the city, yah?

Oh, George, I can hear you now.

I know how. I'll build a good raft, Anna, for me and you.

And you did, George, you built a good raft. I see us on that summer day, gathering lengths of driftwood and cutting down, with that old and rusty metal saw, all else that we needed. Then my stepfather, helping with the details, sweat on his forehead from the long shining sun until there we are, George and I, one glorious summer day, poling our way down the slough.

Wade Daniels

WADE STOOD IN THE QUIET of an early evening, waiting for the southbound train to rumble through and take him with it on its way. His duffle lay like a dead person beside him on the platform, and he felt the pull of the village to his back, wanting him to turn and bid it farewell. He thought he might break if he did. He did not know when or if he would pass this way again.

He told himself the hardest part was behind him, walking away from the cabin he had built with his own hands and the lake that brought him so much joy in the short time he had been blessed to live along its shores. He didn't know what would become of it, his little homestead. The war had robbed him of the chance to prove up on it in a timely manner, and though Fairfield assured him he would follow up on the letter Wade wrote to the office of the territorial governor explaining the situation, Wade worried he would return one day to find his homestead had slipped out of his hands. Despite everything, he realized the homestead was slowly bringing him back with its gentle infusion of all the steady life around him—the magpies in the trees, the young bull moose coming down to the shore, the soft sound of the rain on the roof of the cabin. He was able to feel enough, now, to feel the pain of leaving it all behind.

He was aware of the sound of footsteps on the gravel road behind him, and he found himself in the company of both

Fairfield and the Finn, who came and stood quietly at his side. Shortly after he saw Jake that last time he went to the commissioner's office and told Fairfield everything he knew and everything he thought, though he knew there was little Fairfield could do until some evidence could be found to connect Jake to the hills on the day the Harkers and Nate Peterson were killed. Jake left a week ago, and Wade was able to ascertain through a phone call to his mother's neighbor, Mr. Jones, that Jake went where he was supposed to go and reported to his local draft board.

Beside him the Finn let out a sighing breath, and Wade allowed himself a look at his young friend. The Finn was putting on a brave face, but Wade could see the tightness in the way he held his mouth and narrowed up his eyes. Fairfield, on the other side of him, took out a pipe and lit it, and they all three stared at the tracks that reached over the trestle that crossed one of the three rivers, looking for sign of the train and thinking about the war where Wade was going and the war they felt they had already been through in the past eight months. After a time they heard a whistle—faint, but on its way. As the rumble grew closer and the whistle grew louder and they saw the face of the engine now, coming around the bend, Fairfield turned to Wade and shook his hand.

"Take care of yourself, son," he said and with his free hand gave Wade a hearty pat on the shoulder. The Finn lifted Wade's duffle as the train screamed and lumbered to a stop, and a few other villagers came up to the platform to see if anyone got off. But no one came down the silver steps, and the conductor, clean and precise in his black and white uniform, stood ready and waiting for Wade to board. The Finn swung the duffle up into the baggage car and turned back toward his friend.

"I'll see you over there," he said, nodding and shaking Wade's hand. "You stay safe until I get a chance to catch up."

"Will do," Wade said. "And I'll feel safer as soon as I know you're flying up above me somewhere, giving them hell."

"Won't be long," the Finn said, but Wade wished it would be a long time before this man so much younger than himself got caught up in whatever lay beyond. Wade released the younger man's hand, gave Fairfield a nod, then climbed onto the train. He took a seat by the window and allowed himself the view. There was Fairfield and the Finn, side by side, watching the train slowly start to pull away. There was the Clearwater, down the little rise of the railroad and across the small circle of the village park. There was Main Street, with its haphazard collection of homes and businesses meandering down its length. And beyond the end of the street there would be the river, flowing and open, there at the point where the three rivers became the one that the train would follow south to Anchorage and the sea. Wade watched until the trees took over, then he leaned his head back against his seat and thought about the day he left the family farm to head north. His duffle was packed and waited for him at the bottom of the front porch steps while he stood with his mother and Aunt Dorothy, waiting for Mr. Jones to come over and give him a lift to the bus stop.

"Now don't forget to eat before you get on the plane," his mother said, "and save the sandwiches I made for when you get there in case you can't find a place to grab something right away. And don't forget to call Mr. Jones if you can find a phone so we'll know you made it all right. Oh goodness, here he comes. All right, Wade, now give your mother a hug and kiss, and I'll try not to cry."

She tried, but she cried, and Aunt Dorothy said, "Make sure you save some of those cookies for Jakee, and give my boy a big hug for me." And he left them there, waving on the porch, as he threw his duffle into the back of Mr. Jones's truck and began his journey to the territory of Alaska, where fish and gold filled the streams and the sun shone all night long in the summertime and the winters were what you bragged about when you got old.

He'd turned in the seat of the truck and looked out the window behind him, giving one last wave to the two women on the porch. He was on his way.

Billie Sutherland

IT WAS A SUNNY DAY IN EARLY JUNE, and Billie was rushing through a quick sweep and mop of the roadhouse floors before heading outside. But then she heard the ominous sound of falling pots and something more substantial thudding to the floor. She dropped the mop and ran. Maddie had collapsed by the stove, food flung around her, a strange look on her face, as if one side of it had melted and slid.

"Oh my God." Billie knelt beside her. "Hang on, Maddie." She leapt back to her feet, raced out the door, and ran down the center of the street yelling for help.

Time felt slow and thick as, a short time later, the villagers gathered in the roadhouse and lifted Maddie gently onto a cot, Grandma Millie yelling directions. Billie grabbed her purse on the way out the door and held onto Maddie's hand as the group carrying the cot moved toward the airstrip. Maddie's mouth started moving as if she were trying to speak. Billie leaned down close but failed to understand the words. Then Billie saw that Maddie was looking toward the other side of the cot, where Montana was helping and moving as fast as the others, his cane abandoned in the street. He looked at Billie with a question in his eyes. Billie realized what it was Maddie was trying to say.

"Sorry," Billie said, and the older woman groaned. Billie looked at Montana. "She's telling you she's sorry." And the old man nodded, his eyes blinking fast and hard.

The Finn, forewarned by that same teenage boy Billie had heard yell out "Murderer!" on her second night in the village whose name was Max and who ran like the wind to find the Finn, had the plane started and ready as the cluster around the moving cot turned off Main Street and onto the village airstrip. Billie's ears filled with all the caring murmurings and mumbled blessings for Maddie as she was lifted into the back of the plane, Billie following. "We'll watch over the roadhouse," Grandma Millie shouted above the noise of the plane. "Make sure Maddie doesn't worry about a thing except herself!" The Finn secured the door, and Billie lifted her hand in goodbye.

"You all right back there?" the Finn asked. Billie nodded in the affirmative, and the silver-and-green plane began bumping down the airstrip, rising quickly up into the sky.

"Letter," Maddie said, her speech beginning to clear.

"Oh." Billie silently cursed herself. She had been careless with Fairfield's letter. A week ago she'd had it, and she took it with her to the river where she met Montana, and she'd read it to him to the sound of the tinkling and clinking of the last of the ice swishing through the water. Montana had listened with his eyes gazing downward, then when she finished he lifted his head, his eyes blinking rapidly. "Thank you," he'd said. "That means a lot to me, what Ben thinks. Thank you, Billie." When she returned to her room the letter fell out of her pocket and onto her bed, and that was the last she remembered seeing it, though she was sure it was somewhere in the clutter of the small space. Maddie and Nellie had been in the room this morning, hanging the new curtains and must have stumbled upon it. "You want to know what it says," Billie said now.

Maddie nodded again, and squeezed Billie's hand.

"I've been a bit of a busy-body, I guess you could say," Billie leaned in close so Maddie could hear. "I didn't like my own problems so I meddled in yours." Billie thought for a moment, trying to determine where to begin, what to leave in, what to leave out. She realized she'd better tell Maddie everything, just in case.

Weeks later, as she recovered, Maddie would say to Billie, "Thomas looked for Anna all that winter, but the snow was so deep it was of no use. I went up there too, and we went out to a hill near their old camp and sat in the snow and talked about Anna. It turns out we weren't that far from where she was. If Wade loved her, then I'm glad she was found by someone who did. And if she loved him, then I'm so sorry she never told me. I would have understood. Married life just—well, Henry loved her, but he kept trying to make her someone she wasn't. I could never understand how he couldn't see that if he changed her, then he would lose the woman he fell in love with."

But now, on the way to Anchorage, Maddie could only squeeze Billie's hand. "There's still time," Billie said. "You've still got time." As the plane sped south through the bright blue of the day, she said a silent prayer to a god she could never quite believe in but was gaining definition and shape as a presence in her world, something like an acknowledgment of the grace and beauty of love and life and the power of forgiveness. Amelia Johnson came, as often, into her thoughts. Billie wanted her forgiveness, and asked for it again and again in her little blank book. But to forgive or not to forgive is for the living, Billie realized. In that other world, forgiveness simply is.

Anna Harker

THERE ARE SO MANY THINGS, I have realized—small, quiet things—that will never be known about me. Little moments I had, little things I thought. We keep so much to ourselves, in the quiet corners of our persons, as well as in the moments we live with no witnesses to our actions: the many times I romped through the woods, shotgun in hand, my thoughts drifting as my feet fell on the soft, dusty trail or on a white carpet of snow, or the times I watched my mother, silently, as she worked in the kitchen behind the counter, and I wondered about her life and how I thought she could be in a book, my wonderful mother. My afternoon, on this my last day before the swinging of the ax, will never be shared. But would I have shared it?

While Henry and Nate went down to the operation to finish closing things up, I abandoned my own packing duties, left camp, and walked out across the tundra to where I could see the spread of the rolling hills and all the little streams running like pieces of silver thread through the soft blanket of the reds and oranges of the fall tundra. The mountains were out behind the foothills, bright and clean and pristine, so always and eternal though there was a time, long ago in the history of the earth, when it had not yet been formed by the colliding and shifting of the earth's plates. It was Miss Millie, who married a railroad man and became Mrs. Wilson, who first taught me about that, in the roadhouse where we met because the school had not been built yet, and where we sat at the longest table, big kids and little kids, watching our teacher's eyes grow wide at the immensity of what she was telling us. *Millions of years ago*, she'd said. *Millions!* I'd thought of that, today, as I looked at the mountains. For most of my school years there were so few of us: George and Nellie and the Packard children, whose parents owned the inn back then, and Henry and his sisters, when they were not going to school in Anchorage. There were other children, too, faces that came and went as families tried the life and found it too hard or too lacking, stayed a year or two then moved on. The school was built the year after I married Henry, and when we returned to the village that fall, I would get up early and walk down the street so I could watch the children—still small in number—hurry up the steps of the one-room building. I was happy for them and envious at the same time; I imagined myself among them, going in the door and sitting down at a real desk and watching Miss Millie write the words on a big black chalkboard: *Millions of years ago*. Will anyone ever know that about me?

A steady, cold north wind whipped across the hill and in it I could feel the whispering warning of winter on its way— snow was coming. Soon the hills would be soft and white; we were leaving just in time. I remembered so many days, coming up here with Merkle and soaring across the snow on a sled pulled by our modest little, loyal dog team; I could remember all their names: Grizzly and Wolfie and Brontë and Keats, Uncas and River and Brandy and Jack and Gracie. Tongues out and smiling (or so I thought) as they pulled us along, all long gone now, but so alive still in my thoughts. And for a moment as I remembered the sweet dogs pulling me and Merkle across the thick crust of crystal snow in the vision of all that rolling white, I forgot my current troubles. And when my thoughts shifted and I remembered again the imperfectness of everything that was ever mine, a feeling of peace and acceptance washed across me and settled into me and I thought, how beautiful, how beautiful has my one small life been, and I knew that whatever happened to me and Henry or to me and Wade, that the mountains and the hills would be here and be beautiful and the rivers would run and the streams would trickle and the stars would be there in the dark winter sky. And every wonderful memory that I'd ever had was mine to keep, no matter.

Will those memories go with me now? Will I perhaps be folded into them and live within them as they have lived within me? I could ask for nothing more, nothing more than to let my heaven be my life as I had lived it—my small, imperfect little life.

I can see the red and pink streaks of sunset across the sky. If Henry and Nate still live, they will be returning to the camp soon to find me gone. I wish life for them, though of that I am doubtful, yet I let my thoughts imagine them coming up the trail, wet and tired and dirty, and seeing the twilight coming and no lanterns lit, the two of them, calling out my name as I hear it now—

But I know it is not either of them who is calling.

Anna.

My eye looks longingly at the sky, up up to where it is still blue, my favorite sky.

Anna.

Yes, Uncle Mike. And so there you are.

Wade Daniels

THERE WAS A RAINBOW in the sky over the far end of the field. Wade tried to focus on it to keep his eyes from falling upon the bodies scattered across the tall pale grass. He thought, let me stay here for a while, let me remember for a moment who I am. And he let himself go back to his cabin by the lake, to the vision of Anna there, smiling as the cry of the loon rose from the ice-free water. But he did not let himself be gone long. The war would not wait.

He stood fast, signaling to his men to do the same, while the lead company moved across the field, hunched low in the thigh-high grasses, to ensure the woods beyond were as desolate as they seemed. He was in the south of France, part of a conglomeration of allied forces driving the Germans north and into the mountains. A paratrooper, he had been one of thousands dropped from the sky. There were some missing companies, where the drop had not been right. Perhaps they had found a faction of one of them.

A signal was given, and medics rushed past him and into the field, searching for signs of living among the dead. Wade joined them, gently turning over the bloody broken bodies, all American and all, it seemed, so young, checking for a pulse, for a flicker, a spot of warmth, someone to save. Always he remembered those first bodies shattered by violence, far away in the Harris Hills, which now seemed part of a different life he led in another world. If he knew what the future would bring, just two short years later, would it have been different for him then? No, it couldn't have been, because of Anna. But that was just the beginning of the end of the life he had known. The war had trumped all.

He heard a plane overhead, one of theirs, and as he looked up and saw it in the distance he thought of the Finn, a legendary pilot now in the skies across Europe and he smiled at that. *Go kid,* he thought, wondering where the Finn was at the moment, *and Godspeed.* Would they see each other again, ever, at the end of all this? Survival seemed impossible, with so many soldiers falling every day, but he allowed himself a brief fantasy of seeing the Finn walking down the street of the village they both left behind.

As he knelt beside a soldier, whose helmet had been thrown clear off his head, he noticed a familiar copper hue in the thick hair that waved back off the unseen forehead in a way that, too, was familiar. Coldness gripped his heart as he slowly turned the young man over in the grass. His heart beat again. No, not Jake, and as he looked closer he saw the hair was more brown than copper, the hairline not that familiar. Why did he keep doing this, keep seeing Jake in the faces of the dead? Something he longed for and dreaded at the same time. If Jake died in the war, he would not have to think about what he would have to do about his aunt's only son, his mother's only nephew. He wouldn't have to think about justice for Anna and Henry and Nate Peterson; the war would exact it for them, for all of them. Far better that, he thought, thinking about his mother and his aunt, than the other news that would corrode their lives like acid spilling from a battery. Far better.

"Friend of yours, sir?" A medic knelt by him now, pausing what otherwise would have been a quick grab for the dog tags of this obviously dead soldier so the identification and notification process could begin. It still startled him to be called sir. But promotion came swiftly and unwanted among all this death.

"No," Wade said. He looked at the bloodied face on the ground beside him. "They're all so young, aren't they?"

"They are, sir." The medic looked at the dead man. "We all are, sir."

Wade nodded. The medic reached toward the neck of the dead man's bloody coat. "May I?" he asked.

"Carry on," Wade said. "Any survivors?"

"No—not here, sir. But some could have escaped." The medic pulled the dead man's tags, deftly moved one from the ball chain, to be used for notification, and left the other on the body for identification when conditions allowed for recovery.

"We can hope," Wade said, though he was doubtful. This was a strange world, where lives were taken and lives were spared and everything happened in the blink of an eye. He still knew—had not lost that sense—that every bullet he fired that went where it was meant to destroyed a future that might have been. He had to always think of the people he was saving, or was supposed to be saving, to get him through those moments.

The medic touched his shoulder and continued his grim business. They had to keep moving. Wade lingered, and wondered briefly if there was a prayer he could say for the dead in the field. Nothing came to him. His thoughts went instead to the Harris Hills, to the flutter of Anna's dark hair in the wind. "God have mercy," he said to the young man, then he stood and walked away.

Later, as they camped for the night on a wooded hill that allowed good views, Wade sat in the last of the light and attempted to write a letter home. But his thoughts were in Alaska, and he took another piece of wrinkled worn paper and began a letter to Madeline and Thomas Merkle.

It is nearly two years now, since that awful day in the hills that took the life of your beloved Anna. I'd always meant to tell you how very sorry I was, and still am, but I have never been able to find the words. Your daughter was someone I very much admired, and I think of her often here while in the midst of war, of how brave I'm sure she was when she met her end, and perhaps she can send some of that bravery to me while we press onward into Europe.

But here he stopped, unable to continue. What could he say to them? He had asked Fairfield to keep on the case and try to find some shred of evidence that could connect Jake to the murders. And he asked him to try to clear Montana so the man could have his life back. But how and if he could accomplish that, Wade did not know.

He could see a farmhouse in the distance, barely visible in the fading of the day. He put down his pen and imagined the lives lived there, for generations perhaps, before the advent of this awful war. Mothers, fathers, children, husbands, wives, lovers, and friends. He wished the empty dwelling could speak to him, to tell him stories of all the life and lives it had known. Tales of life and love, not death and hate. Once upon a time. Once upon a time he was a young man new to the wilds of Alaska, and he stood on the shores of a tree-fringed lake and saw a beautiful girl. The story of him. Now here he was, in the south of France, in the chaos of war. He let his thoughts travel to the Alaska rivers beyond the village he once knew and saw a rainbow breaking water at the end of his line. It's a long way, he thought; such a long, long way that I have come.

Billie Sutherland

"CAN YOU HELP ME, BILLIE?"

Billie looked up from the bread she was kneading, flour down her front and trailing up her arms. Maddie was in the dining room threshold, in the wheelchair she hated, holding her old brown sweater. "I'm about done," Billie said. "What have you got in mind?"

"I'd like to go down to the river today."

Billie paused, smoothed the surface of the dough, and looked at it with a furrowed brow.

"It looks fine, Billie," Maddie said. "Now put a little oil in the bowl and coat the dough with it, cover it with a clean cloth and leave it someplace warm."

Billie smiled and nodded, though Maddie had instructed her in this several times before. They were all pitching in to keep the roadhouse going—Billie, Nellie, and Grandma Millie, all doing the cooking and cleaning and baking. The Finn came in every evening to wash all the dishes while Billie sat on the counter after closing and watched him. One such evening while Maddie was out in the garden supervising Montana as he weeded and planted, the Finn stepped over to her, placed his warm, wet, and soapy hands on her thighs and kissed her down the stretch of her neck. "Marry me, Billie," he whispered, and when she caught her breath, she said, "Keep washing and I'll think about it," an answer that seemed to satisfy him enough for the time being.

Now Billie set the covered dough on a shelf near the stove, washed the flour off her hands and arms, and came around the counter. "Should I lock the door?" she asked.

"No need," Maddie said. "We won't be too long. If anyone comes in, they can help themselves to coffee and wait."

Billie grabbed the can of mosquito spray and tossed it to Maddie, then pulled on a plaid flannel shirt. "They're sure to be out today," she said, and Maddie grimaced but complied, then wheeled the chair over toward the door. "All set?" Billie asked, and Maddie nodded. Billie grabbed the chair's handles and maneuvered it over the threshold, holding the door open with her leg as she did. As she pushed it toward the street Maddie said, "Wait. Can you take me over there? By the rosebush?"

"Of course," Billie said, noting the controlled frustration in the older woman's voice. Hang in there, she wanted to say, but she had said it so often these few weeks since Maddie's release from the hospital she figured her friend was sick of hearing it. Maddie would eventually get her strength back, and she would be able to walk again, a little bit at a time. Billie turned the chair toward the thick bushes that grew beside the front corner of the building. Maddie sat quietly for a moment, staring at the bush, which was now in full bloom, a jungle of green leaves and pink flowers. Wild roses—so beautiful and so swiftly passing, so everywhere for such a short time, filling the woods with color and scent. Then Maddie reached forward, took a small pocketknife from the pocket of her shirt, and cut a single, perfect rose. That's when Billie realized. Today was Anna's birthday. "All right, let's go now, please," Maddie said, and Billie pushed the chair out onto the dusty road.

Things got a little trickier when they reached the trail that linked the end of the street to the river shore. Billie leaned her weight into the chair, wishing the Finn or Montana or Nellie were there to help. Then there was a small stream of water, the tail end of a slough, that they had to get across, and Billie watched as the water licked the bottoms of Maddie's shoes at the same time she felt it seeping into her own. The hardest part was getting up a slight rise to the shore proper, and Billie gave it everything she had in the hope she would succeed before Maddie started apologizing. And they made it, Billie panting and smiling and trying not to let Maddie hear her labored breathing. Getting the chair across the silty beach was no picnic, either, and again Billie leaned her weight into the chair, but they could see the river now, slow and gray, and in the distance the light cover of clouds thinned around the mountains, revealing bits of the bright white peaks. Billie pushed the chair as close as she dared to the great rushing water, then eased her grip on the handles and wiped the sweat off her forehead.

"Thank you," Maddie said, and reached back a hand that Billie took in hers. *I will be here someday too,* Billie thought, and suddenly pictured herself old and still here and coming down to this river that stays on like the mountains it comes from, flowing down from the glaciers and across the miles to spill into the sea. The river will be here when Maddie is not. The river will be here when Billie, too, ceases to be, but before that—God willing—there would be old age preceded by a long trail lined with a forest of all the small good things that make a life. Yes, she will marry the Finn, that rascal of a man, and get him to seed her some children before he flies out of the sky, and she'll take those children and pull them on a sled through the woods near the cabin by the lake where they will live, and maybe spin the sled around and around on the ice until the children are old enough to skate beside her. And when the children are grown and the Finn is gone perhaps she'll meet someone who will be to her what she is to Maddie, and that someone will help her down to the river when she is old and she will throw a rose into the river for Maddie for Anna because she is still, at that moment, here.

On this day the river was full and opaque, the glaciers melting under the summer sun. Maddie leaned forward in her chair and tossed her rose. It landed lightly on the gray surface, spun a moment, then rushed on its way.

Epilogue

"YOU WERE RIGHT, BEAUTIFUL," he said as he walked in the door. She had seen him through the side window of the cabin, the one that faced the trail to the village, walking swiftly with a back still straight despite the onslaught of age.

She would have said, "Of course I'm right," without knowing what it was he was talking about, but there was something in his face that held her back. He set the newspaper onto the table in front of her. He had folded it neatly to a certain page.

It only took her a moment, then she knew: Hikers. Skeleton. Ax marks on the skull. Martin Bell.

"Oh my God," she said. Her mouth went dry and she tried to swallow. She lifted her eyes from the page. "It's over then, isn't it? It's over!"

"I'll say."

"It's about damned time!"

He nodded. "It's about damned time."

Then she felt her chest heaving against her will, and she clasped her shaking hands to her mouth to stifle a sob.

"Hey," he said, reaching across the table, gently pulling her hands away from her face. "Hey. This was wanted, remember? This is good."

"Yes," she said, tears now stinging her eyes. She took a deep breath. "But it's so many years too late."

"No," the Finn said. "Not too late. The truth turns at its own speed, that's all."

Billie blinked fast and looked out the window at the lake, a thin layer of newly formed ice laying clear and clean across the surface. She had walked on it yesterday—carefully—and was able to see clear down to the bottom, a strange floor of rocks and mud and algae, unmoving in its sealed state. Is the past, she now wondered, like the bottom of a lake in winter? Set in place just before the freeze, all the pieces and the layers held still, waiting.

Acknowledgments

I am deeply indebted to both Roberta Sheldon and Ken Marsh for their wonderful books on the history of Alaska's northern Susitna Valley: Roberta Sheldon's *The Mystery of the Cache Creek Murders* (Talkeetna Editions, 2001) and *The Heritage of Talkeetna* (Talkeetna Editions, 1995), Ken Marsh's *Alaska's Sealed Book* (Trapper Creek Museum, 2015) and *A River Between Us* (Trapper Creek Museum, 2002). It is with thanks to them that much of the history of the area has been preserved and the stories made available for all. Though I grew up hearing renditions of the 1939 murders in the Cache Creek mining district, Sheldon's gripping investigation of this horrendous crime brings the story to life with vivid detail. Similarly, Marsh's *Alaska's Sealed Book* recreates the epic story of the settling of the northern Susitna Valley, and I could not have written *Wild Rivers, Wild Rose* without either of these rich resources.

One specific scene in *Wild Rivers, Wild Rose* was directly influenced (though highly fictionalized) by a passage featured in *Alaska's Sealed Book*: the story Montana tells Billie of the dead miner, which was inspired by a section from the Dorothy Wolfe recollections held by the Talkeetna Historical Society and reprinted in part in Marsh's book. The scene where Anna and Merkle capture the shrews in a can while in their trapping cabin was inspired by a story from Marsh's interview with long-ago Talkeetna resident Gale Weatherell, likewise in *Alaska's Sealed Book*. Additional thanks go to the Talkeetna Historical Society for preserving the Dorothy Wolfe papers in their archives and for the wealth of information I gleaned from their collections over the years.

I would also like to acknowledge the trustees of the Wilfrid Gibson estate for permission to reprint Gibson's haunting 1915 poem, "Back." The song "The Braes of Balquhither" was written by the Scottish poet Robert Tannahill (1774–1810), the lyrics of which can be found in Tannahill's *The Works of Robert Tannahill, with Life of the Author and a Memoir of R. A. Smith.*

I researched numerous websites about World War II, including historyextra.com, nationalww2museum.org, and warpoets.org. Though I grew up hearing different versions of the three traditional folk ballads featured in the book, I referred to fresnostate.edu and mainlynorfolk.info as well as Jerry *Silverman's Folk Song Encyclopedia Volume I* (Chappell & Co. Inc., 1975) to glean additional information.

Thanks go as well to Lew Freedman for his wonderful book *Bad Friday* (Epicenter Press, 2013) that helped me get a feel for what Alaska's 1964 earthquake was like for those who lived through it. I also spent hours scouring the photographic collections in Alaska's Digital Archives (vilda.alaska.edu) to get a sense of historic Anchorage both before and during 1964. James Kari and James A. Fall's *Shem Pete's Alaska* (University of Alaska Press, 2003) and Kari's *Dena'ina Topical Dictionary* (Alaska Native Language Center, 2007) were both invaluable aids to my understanding of the northern Susitna Valley's Dena'ina population: their lifestyle, their struggles, and their language.

I am also extremely thankful to Alaska's Rasmuson Foundation, which, in 2015, awarded me an Individual Artist Project Award grant based on the work I had completed on *Wild Rivers, Wild Rose.* Though I am ever grateful for the funding for a small writing studio, what I am most grateful for is their show of support for the project, which inspired me to complete a draft within nine months. Thank you!

I am indebted as well to Peggy Shumaker of the University of Alaska Press for picking *Wild Rivers, Wild Rose* out of the pile and to everyone at UA Press for bringing *Wild Rivers, Wild Rose* to beautiful life.

I would like to thank Joeth Zucco for her excellent editing, as well as 590 Design for the lovely production work and patience with my many requests.

Thank you to William Barstow for his steady belief in my creative worth and whose own creative endeavors inspire mine. Thanks as always to Sondra Porter for the early encouragement that made all the difference.

Love, thanks, and gratitude to my late mother, Carol L. Durr, and to my family—Chris, Jenny, and all the Durrs, Barstows, Birdsalls, and Kays. Love, thanks, and gratitude as well to the members of the WACBABS book club and my other dear friends in Talkeetna and elsewhere, including my darling furry friends, Jack Shephard and Lola Burger. You make life wonderful!